Valor of Many Stripes

Valor of Many Stripes

Remarkable Americans in World War II

SCOTT BARON

McFarland & Company, Inc., Publishers
Jefferson, North Carolina

ALSO OF INTEREST

BY SCOTT BARON AND JAMES WISE, JR.
*Conduct Unbecoming: Fifteen Military
Criminals, Rogues and Victims of Justice
from the Revolutionary War
to Vietnam* (McFarland, 2016)

BY JAMES WISE, JR. AND SCOTT BARON
At the Helm of USS America:
*The Aircraft Carrier and Its 23 Commanders,
1965–1996* (McFarland, 2014)

ISBN (print) 978-1-4766-7441-4
ISBN (ebook) 978-1-4766-3508-8

LIBRARY OF CONGRESS CATALOGUING DATA ARE AVAILABLE

BRITISH LIBRARY CATALOGUING DATA ARE AVAILABLE

© 2019 Scott Baron. All rights reserved

No part of this book may be reproduced or transmitted in any form
or by any means, electronic or mechanical, including photocopying
or recording, or by any information storage and retrieval system,
without permission in writing from the publisher.

Front cover photographs: U.S. soldier crosses a road cautiously under
the cover of a light tank in the Hedgerows of Normandy, July 1944,
Normandy Campaign, France (© 2019 Everett Historical/Shutterstock);
Major General William "Wild Bill" Donovan presents Virginia Hall
with the Distinguished Service Cross (Central Intelligence Agency);
SSgt. Maynard "Snuffy" Smith receives the Medal of Honor
from Secretary of War Henry Stimson,
July 15, 1943 (U.S. Air Force Historical Society)

Printed in the United States of America

*McFarland & Company, Inc., Publishers
Box 611, Jefferson, North Carolina 28640
www.mcfarlandpub.com*

To my friend and mentor James E. Wise, Jr. (1930–2013).
Gone, but never forgotten. Scholar, Vietnam veteran,
coauthor, mentor and friend. Most importantly,
a living example of honor.

And to my wife Marisela, who knows
everything about me and loves me anyway!
Forty-two years and still in love.
Thank you for keeping me humble.

Acknowledgments

This book would not have been possible without the knowledge, goodwill and generosity of numerous individuals whose patience and willingness to assist made the task of researching and writing the stories enjoyable and easier to achieve.

First and foremost among that distinguished company is Douglas Sterner and his phenomenal and, to the military researcher, essential website Home of Heroes at http://www.homeofheroes.com/.

Doug's knowledge, expertise and assistance proved invaluable in the selection and researching of many of these stories, and he generously shared resources and pointed me in the right direction. A successful author himself and a Vietnam veteran, Doug's efforts made this book better.

Also worthy of note are Kevin Reem, Tyrone Brown, Murray Mullins, Scurgeon Cruz, James Falk, Bill Marshal, Scott Johnson, Madlyn Stokes and the staff of the Watsonville (California) Public Library.

Table of Contents

Acknowledgments	vi
Introduction	1
Kemp Tolley: The Man Who Almost Started World War II	3
Kermit Tyler: Pursuit Officer, Fort Shafter, Oahu, Hawaii Territory	8
Edwin P. Ramsey: The Last Horse Cavalry Charge in U.S. Military History	14
James R. Roosevelt: Second Marine Raider Battalion at Makin Island	24
Douglas Munro: Only Coast Guard Medal of Honor	39
Demas T. Craw and Pierpont M. Hamilton: Operation Torch	44
The Niland Brothers: Inspiration for *Saving Private Ryan*	55
The Borgstrom Brothers: Further Inspiration for *Saving Private Ryan*	60
The Stokes Twins: Awarded the Silver Star for the Same Action	65
Guy "Gabby" Gabaldon: The "Pied Piper of Saipan," from Hell to Eternity	78
Eugene B. Fluckey: Only Sub Commander to "Torpedo" a Train	86
John C. "Jack" Lee, Jr.: Joint German American Force at the End of World War II	97
Operation Ginny II: Execution of 15 American Commandos	109

Matt Urban: Most Decorated Soldier in American History	124
Maynard H. "Snuffy" Smith: First Enlisted Airman Medal of Honor (Europe)	131
Joseph T. O'Callahan: Only Chaplain Awarded Medal of Honor in World War II	138
Silvestre S. Herrera: Medal of Honor Awarded to a Mexican National	144
Isadore S. Jachman: Native-Born German Who Won the Medal of Honor	148
Richard Nott Antrim: Only Medal of Honor Awarded to a POW During World War II	153
Roddie Edmonds: First U.S. Serviceman Named "Righteous Among the Nations"	164
Charles Valentine August: Twice a POW in the Same War	169
Virginia Hall: World War II's Most Dangerous Spy	175
Moe Berg: Catcher, Scholar, Intelligence Officer	183
Bert Shepard: One-Legged Major League Pitcher	189
William Augustus Read, Jr.: Coconuts and the Navy Cross	195
Bruce Ward Carr: Departed in a Mustang, Returned in a Focke-Wulf	202
Chips: U.S. Army War Dog Awarded the Distinguished Service Cross	208
Index	215

Introduction

The award of a military decoration or medal does not define valor; it only recognizes it. Many acts of unbelievable courage and self-sacrifice occur on the battlefield but are often obscured in the fog of battle, to remain unrecognized and unheralded.

The men and women in these stories did very unusual things, and although in many cases there was the official awarding of medals, including several Medals of Honor, their stories remain unknown and untold. This book is a modest attempt to correct that oversight.

Their stories comprise a cross section of participants that includes airmen, tankers, sailors, Marines, spies, POWs and a chaplain. They are male and female, military and civilian, and a dog.

Their stories stretch from the first attack at Pearl Harbor to the first war crimes trial in Italy, from Operation Torch to the beaches of Saipan, from the early first battles in the Philippines to the last battle in Austria during the closing days of the war in Europe.

Their stories are of the man who almost started World War II and the woman considered the war's "most dangerous spy." They recount the experiences of the son of a sitting U.S. president, a native-born German and a Mexican immigrant.

Their stories include the last cavalry charge, the only one-legged pitcher in Major League Baseball, a Navy Cross awarded for a coconut fight and a submarine that torpedoed a train. They include U.S. tank drivers who fought side by side with German soldiers against a common enemy, a POW who was awarded the Medal of Honor, and the only private first class to bite Gen. Dwight D. Eisenhower.

These are not the stories of heroes. These are the stories of people who through choice or circumstance accomplished heroic tasks. Often, they are the "first" or "only"; sometimes they are the "last." They inspire and awe us. Their stories amaze us and cause us to reflect on ourselves. Some have humor, some irony. But in the end, they all are the stories of people.

It has been said that war brings out the best and worst in people. I believe these stories give ample evidence of the former.

Kemp Tolley

The Man Who Almost Started World War II

On the morning of December 7, 1941, Lt. Kemp Tolley USN set sail from Manila Bay with a 19-man crew aboard the USS *Lanikai*, a wooden two-masted schooner. Under top secret orders from the president of the United States, Franklin D. Roosevelt, its mission was to patrol in the vicinity of Camranh Bay, French Indochina, hoping to provoke an attack by Japanese forces and provide a justification for FDR to declare war on Japan. Tolley was instructed to imitate a pirate vessel and provoke the Japanese to fire on him. In essence, his mission was to give the United States justification for entering the war. It would begin a 4,000-mile, three-month voyage to evade the Japanese.

Born to a U.S. Army officer at Fort McKinley, Manila, in the Philippines on April 29, 1908, Tolley entered the U.S. Naval Academy at Annapolis in 1925, at the age of 17. While in his senior year, in February 1929, Midshipman Tolley was assigned as a watch officer aboard the battleship USS *Florida* (BB-30).

After graduating in June 1929, Tolley was commissioned into the U.S. Navy as an ensign (serial no. 062657) and assigned to navy headquarters, attached to the U.S. Navy Rifle Team and competing in the National Matches. He returned to the *Florida* in September, remaining there until assigned to a staff position with the commander in chief (CIC) of the U.S. Fleet in April 1930.[1]

In December 1931, Tolley was transferred to the submarine tender USS *Canopus* (AS-34) where he served as a watch and division officer until April of 1933, when he served briefly on the staff of the CIC-Asiatic Fleet. In August 1933, Tolley was assigned to the Yangtze River

Patrol as communications officer aboard the USS *Mindanao*, a river gunboat.

In May 1934, Tolley began a two-year study of the Russian language, first in Shanghai, then in Riga, Latvia, becoming one of the few naval officers fluent in Russian. By June of 1936, he was back at sea aboard the battleship USS *Wyoming* (BB-32), before serving as an aide to the South Seas Patrol commander from May 1937 until July 1938. In August 1938, he took over as executive officer of the gunboat USS *Wake* as part of the South China Patrol.

After another nine months studying Russian in Shanghai, Tolley returned to the United States where he served as a French instructor at his alma mater, Annapolis, from September 1940 until August 1941, when he returned to the USS *Wake* as executive officer. Evading Japanese forces aboard the river gunboat USS *Oahu*, Tolley arrived in Manila on December 4 and took command of the USS *Lanikai* the following day, December 5.

The *Lanikai* itself had an interesting history. Built by W. F. Stone and Company in Oakland, California, in 1914, it was a 67-ton two-masted wooden-hulled motorized schooner. Sold to a Hamburg businessman, it was used for trade among German-governed islands in the Pacific until confiscated in Hawaii by U.S. military authorities after America's entry into World War I.

Commissioned as the USS *Hermes* on April 1, 1918, it patrolled the west coast of Hawaii for the remainder of the war, was decommissioned on January 23, 1919, and remained on the navy rolls as a depot ship until July 1926, when it was sold to the Lanikai Fish Company and renamed.

Converted to a fishing boat, it spent the next 11 years catching salmon in Alaska and as a charter yacht. Sold to MGM Studios in 1937, it was used in the film *Hurricane*, starring Dorothy Lamour, and then sold to an American businessman in Manila on April 6, 1939, where it remained until being chartered by the U.S. Navy for one dollar a year on December 4, 1941.

Commissioned the USS *Lanikai* as an auxiliary schooner the following day, it was equipped with a three-pound gun of Spanish-American War vintage and two Lewis machine guns from World War I and placed under the command of Lieutenant Tolley. It thus became an official U.S. warship.

With the majority of the country still opposed to U.S. involvement in the war and the country still officially neutral, FDR had made a "sacred promise" to American fathers and mothers that the United States would not enter the war unless American forces were attacked, a promise he had incorporated into the 1940 Democratic platform.

However, on December 1, FDR had directed Admiral Stark, chief of naval operations, to charter "three small vessels" to form a "defensive information patrol" for the purpose of observing and reporting on Japanese movements in the South China Sea and Gulf of Siam. The minimum requirements to establish an identity as a U.S. man-of-war would be "command by a naval officer" and the presence of a "small gun and one machine gun."

According to Tolley in his book *Cruise of the Lanikai*, the real purpose of his mission was to devise an incident whereby Japan would fire on a U.S. warship, providing the justification for the United States to enter the war. His orders from Admiral Hart, commander of the Asiatic Fleet at Manila, were to put his ship in the path of Japanese convoys, attract their attention, and raise the colors only after being fired upon.

This is supported by a communication between FDR and Winston Churchill on December 3 in which the president assured the British prime minister that England could expect "armed American direct support very soon" and also by the fact that the *Lanikai* had no working radio, highly unusual for a "reconnaissance" mission.

The *Lanikai* was waiting off Corregidor on the morning of December 7, preparing to depart on what Tolley characterized as a "suicide mission," when news of the Japanese attack on Pearl Harbor made the mission unnecessary.

The *Lanikai* remained in the area as part of the inshore patrol until December 26, when it departed the Philippine Islands for the Netherlands East Indies, arriving in Java on January 22, 1942. After refitting, it departed with passengers on February 26, just prior to the Dutch surrender. Dodging Japanese patrols, it arrived in Australia on March 18, escaping from under the noses of the Japanese Navy.

The *Lanikai* then patrolled the north coast of Australia, watching for Japanese activity until April 27, when Tolley, now a lieutenant commander, was detached from the *Lanikai* for other duties.

The *Lanikai* was transferred to the Australian Navy on August 22, 1942, and commissioned His Majesty's Australian ship *Lanikai* on December 9.

Tolley served as the assistant naval attaché at the U.S. embassy in Moscow from May 1942 until May 1944. There, he met Vlada Gritzenko, whom he married in 1943. She later became a professor of Russian at Goucher College when the couple returned to Maryland.

In September 1944 he reported to the battleship USS *North Carolina* (BB-55) as a navigation officer. The *North Carolina* saw action at Leyte, Luzon, Iwo Jima, and Okinawa and participated in attacks on the Japanese home islands.

In September 1945, Tolley was transferred to the Office of Naval Intelligence, where he remained until May 1947. In June of 1947, he was transferred to the USS *Vermilion* (AKA 107), an attack cargo ship, followed by command of an LST (landing ship, tank) squadron in September 1948.

Transferred to the Armed Forces Staff College in August of 1949, he served as director of the intelligence division until July 1952 when he was appointed operations officer of Amphibious Group Two. In December 1954 he became commanding officer of Amphibious Squadron Five.

In August 1956, Tolley, now an admiral, served first as chief of staff, then later (June 1957) as commander of Fleet Activities at Yokosuka, Japan. He retired from the navy at the Philadelphia Naval Station as a rear admiral on June 30, 1959. His awards included the Bronze Star and Purple Heart.

After Admiral Tolley retired to Monkton, Maryland, he became an active writer on naval subjects and produced four books: *Yangtze Patrol—The U.S. Navy in China* (1971), *Cruise of the* Lanikai (1973), *A Biography of Ed Heinemann* (1980) and *Caviar and Commissars: The Experiences of a U.S. Naval Officer in Stalin's Russia* (1983).

Tolley was a colorful figure in navy lore. As Capt. James M. Wylie, who knew him, recalled, "The admiral was a Navy legend. He regaled us with sea stories of the China coast and old Japan. He talked, and we listened." Tolley died at home from a massive stroke on October 28, 2000, at the age of 92.

NOTE

1. The *Florida* was decommissioned in 1931.

Rear Adm. Kemp Tolley, unknown date (U.S. Naval Academy).

Sources

Harding, Stephen. "The Little Navy Ship That Sailed 3,000 Miles to Escape the Japanese." http://www.thedailybeast.com/articles/2016/04/16/the-little-navy-ship-that-sailed-3-000-miles-to-escape-the-japanese.html.
Kelly, Jacques. "Kemp Tolley, 92, Retired Rear Admiral, Linguist and 'Legend.'" *Baltimore Sun*, November 1, 2000.
Tolley, Kemp. *Cruise of the* Lanikai. Annapolis, MD: Naval Institute Press, 1973.
Tolley Obituary. http://www.oocities.org/songkhla.geo/Tolley.html.

Kermit Tyler

*Pursuit Officer, Fort Shafter,
Oahu, Hawaii Territory*

It was about 7:15 a.m., and 1st Lt. Kermit Tyler, U.S. Army Air Corps, was nearing the completion of a four-hour tour of duty as pursuit officer at the Radar Information Center, Fort Shafter, Hawaii Territory.

The duty of a pursuit officer was to assist the controller in ordering planes to intercept suspected enemy planes. Tyler was the only officer present, in command of eight enlisted men. The information center was the hub of six mobile radar stations on the island of Oahu. The commanding general at Wheeler Field wanted his pilots to learn about this new technology and had ordered them to rotate through the center as observer-trainees.

Tyler, a fighter pilot and the executive officer of the 78th Pursuit Squadron at Wheeler Field, had been the first officer on the duty roster on December 3, four days earlier, and was now completing his second familiarization tour as the center struggled with getting up and running.

The center was normally staffed by six spotters, a telephone operator and one man to keep a historical record of all plots made by radar. The spotters were in contact with the six mobile radar sites, and they displayed radar plots on the center's display board. But at 7 a.m., the plotters shut down their equipment and left for breakfast, and Tyler was alone, waiting for his tour to finish.

At one of the mobile sites, the Opana Station at the north tip of the island, Privates George Elliott and Joseph Lockard were also shutting down, but Elliott, wanting more training time, continued to monitor the radar.

The radar, an SCR-270B, had an antenna that sent an electrical pulse into the sky. If anything interrupted the electrical beams, the radar's oscilloscope reflected the object as an echo. The radar was new technology and classified secret, and the personnel of the Signal Aircraft Warning Company, Hawaii, were still in training.

Some echoes were constant, such as those from the nearby hills and cliffs, but others were intermittent, and those were the ones to be alert for. They showed and tracked planes intersecting the radar transmitter's beams.

At 7:02 a.m., Elliott detected a large blip in the upper corner of his oscilloscope and reported it to Tyler at 7:15 a.m., after he was located by Private Joseph McDonald, the telephone operator. Elliott reported "a large number of planes" coming in from the north.

Aware that a flight of army B-17 bombers were due in from Hamilton Field, near Novato, California, and would be approaching from the north, Tyler advised them, "Don't worry about it."

They were just four words, but they would haunt him the remainder of his days.

Kermit Arthur Tyler was born in Oelwein, Iowa, on April 13, 1913, and the family moved to Long Beach, in Southern California, while he was still young. Interested in aviation and flying from an early age, after seeing a barnstormer land near his home, Tyler enlisted in the U.S. Marine Corps Reserve in 1932, where, after duty hours, he helped out at the airfield cleaning parts and working on planes in the hope of getting a ride. His enthusiasm waned after he was among those tasked with cleaning up the crash site of a dive bomber.

Tyler joined the Civilian Conservation Corps in 1934 where he renewed his interest in flying. Tyler was a junior at University of California, Berkeley, and by his own admission struggling academically when he learned from the Army Air Corps that he had been accepted into the cadet program. On October 9, 1936, Tyler enlisted again, this time as a flying cadet at Hamilton Field, California, and he departed for San Antonio, Texas, that same day.

Tyler took primary and basic training at Randolph Field and then advanced training at Kelly Field, outside San Antonio, initially flying primitive biplanes and transitioning to the BT-9, a low-wing monoplane.

Out of his class of 100 cadets who began training, three were killed and others washed out, and only 49 graduated. Commissioned a second lieutenant in October 1937, Tyler requested observation flying and was assigned to Moffett Field, California, where he towed targets which allowed for the adjustment of artillery fire.

While at Moffett, Tyler transferred into the 35th Pursuit Group on October 1, 1940, stationed at Hamilton Field as a fighter pilot.

In early February 1941, Tyler was offered a transfer to Hawaii. He took it. He and the 30 other pilots transferring to Hawaii were loaded aboard the carrier USS *Enterprise* (CV-6) with their 31 P-36 Mohawk fighter planes and shipped to Hawaii to reinforce the 14th Pursuit Wing. Fifteen miles from Oahu, they took off from the deck of the carrier in their P-36 fighters.

Tyler found Hawaii good duty, flying OA-9s and P-40s as he oversaw training for pilots transitioning from the P-36 Mohawk to the P-40 Warhawk. In addition to checking out pilots in P-40s, Tyler spent his time developing his skills as a pilot, surfing and seeking female company in the tropical paradise.

All that came to an end that Sunday morning, the 7th of December 1941. Not especially alarmed at the report from Opana, Tyler, like the rest of the staff, went to breakfast.

Back at the Opana site, Elliott and Lockard continued monitoring the blip until 7:40 a.m., when background interference caused them to lose the signal. They secured the site and went to breakfast a little before 8 a.m.

At 7:48 a.m., the first bombs began falling on the Naval Air Station at Kaneohe and were followed quickly by attacks on Wheeler and Hickam Army Air Fields, Ewa Marine Corps Air Station, Bellows Field and Battleship Row, announcing to the world the United States' entry into World War II.

In 110 minutes, two waves of more than 350 Japanese aircraft—high-level bombers (103), torpedo bombers (40), dive bombers (131) and fighters (79)—attacked. In what was hoped to be a knockout blow to the U.S. Pacific Fleet, 21 vessels were damaged, including eight of nine battleships (the USS *Colorado* was at Puget Sound in Washington State), sinking four; 164 aircraft destroyed and another 159 damaged out of approximately 400 aircraft in Hawaii; and 1,999 sailors, 233 soldiers and 109 Marines as well as 49 civilians were killed. Japanese losses were 29 aircraft and five midget submarines. Sixty-four servicemen were killed and one captured. Sources vary as to numbers.

Even before the fires were out, there was a scramble to assess responsibility and assign blame. Fingers were pointed, and many of them pointed at Lieutenant Tyler for blithely ignoring the radar warnings. He has been vilified as the man who could have prevented Pearl Harbor. But could he?

That Sunday morning, the United States was at peace, and none of the military commands were on alert. A flight of B-17s was expected that morning, and the radio station KGMB had been broadcasting all night, a further indication that the bombers were expected from the north. And there was no way that the radar could distinguish between friendly and hostile aircraft.

Even had the large blip caused him alarm, it is questionable as to how much Tyler could have done to raise the alarm. He had been given no instructions. He and Private McDonald were the only ones on duty; the plotters were off duty, the radar shut down. He was not in the chain of command, and it was only his second tour of duty training as a pursuit officer. There was no established line of communication, nor was the air defense system fully integrated between the radar sites, the information center and the pursuit squadrons.

A little after 8 a.m., Tyler stepped outside for some air and saw planes dive-bombing Pearl Harbor and heard anti-aircraft fire. It was only then that he realized that they were under attack, a fact confirmed moments later in a call from Wheeler Field.

All personnel were recalled, Major Tindal, a controller, arrived from Hickam Field to take charge of operations, and Tyler remained there assisting as he could until 3 p.m. the following afternoon.

After the attack Tyler's squadron remained on alert but didn't fly any missions, while Tyler was assigned temporary duty as a controller.

Tyler flew a number of combat missions over Guadalcanal from Henderson Field, assigned to the 44th Fighter Squadron, serving as its commanding officer from September 9, 1942, until May 24, 1943, and again later in the Philippines.

Lt. Col. Kermit Tyler circa 1950s (U.S. Air Force photograph).

On June 15, 1943, Tyler was promoted to lieutenant colonel and became operations officer of Fighter Command. He remained at this post until May 5, 1944.

Tyler returned home but, in February of 1945, was sent back to the Pacific as a representative of the Air Force Board. It was a freelance assignment and Tyler had additional missions flying a P-38 Lightning. He finished the war with the award of a Legion of Merit.

Although he testified before the Roberts Commission, the Navy Board of Inquiry, and the Army Pearl Harbor Board, all of which cleared him of any wrongdoing, and no disciplinary actions were taken, the stigma followed him the remainder of his career. As one lieutenant general wrote in the endorsement of his fitness report, "This officer has shown an inability to recognize operations or emergencies which might affect his operation."

Tyler finished his career with a series of low-profile assignments: commanding the 999th Army Air Force Base Unit in Orlando, Florida; serving three years as senior air instructor for the Utah National Guard; and being assigned to the Air Defense Command at Colorado Springs, Colorado, in the mid-1950s.

Tyler retired from the military on July 31, 1961, still a lieutenant colonel after 18 years in grade. He put in a total of 25 years in the air force and four years in the Marine Corps. Following his discharge, he earned a degree in business and had a long, successful career in real estate. He passed away at his home in San Diego on January 23, 2010, at the age of 96.

As for Lockard and Elliott, Lockard was promoted to staff sergeant, awarded the Distinguished Service Medal and early in 1942 was sent to Fort Monmouth, New Jersey, to attend officer candidate school. As a second lieutenant, Lockard went to advanced radar school in Florida and then to Alaska and the Aleutian Islands. After the war, he worked for a railroad and then in the electronics industry, ultimately securing 40 patents.

Elliott didn't fare so well. In the aftermath of the attack, Lockard was given almost complete credit for spotting and reporting the approaching Japanese aircraft. Elliott was initially a footnote to the event until lobbying from senators in 1946 convinced the army to award Elliott the Legion of Merit for his actions, an award he declined, stating that he should not receive a lesser award than Lockard. After the war, Elliott lived in Long Branch, New Jersey, where he worked for New Jersey Bell Telephone for 33 years.

As for Tyler, as he explained in an interview, "I wake up at night and think about it. But I don't feel guilty. I did all I could that morning."

Sources

Goldstein, Richard. "Kermit Tyler, Player of a Fateful, If Minor, Role in Pearl Harbor Attack Dies at 96." *New York Times* February 25, 2010.

McWilliams, Bill. *Sunday in Hell*. New York: Open Road Media, 2014.

National Park Service Oral History 220. http://NPS.gov/vair/learn/historyculture/upload/KermitTyler.pdf.

National WW II Museum. http://www.ww2online.org/view/kermit-tyler/segment-1.

Wels, Susan. *Pearl Harbor: America's Darkest Day*. San Diego: Tehabi Books, 2001.

Edwin P. Ramsey
The Last Horse Cavalry Charge in U.S. Military History

On the morning of January 16, 1942, the United States had been at war a little more than a month, and First Lieutenant Ramsey had his orders. He was to lead his mounted troops, a composite of E and F Troops, 26th Cavalry, west to occupy the village of Morong on the upper west coast of the Bataan Peninsula on the island of Luzon in the Philippines.

The first Japanese troops had landed on the north coast of Luzon on December 10, two days after the attack on the U.S. fleet at Pearl Harbor on December 8, 1941 (December 7 in Hawaii). A second landing of a much larger force of over 43,000 troops of the 48th Division, supported by artillery and 90 tanks, landed at Lingayen Gulf northwest of Manila, the Philippine capital, on December 22.

Slowly, but inexorably, the battle-hardened veterans of Gen. Masaharu Homma advanced toward Manila, pushing back the ill-equipped and poorly trained North Luzon Force, comprised of the 11th and 71st Divisions of the Philippine Army, who seemed unable to repel or contain the Japanese advance.

The 26th Cavalry Regiment PS (Philippine Scouts) was an exception. Formed October 1, 1922, the regiment of native Filipinos, led primarily by American officers, was highly trained and motivated by a high "esprit de corps" and the regiment's motto "Our strength is in loyalty."

Under the command of Col. Clinton A. Pierce, the regiment stood at 52 officers and 784 enlisted men at the outbreak of the war.

On December 24, Gen. Douglas MacArthur, commander in the Philippines, invoked WPO-3 (War Plan Orange 3), which provided for a withdrawal to defensive positions on the Bataan Peninsula.

Lt. Edwin Ramsey, mounted on his charger Bryn Awryn, in the Philippines, circa 1940.

The exodus of the military headquarters and Philippine government as well as 80,000 troops and 26,000 refugees far exceeded the numbers anticipated by the plan and provided for, putting a strain on existing resources and supplies.

Following the first Japanese landings, the 26th Cavalry had aggressively harassed and counter-attacked the advancing Japanese. Skillfully fighting a rearguard action, the regiment delayed and slowed the enemy advance, covering the withdrawal to Bataan, but it paid a high price with the loss of a quarter of the men and half the horses in the first five days of combat.

By December 27, the Japanese 48th Division had the North Luzon Force in full retreat. Fighting mounted and on foot, the 26th worked to slow the pursuit as troops withdrew from south and central Luzon, and they scouted and fought a rearguard action, at one point attacking tanks with gasoline-filled bottles.

On January 2, 1942, the Japanese entered Manila, and by January 6, the withdrawal to Bataan was complete. Exhausted, the regiment rested and refitted, but conditions were harsh, with troops reduced to half rations and little to no forage available for the horses.

It was a holding action, complicated by ever-shrinking stocks of ammunition, food and medicine and shortages of everything else. The 26th was assigned various missions, performing reconnaissance, sleeping little, and being in the saddle almost continuously for a week as the Japanese forces tightened the noose.

On January 16, Gen. Jonathan Wainwright arrived, furious that the First Philippine Division had withdrawn from Morong. He believed the village to be a good defensive position, located south of the Batolan River, the only river remaining between them and the Japanese.

There were reports that the Japanese had landed a force of infantry and tanks at Olongopo and were planning a flanking move toward Mauban.

Wainwright ordered Gen. Fidel Segundo to move forward with the First Division to reoccupy Morong, and the 26th Regiment was tasked with acting as an advance guard to reconnoiter and secure the village until the division could move up into the line.

Wainwright, a cavalryman, noticed Ramsey standing nearby and, recognizing him, called, "You played in the polo match at Stotsenberg?" When Ramsey replied in the affirmative, Wainwright ordered, "You take the advance guard. Move out."

Ramsey had just returned from a two-day reconnaissance, but he saluted wearily and mounted up.

When G Troop had been sent to the rear to rest, Ramsey, who was familiar with the terrain, had volunteered to remain to assist Capt. John Wheeler, now in command of the remains of E and F Troops, who had gratefully accepted the offer. Ramsey was granted permission to stay and detailed to Wheeler's command.

Now in command of 27 troopers of E Troop's First Platoon, Ramsey took the lead, followed by the Second and Third Platoons under Wheeler's command. They advanced in two columns north along the coastal road, a deeply rutted jungle track, thick with dry-season dust, a gray powder that irritated both man and horse.

The men were fatigued, suffering from malaria, dysentery, beriberi and malnutrition, with the horses in even worse condition, but still they stubbornly fought on. Arriving at the eastern edge of Morong, Ramsey halted his men and prepared to enter the village.

At 24, 1st Lt. Edwin Price Ramsey was a good choice to lead the advance. Born in Carlyle, Illinois, on May 9, 1917, Ramsey moved with his family to El Dorado, Kansas, when he was two and then to Wichita at age 12, after the suicide of his father. Spending summers at an uncle's farm in Illinois, Ramsey spent whole days on horseback and was a natural, instinctive horseman.

His sister Nadine, five years older, shared his love of adventure and was one of the first female pilots in Kansas. A stunt-racing pilot, she was the first woman to fly the air mail and would be one of only eight women qualified to fly fighter planes during World War II.

Growing up without a father and with a working mother, Ramsey gained a reputation as "wild," and by age seventeen, he was smuggling moonshine into Wichita. Worried, his mother arranged for him to finish his senior year of high school at the Oklahoma Military Academy (OMA). Motivated both by his desire to get his life back on track and by OMA being a cavalry school, Ramsey agreed.

Ramsey attended OMA for three years, where he excelled on the academy's polo team and graduated in May 1938 with a degree and a reserve commission as a second lieutenant of cavalry. He enrolled at the University of Oklahoma School of Law but had to drop out in September of 1940, his senior year, to care for Nadine, who had been seriously injured in a plane crash. Remarkably, despite a broken back, broken ribs and other injuries, she returned to flying the following February.

With Europe and Asia already at war, and at loose ends, Ramsey traveled to Los Angeles and applied for active duty, and in February 1941, Ramsey reported to the Second Squadron, 11th Cavalry Regiment at Camp Moreno, in the hills above San Diego, California, assigned as a remount officer training draftees and horses.

By 1941, the cavalry was mechanizing, so in April, Ramsey volunteered for transfer to the 26th Cavalry Regiment in the Philippines, primarily because they were rumored to have the best polo team in the entire U.S. Army and not taking into consideration that if war broke out in the Pacific, the Philippines would be the first target of attack.

He reported to the Presidio of San Francisco on June 5, 1941, and embarked the following day aboard the *President Pierce*, a passenger liner converted to a troop ship with 1,500 officers, 3,000 enlisted men and a dozen nurses.

On June 23, the *President Pierce* docked at Manila and those assigned to the 26th were taken to the Army-Navy Club, across the street from the Manila Hotel, where on the fourth floor, Gen. Douglas MacArthur had his quarters.

The Philippines was considered the country club of the U.S. Army, the last vestige of the American colonial army. Officers had native orderlies, starched white dress uniforms were worn to dinner, and cocktails were served on the veranda under a tropic moon. And training for the polo season began in September.

Even as war clouds grew darker on the horizon and Japanese aggression increased, practice continued, along with mounted drill and maneuvers. The opening match, between the 26th and the Manila Polo Club was scheduled for December 7, a clear, sunny day.

General Wainwright kept score, and despite losing the match, the 26th's commanding officer threw a post-match party with plenty of alcoholic beverages and pretty young ladies, and the party stretched into the early hours of the morning.

Ramsey awoke the next morning, hungover, to discover that across the international dateline, in Hawaii, the Japanese had attacked American military installations at Pearl Harbor. America was at war.

Ramsey rushed to regimental headquarters, where General Wainwright ordered Troop G north to move 120 miles northeast to the village of Bongabong in the foothills of the Sierra Madre to relieve Troop B. At noon, just as the convoy was preparing to move out, the Japanese attacked, flying low overhead but ignoring the column for the important targets at Clark Field, destroying the aircraft and damaging the base.

They arrived at Bongabong around sunset, and Ramsey was ordered to take 27 mounted troopers, two machine guns and a staff car with radio to Baler Bay and take command of the local constabulary and organize a defense. They also carried crates of TNT to blow up the mountain bridges as they withdrew.

Although the invasion was expected at any minute, it wasn't until December 17 that Ramsey came under attack as Japanese Zeroes strafed and bombed their position, and air raids continued intermittently until Christmas. On the 26th, he was ordered to withdraw back to Bongabong.

Arriving at Bongabong, Ramsey learned that the Japanese had landed at Lingayen Gulf and that they were advancing on Manila. Troop G had been ordered south to rejoin the regiment, which had suffered heavy casualties in delaying the advance, and Ramsey had found himself almost continuously in action thereafter as U.S. and Filipino forces withdrew to Bataan.

Now, as Ramsey led his platoon into the village of Morong, a community of woven huts and a stone church, they began taking small-arms fire from the center and northern edge of the village. Ramsey saw that a large advance guard of Colonel Yunosuke Watanabe's 122nd Infantry Regiment had already crossed the river into the village center and that an even larger force, the main body numbering in the hundreds was beginning to wade across, Ramsey, clearly outnumbered, did the only thing he could do; he ordered, "Charge!"

Pistols raised, Ramsey and his men galloped into the enemy, sowing panic and confusion and initiating the last horse cavalry charge in U.S. military history.

As he recalled in his 1990 memoir *Lieutenant Ramsey's War*,

> I brought my arm down and yelled to my men to charge. Bent nearly prone across the horses' necks, we flung ourselves at the Japanese advance, pistols firing full into their startled faces. A few returned our fire, but most fled in confusion, some wading back into the river, others running madly for the swamps. To them, we must have seemed a vision from another century, wild-eyed horses pounding headlong; cheering, whooping men firing from the saddles.

The charge broke through the advance force to the swamp where they dismounted and, retrieving their rifles from their scabbards, set up a skirmish line along the river to hold back the main force, while Ramsey took the rest back into Morong to clear the village of snipers. It was a hazardous position; Ramsey's force was between the advance and main Japanese forces and taking fire from both.

Ramsey and his men moved from hut to hut, clearing out the remaining Japanese, even as the main force began lobbing mortar shells into the village, causing casualties to both horses and men.

Captain Wheeler arrived with the other two platoons, sending one forward to reinforce the skirmish line and putting the other to work assisting in clearing the village. The fighting continued until late afternoon, when General Segundo arrived with the First Philippine Division and secured the village.

Only after the battle did Ramsey notice that he had taken a shrapnel wound to the left knee. The troop was ordered to the rear to regroup and receive medical treatment, as well as get much-needed rest. He'd had one trooper killed and six wounded, in addition to losing several horses.

Outnumbered, with no air support, shortages of everything and under a Japanese naval blockade, the situation for the defenders worsened daily as they prayed for the promised relief, but none came, affecting morale.

Ramsey contracted jaundice in early February and was sent to Hospital Two in Mariveles, at the southern end of Bataan, where he remained until the first week in March. While Ramsey was in the hospital, the quartermaster had confiscated the remaining horses and butchered them to supplement the starvation rations.

Ramsey returned to the regiment, which was being held in reserve, and the remainder of G Troop was assigned as security for I Corps Headquarters, under the command of Capt. Joe Barker, a West Point graduate from Alabama.

On March 12, President Roosevelt ordered MacArthur to Australia, leaving General Wainwright in command. Philippine president Manuel Luis Quezon soon followed, as the Japanese rested and consolidated their forces for the final assault.

The resistance at Bataan embarrassed General Homma, destroying the Japanese timetable and extending the anticipated 50 days to over 100 as American and Filipino sailors, airmen and policemen were put into the line, while Japanese troops, fresh from victories in Singapore and Hong Kong arrived to reinforce the invaders.

Sick, starving and exhausted but still defiant, they fought on against increasingly overwhelming odds. As Ramsey recalled, "As far as we knew, we were the Allied war effort in the Pacific, and we would not give up without a fight."

On April 3, General Homma sent a polite note to the Allied commander, requesting that he surrender. When no reply was received, Homma ordered the most massive artillery and air strikes in the war to that point.

On April 6, Wainwright ordered a counterattack, but the line broke and the 26th withdrew to Limay, south of Orion, under constant air attacks as they passed abandoned and destroyed equipment. One attack blew up the truck carrying their remaining ammunition. Another attack killed most of the staff and rearguard.

Surrounded on three sides, the survivors withdrew into the jungle, and Ramsey found himself with Barker and about 60 others cut off from their lines. Ramsey and Barker made a pact not to surrender.

On April 9, the bombing and artillery ceased, and the next morning they learned that Bataan had surrendered. The ranking officer, Major Blanning, said that since they had never received an order to surrender, they were technically missing in action and gave them the option of going into Mariveles and surrendering or breaking into groups and trying to escape. No one chose to surrender. In hindsight, considering the subsequent Bataan Death March, it was a wise choice.

Ramsey and Barker, armed only with .45 automatic pistols, too weak to carry anything heavier, set off for the summit of Mt. Mariveles and were soon joined by Private Gene Strickland of the 31st Infantry Regiment.

The three met up with numerous groups of Americans and Filipinos who had refused to surrender as they made their way north, assisted by local farmers and others. They heard tales of the Bataan Death March and rumors of resistance groups forming in the hills, specifically that Lt. Col. Claude Thorpe, a staff officer with U.S. Army Forces in the Far East and a former cavalryman, was recruiting a guerrilla force in the hills above Fort Stotsenberg.

Weak from hunger, exhausted, and sick with malaria, dysentery and sores, they made their way to the barrio of Timbo, Thorpe's advance camp, but Strickland, weakened, died on April 23. Aware that if captured by the Japanese, they would be considered as criminals and summarily executed, they still refused to surrender, finally making contact with Thorpe's group.

Thorpe was authorized by MacArthur in January 1942 to escape from Bataan and proceed to Mt. Pinatubo, 5,248 feet above sea level, there to organize resistance and provide intelligence. He divided Luzon into four areas of operations; North Luzon, East Central Luzon, Western Luzon and Southern Luzon. Barker was given command of the East Central Luzon Guerrilla Area with Ramsey as his deputy, an area that stretched from Manila north to Lingayen Gulf. The force grew to eventually consist of 3,700 officers and 38,000 enlisted men and women. Barker and Ramsey finally made contact in May 1942.

Engaging in intelligence gathering, sabotage and ambushes, the guerrillas were constantly hunted by the Kempei Tai, the Japanese secret police, and the danger of betrayal was ever present. One by one, most of the commanders were hunted down or betrayed and captured.

Thorpe was captured on October 29, 1942, and with other leaders was held at Fort Santiago in Manila, where he and the others were interrogated, tortured and eventually taken to La Loma cemetery, where they were forced to dig their own graves before being beheaded on November 1, 1943.

Barker, who had traveled to Manila disguised as a priest in December 1942, was betrayed the next month and captured on January 13. He was executed around the same time as Thorpe and the others in late October or early November 1943.

In early 1944, Ramsey, promoted to major, traveled three hundred miles to Mindoro to get a radio so that he could establish direct contact with MacArthur's headquarters. There was no radio, but he was offered to be taken by a U.S. submarine to Australia.

When he declined, he was given a folded piece of paper. "My instructions were to show it to you only if you decided to leave," the person who gave it to him said. He opened the paper and read it. It was a radio signal from MacArthur to Ramsey that read "Request that you return to Luzon and command of your resistance forces." It was signed by General MacArthur himself. Ramsey returned to take command of the guerrilla group. Ramsey evaded capture despite several close calls and being placed at the top of the Kempei Tai's most-wanted list.

In mid-1944, Ramsey and the other guerrillas were ordered to ramp up sabotage against the Japanese in anticipation of the Allied invasion of the Philippines.

On the morning of January 9, 1945, MacArthur's forces landed at Lingayen Gulf, where the Japanese had landed four years before, and on January 31, Ramsey received a message from MacArthur putting all guerrilla forces under the command of Lt. Gen. Walter Krueger's Sixth Army.

For three years, Ramsey had battled both Japanese troops and communist Huk guerrillas, escaped an assassination attempt, underwent an emergency appendectomy without anesthesia, and helped build a resistance network that came to number an estimated quarter million men and women.

On June 13, 1945, MacArthur personally presented Ramsey with the Distinguished Service Cross for, as the citation noted, "extraordinary heroism in connection with military operations against an armed enemy … from 21 April 1942 to 30 April 1945 in the Philippine Islands."

Ramsey was suffering from malaria, amoebic dysentery, anemia, acute malnutrition and fatigue, and MacArthur ordered him home three days later. After almost a year in a stateside hospital, Ramsey, now a lieutenant colonel, was medically retired from the U.S. Army.

He went on to earn a law degree from the University of Oklahoma and had a successful business career with Hughes Aircraft in Manila, Hong Kong, and Tokyo before retiring to Los Angeles, where he died on March 7, 2013, at the age of 95.

Besides the Distinguished Service Cross, Ramsey was awarded a Silver Star and Purple Heart for his actions on January 16, 1942, at Morong, as well as the Philippine Medal of Honor, the Distinguished Conduct Star, and the Distinguished Service Star from the Republic of the Philippines and was recognized with other resistance leaders by the U.S. Army John F. Kennedy Special Warfare Center at Fort Bragg, North Carolina.

SOURCES

Ramsey, Edwin Price, and Stephen J. Rivele. *Lieutenant Ramsey's War–From Horse Soldier to Guerrilla Commander.* Washington, D.C.: Brassey's, 1990.

Seals, Bob. "Lieutenant Colonel Edwin P. Ramsey, USARet." *Soldier Magazine*, Summer 2011.

Stevens, Peter F. *The Twilight Riders: The Last Charge of the 26th Cavalry.* Guilford, CT: Lyons Press, 2011.

Woo, Elaine. "Edwin Ramsey Dies at 95; WWII Army Cavalry Officer in Philippines." *Los Angeles Times*, March 16, 2013. http://www.latimes.com/local/obituaries/la-me-edwin-ramsey-20130317-story.html.

James R. Roosevelt
Second Marine Raider Battalion at Makin Island

At 3:30 a.m. on the morning of August 17, 1942, under cover of darkness, 221 Marines came up onto the decks of the submarines USS *Argonaut* (SS-166) and USS *Nautilus* (SS-168) and began loading into the rubber boats bobbing crazily in the rough seas. They were happy to be in the fresh air, even if it was raining.

Having arrived offshore the previous evening, the men were happy to escape the odorous confines of the sub, many having spent the eight-day cruise from Pearl Harbor violently seasick, and struggled to load weapons, ammunition and themselves into the boats in the high waves.

The 13 officers and 208 enlisted men were the headquarters section and Companies A and B of the Second Marine Raider Battalion, an elite unit of volunteers established to conduct special amphibious operations behind enemy lines, the forerunners of today's special operations troops.

Under the command of Lt. Col. Evans Carlson, the Marines were making a raid on Makin Island in the Gilbert Islands. The mission was unique in many ways. It was the first commando raid launched by submarines and one of the earliest offensive operations conducted by the Marine Corps in the Pacific war. It was the baptism under fire for the Second Marine Raider Battalion. And the battalion's executive officer, Maj. James R. Roosevelt, was the son of the current president, FDR.

James "Jimmy" Roosevelt was born in the family home in New York City on December 23, 1907, the oldest of four boys born to Franklin Delano and Eleanor Roosevelt, members of one of America's most prominent families.

Educated in private schools, he attended Harvard University, where he enrolled in the Naval Reserve Officer Training Corps, graduating in 1930. He entered Boston University School of Law, only to drop out a year later to partner with John A. Sargent to form the rapidly successful Roosevelt and Sargent Insurance Agency.

Roosevelt also became active in politics, playing a major role in his father's successful campaign for the presidency in 1932. When he resigned from the business to take a job in the White House in 1937, the agency was valued at $500,000.

In 1936, Roosevelt was given a direct commission as a lieutenant colonel in the U.S. Marine Corps Reserve, and he served as a military aide to the president during his father's attendance at the Inter-American Conference in Buenos Aires, Argentina in December 1936.

On January 6, 1937, Roosevelt was appointed as an administrative assistant to the president and on July 1 of that year he was promoted to secretary to the president. By October, he was overseeing 18 federal agencies.

Roosevelt's time in the White House was marked by scandal and accusations that he was using his political position for financial gain. Despite his denials and making his tax returns public, he resigned from the White House in November 1938.

Moving to Hollywood, California, Roosevelt took a position as a personal assistant to studio head Samuel Goldwyn at MGM Studios, where he remained until November 1940, setting up his own production company, Globe Productions, in 1939.

In September 1939, war broke out in Europe, and on October 3, possibly because of public criticism regarding his commission as a lieutenant colonel, Roosevelt resigned his commission, taking instead a commission as a captain in the Marine Reserves on November 24, 1939.

On November 7, 1940, Roosevelt was called up for extended active duty when his unit was mobilized, and he commanded an artillery battery in the Second Battalion, Tenth Marine Regiment, Second Marine Division at Camp Elliott, California. He was present when his father was sworn in for his third term as president on January 20, 1941.

Shortly thereafter, FDR called his oldest son to the White House for a meeting in which he told James that he was sending him on a secret mission. Ostensibly, he would be accompanying Marine Maj. Gerald Thomas to the Orient and the Middle East to report on the state of military preparedness of various Allied nations.

The real purpose, unknown even to Major Thomas, would be to assure the leaders of those countries that the United States, although officially neutral, would do everything it could to support those countries already at war, a message FDR hoped to keep secret from his isolationist critics in the Congress and the press.

Roosevelt married his second wife, Romelle Theresa Schneider, on April 14, 1941, and three days later he and Major Thomas departed San Diego aboard a Clipper to Hawaii to begin their mission.

The tour would take him from Hawaii to the Philippines, China, Burma, India, Iraq, Crete, Palestine and North Africa, and during the course of his "inspections," Roosevelt met with Chiang Kai-shek in China; King Farouk of Egypt; King George of Greece; King Peter of Yugoslavia; Sir John McMichael, the high commissioner of Palestine; and Abdul, the regent of Iraq. He also held meetings with senior British military officers like Gen. William Slim in Basra, Iraq; Vice Marshal Arthur Tedder and Gen. Sir Archibald Wavell in Cairo, Egypt; Free French general Charles de Gaulle; and Captain, Lord Louis Mountbatten in Lisbon, Portugal.

During the tour, Roosevelt and Thomas came under hostile fire, including an air raid while visiting Chungking on April 29 and when German paratroops invaded Crete on May 20, 1941. Roosevelt evacuated with British forces aboard a Sunderland flying boat. On May 26, a car he was riding in was strafed by German fighters.

As the Australian newspaper the *Examiner* reported on May 27,

> The British United Press correspondent at Cairo says apparently the Germans made a dead set to get President Roosevelt's son, Captain James Roosevelt, who is visiting Iraq.
> Twice at Habbanlyah, German planes attacked Captain Roosevelt's car. The first time three Heinkels swooped and rained bombs on the car, which was forced to turn back and dash to safety. Later four Messerschmitts dived to 200 feet, spraying machine-gun bullets around the car. Roosevelt jumped out, ducked, and flung himself flat on the sand.

By June 23, Roosevelt and Thomas were back in Washington, D.C. Major Thomas made his report to Admiral Harold Stark, chief of naval operations and Gen. Thomas Holcomb, commandant of the Marine Corps, and Captain Roosevelt reported to his father.

In August 1941, Roosevelt was assigned as military liaison to the Office of the Coordinator of Information working for the director, William J. "Wild Bill" Donovan, a lawyer who was awarded the Medal of Honor as a major with the Fighting 69th during World War I. A personal friend of FDR, Donovan would later serve as director of the Office of Strategic Services, precursor of the Central Intelligence Agency (CIA), during World War II.

Following the Japanese sneak attack on the U.S. naval fleet at Pearl Harbor on December 7, 1941, Roosevelt requested to be assigned with the troops, and on December 19, Roosevelt and his wife departed for the West Coast, returning to Camp Elliott and the Second Marine Division.

At Camp Elliott, Roosevelt was reacquainted with another Marine officer, Maj. Evans F. Carlson with whom he had become friends when Carlson was the executive officer of the Marine security detail guarding the presidential retreat at Warm Springs, Georgia.

The two discovered they shared an interest in unconventional warfare and special operations behind enemy lines, similar to the British commandos and the Chinese Eighth Route Army. They advocated for the United States to develop such a unit, an idea supported by Admirals Chester Nimitz and Ernest J. King, William Donovan and the president himself although not enthusiastically embraced by the upper ranks of the Marine Corps.

In a letter to the commandant on January 13, 1942, Captain Roosevelt strongly advocated for a Marine unit that could conduct guerrilla operations behind enemy lines. Titled "Development within the Marine Corps of a Unit for Purposes Similar to the British Commandos and Chinese Guerrillas," the proposal outlined Carlson's ideas, including dispensing with conventional rank structure in favor of the more democratic terms of "leader" and "fighter" and suggesting that "discipline should be based on reason and designed to foster individual volition."

Such unorthodox ideas were not warmly received by the Marine leadership, who nonetheless were powerless to oppose the president's desires.

On January 23, 1942, General Holcomb authorized the formation of Marine Raider units, with the First Marine Raider Battalion formed on the East Coast, on February 16, with Lt. Col. Merritt Edson in command and the Second Marine Raider Battalion formed on the West Coast three days later, on February 19, under the command of Maj. Evans Carlson.

Carlson's background made him both an ideal candidate for that command and a concern to his superior officers. He was not the traditional career Marine officer.

Born February 26, 1896, in Sidney, New York, the son of a Congregationalist minister, Carlson ran away from home when he was 14 and lied about his age to enlist in the U.S. Army in 1912 at age 16, serving in the Philippines and Hawaii. He was discharged as a first sergeant in 1916 but almost immediately reenlisted to chase Pancho Villa as part of the Mexican Punitive Expeditionary Force under Brig. Gen. John J. "Black Jack" Pershing.

Carlson went overseas to France during World War I, serving with the American Expeditionary Force, where he was wounded in combat. He was promoted to second lieutenant in May 1917 and to captain that December.

Carlson served with the Army of Occupation in Germany until his discharge in 1921. After an unsuccessful stint as a salesman, Carlson reenlisted, this time as a private in the Marine Corps in 1922 and was commissioned a second lieutenant the following year.

He served in Shanghai, China, from 1927 to 1929, and then was sent to Nicaragua in 1930 where he was awarded the Navy Cross for leading 12 Marines in a night attack on 100 bandits. He would subsequently be awarded the Navy Cross two more times, at Makin Island and Guadalcanal. He was commended for his actions following the 1931 earthquake at Managua and for his performance as chief of police in 1932 and 1933.

After serving at Warm Springs, Carlson was sent back to China as an intelligence officer with the Fourth Marines in Shanghai and later was with the Marine detachment of the American legation in Peiping (today's Beijing), China, where he served as adjutant and studied the Chinese language.

In 1936, he returned to the States to attend Marine Corps schools in Quantico and study international law and politics at George Washington University in Washington, D.C.

Carlson returned to China for the third time in 1937 as a military observer with Chinese forces, where he had the opportunity to learn the tactics of the Japanese soldier.

He visited the Chinese communist troop headquarters in northern China, where he met Chinese communist leaders such as Mao Zedong, Zhou Enlai and Deng Xiaoping. Traveling through the interior of China with the communist guerrillas, often on foot and horseback, he lived under the same primitive conditions.

Impressed by the tactics used by Chinese communist guerrillas, Carlson often expressed left-wing political views, prompting Gen. David M. Shoup to observe, "He may be red, but he's not yellow."

Carlson was so concerned about the danger of Japanese aggression in the Far East that he resigned his commission in 1939 to be able to speak freely, going on speaking tours and appearing on radio programs. In April of 1941, realizing that war with Japan was imminent, Carlson reapplied to the Marine Corps and was commissioned a major in the reserves.

Now in command of the Second Raider Battalion, he selected Roosevelt to be his executive officer and set about putting his ideas into practice. In the process, he created a Marine Corps legend.

The Raiders were designed to be a flexible, mobile force capable of maximum firepower. To accomplish the latter, the battalion was organized into a headquarters company and four companies, A, B, C, and D, each comprising ten-man squads. Each squad would consist of three fire teams of three men each and an NCO.

Unlike conventional Marine squads, which early in the war were armed with one Browning automatic rifle and eight Springfield bolt-action rifles, each Raider squad was armed with three Thompson submachine guns, three Brownings and six of the new M-1 Garand rifles. This gave a Raider squad a tremendous amount of mobile firepower. Carlson would later admit that having the president's son as his executive officer had certain logistical advantages.

Carlson and Roosevelt personally interviewed over 500 volunteers, seeking candidates that were physically in top condition and mentally tough to carry the fight to the Japanese. Over 8,078 men, including 368 sailors, would become Raiders during the war, and of them, seven would receive Medals of Honor and 136 received the Navy Cross.

The Second Raiders underwent intensive physical conditioning as well as weapons and close-combat training and from March 25 until April 18, 1942, participated in amphibious training exercises off San Clemente Island. Two additional companies, E and F, were organized at Camp Elliott on April 1.

On May 8, the battalion departed San Diego for Pearl Harbor, Hawaii Territory, aboard the USS *J. Franklin Bell* (APA-16) arriving May 18. Three days later, Companies C and D departed for the Midway islands and were present for the air and sea battles there, June 4–7.

On August 8, Companies A and B and a headquarters component boarded the submarines *Argonaut* and *Nautilus*, headed for the Gilbert Islands and a raid on the Makin Atoll. Makin, now known as Butaritari, is a tiny triangular atoll at the northern tip of the Gilbert Islands, located just north of the equator, between Hawaii and Papua New Guinea.

The raid's objectives included destroying a seaplane base located there, taking prisoners, gathering intelligence on the Gilbert Islands, and most important, diverting Japanese troops from the American invasion of Guadalcanal.

The submarines traveled submerged for the majority of the trip, surfacing only for brief periods, and the inadequate ventilation and high temperatures made the cramped voyage especially unpleasant.

There were high winds and the seas were rough as the Marines struggled to load their LCRLs (landing craft rubber, large), inflatable boats that could carry ten men. The first two boats, loaded with several machineguns and medical supplies, were lost in the high waves. The small outboard motors had swamped and failed to start. Worse, the sub commanders advised Carlson that the tide was moving the subs toward the reef, and they would have to withdraw, making the planned assembly before departure impossible.

The plan was changed to one, rather than two landing sites, but Lt. Oscar Peatross, the B Company commander, and 11 Raiders didn't get the word and landed on the western side of the island, separated from the main force about a mile away. Paddling through the rough surf, 18 boats containing the exhausted Raiders made shore at 5:30 a.m. They quickly concealed the boats with sand and palm fronds. Two boats landed north of the main party.

As they reorganized on shore, the element of surprise was lost when PFC Vern Mitchell of A Company accidentally fired his Browning automatic rifle. Company A advanced with Company B following in reserve.

Sources disagree as to the number and type of Japanese troops garrisoning the island. Naval intelligence had briefed the Raiders that the number could be as high as 250. Friendly natives advised Carlson that the garrison numbered 75–200. Most current sources place the number between 71 and 75, made up of mostly seaplane support personnel and a detachment of 43 Special Naval Landing Force Marines under the command of Sergeant Major Kamemitsu. All sources agree they were alerted to the Raiders' presence and they radioed for reinforcements.

As the Raiders advanced inland, first contact was made shortly after dawn, at about 6:30 by 2nd Lt. Wilfred S. LeFrancois's First Platoon, A Company.

Advancing down the Lagoon Road in a V formation, they moved toward the native hospital, clearing every hut and building along the way. A truck carrying approximately 20 Japanese soldiers stopped 300 yards down the road, and the men jumped out, planted a flag, and moved into the surrounding brush and undergrowth on both sides of the road. More Japanese arrived on foot.

Sgt. Clyde Thomason deployed his squad into a horseshoe formation to ambush the oncoming Japanese.

The Japanese advanced across open ground with fixed bayonets straight into Sergeant Thomason's ambush, a deadly, well-prepared killing ground. After Thomason opened fire with his shotgun, the whole platoon opened fire with Thompsons, Brownings and rifles, killing most of the oncoming Japanese. A Boys anti-tank gunner destroyed the truck engine with one shot.

About the same time, a 3,500-ton troop transport, carrying 60 reinforcements, and a small patrol boat entered the lagoon. Carlson radioed the subs requesting that they surface and engage the boats with their six-inch deck guns.

In an extraordinary feat of marksmanship, or blind luck, the *Nautilus*, shooting blindly and using only compass bearings radioed by Carlson, sank both vessels.

As the Raiders moved inland, they met stiff resistance from snipers and machine-gun teams, stalling the advance. It took Second Platoon, B Company, over 30 minutes to swing right and flank the machine-gun positions and destroy them, taking casualties, including nine killed, in the process.

Sniper fire continued to be a problem, pinning down the Raiders until almost 11:30 a.m. At one point, Sergeant Thomason exposed himself to draw fire away from his men and was killed by a sniper's bullet, actions for which he would later be awarded a posthumous Medal of Honor, the first Marine in World War II to be so honored.

At about that time, accompanied by shouts of "Banzai" and bugles, the Japanese charged the Raiders in what would become known as the Battle for the Breadfruit Trees, but the Raiders' superior firepower decimated their ranks, and a second Banzai charge proved no more successful. Although Carlson was unaware of it, he had killed most of the Japanese garrison on the island.

Elsewhere, Lieutenant Peatross and his 11 men found themselves isolated from the main body and unable to make radio contact, so he sent two runners to make contact with Carlson, both arriving to advise him of Peatross's disposition. But Carlson sent no runner back with additional orders. In the meantime, Peatross's Raiders had engaged and killed eight Japanese soldiers, including Sergeant Major Kamemitsu, the garrison commander.

Peatross moved his men closer toward the Japanese positions, killing eight more Japanese and destroying the radio station and a moving vehicle, while losing three killed and two wounded, all the time keeping pressure on the Japanese rear. Peatross would subsequently be awarded the Navy Cross.

All through the day, Carlson moved back and forth between the command post and the front lines, while Roosevelt remained at the command post, coordinating care to the wounded at a makeshift aid station and maintaining communication between the Marine units and the submarines.

On one occasion, when snipers infiltrated the command post area, Roosevelt returned fire, and was wounded slightly when a bullet grazed his finger, for which he would later reject the award of a Purple Heart.

At about 11:30 a.m., two Japanese Nakajima E8N "Dave" reconnaissance aircraft, a single-engine, two-seat biplane, flew over the island, circling for 15 minutes before dropping two bombs and departing. No Raiders were injured.

Having submerged during the air attack, the *Nautilus* surfaced at 12:55, only to pick up a large number of planes approaching on radar. It tried unsuccessfully to raise the Raiders by radio before submerging again.

At 1:20 p.m., a flight of 12 aircraft consisting of four Kawanishi E7K Type 94 "Alf" reconnaissance float planes, two Nakajima E8N Type 95 "Dave" seaplanes, two Kawanishi H8K "Emily" flying boats and four Mitsubishi A6M Type 0 "Zero" fighters attacked the island, bombing and strafing for 70 minutes, again with no U.S. casualties.

Attempting to reinforce the garrison, two aircraft attempted to land in the lagoon off Kings Wharf and were greeted by intense machine-gun and Boys anti-tank rifle fire from A Company. A Dave seaplane burst into flames as it taxied in, quickly sinking. Trying to avoid a collision, the Emily flying boat tried to pull up too sharply, stalled, and crashed into the lagoon, exploding into flames. Opinions differ as to whether any Japanese troops made it to shore.

The plan called for Carlson's Raiders to rendezvous with the subs after 6:30 p.m. but not later than 9 p.m., and given that he had no idea how many of the enemy remained and certain that they'd be reinforced the following morning, Carlson ordered the men to prepare to withdraw back to the beach.

Japanese aircraft returned at 4 p.m., but the Raiders' withdrawal had caused the Japanese to advance, and they fell victim to friendly fire when the planes bombed the Raiders' former positions for 30 minutes.

At 5 p.m., Carlson sent men to the beach to prepare the LCRLs as the Raiders began pulling back. The withdrawal was orderly. Carlson and Roosevelt said goodbye to the natives who had helped them and arranged with the police chief, a native named Joseph Miller, to have the dead Raiders buried.

By 7:15, leaving a small guard force to cover the withdrawal, 18 boats went into the water, with those on either flank entering the water first. The plan was that under cover of darkness and with high tide, the subs could come closer to the shore, making it easier for the Raiders to reach the subs.

What wasn't planned for was the rapid succession of breaker waves and high surf, which capsized the boats, spilling men, equipment and weapons into the roiling water, and after several hours of struggle, many of the boats were forced back to shore, the survivors exhausted, half naked and in many cases, without weapons.

Lieutenant Peatross, unable to contact Carlson, had returned with eight Raiders to the *Argonaut* in late afternoon. Of the 18 boats of the main force, four boats carrying 53 Raiders made it to the *Nautilus*, and three boats carrying 27 Raiders made it to the *Argonaut*.

The remaining Raiders, including Carlson and Roosevelt, were stranded on the island, so they prepared a defensive line with their few weapons and set in for a long, cold rainy night. One controversy that continues, with differing accounts, is whether Carlson attempted to surrender to the Japanese. It is almost certain it was considered. That task was complicated by the fact that, unknown to Carlson, they had killed almost the entire garrison and there were no Japanese to surrender to.

At 7:40 a.m. on August 18, the captain of the *Argonaut* sent two reserve landing boats ashore to assist with the extraction, carrying five Marine volunteers and all the available arms they could gather. He also sent a message to the Marines that they would remain indefinitely until all the men were extracted. They would submerge during the day to avoid air attacks and surface at 7:30 the following night after dark.

While the two boats headed for shore, four boats managed to get through the surf to the two submarines, including several wounded and Major Roosevelt, but Japanese planes arrived as they were unloading and began attacking, forcing the *Argonaut* into a crash dive.

As the *Argonaut*'s captain, Lt. Cmdr. John Pierce, later recalled, "Roosevelt was the last man out of the boat and had just barely gotten his tail feathers down when the first Jap plane came over and the *Argonaut* had to go under. If the plane had appeared fifteen or twenty seconds earlier, I'm afraid Major Jimmie would have been swimming around in the Pacific."

The planes strafed the volunteers' boat, but one man managed to get his message through to Carlson by swimming to shore. The submarines remained submerged throughout the day.

Waiting for darkness, Carlson sent out patrols who counted 83 enemy dead. Their bodies were searched for papers and weapons to rearm themselves. Two additional snipers were killed during the day.

At dusk, Carlson signaled the subs to pick them up in the lagoon at

9:30 p.m., and after lashing the remaining boats to two native outriggers, the 70 remaining Raiders were aboard the subs by midnight.

Casualties for the two days of fighting totaled 51, with 18 killed in combat, seven drowned in the surf, 14 wounded and 12 missing.

The subs departed for Pearl Harbor, splitting the 14 wounded evenly between the two subs with all 14 surviving, and they returned on August 26 to a hero's welcome. The raid made headlines across the world, and the Raiders were hailed as national heroes, the raid a resounding success.

Besides Thomason's Medal of Honor, 23 Navy Crosses were awarded, including to Carlson and Roosevelt. Five of the awards were posthumous. A movie based on the raid, *Gung Ho*, was produced in 1943, starring Randolph Scott and Robert Mitchum.

Modern historians have been less generous in assessing the success of the mission. Critics claim that while most of the garrison was killed, no prisoners were taken, no significant intelligence was obtained, and few resources were diverted from the Solomon Islands. Additionally, the island's garrison and fortifications were strengthened, making a subsequent invasion necessary and more difficult.

Lt. Col. Evans F. Carlson and Maj. James Roosevelt with captured Japanese flag upon return from Makin Island raid (National Museum of the Marine Corps).

Champions point out that the raid destroyed the island's seaplane base and radio station, field-tested new strategies and tactics, including insertion by submarine, and was a tremendous boost to American morale.

Most disturbing was the subsequent discovery that nine of the 12 missing Marines were inadvertently left behind in the confusion of the withdrawal:

Sgt. Robert V. Allard, Sgt. Dallas H. Cook, Cpl. Joseph Gifford, PFC Richard E. Davis, PFC Richard N. Olbert, PFC William E. Pallesen, Pvt. John I. Kerns, Pvt. Alden O. Mattison, and Pvt. Donald R. Robertson. Five of them, Allard, Cook, Kerns, Olbert and Robinson would be awarded the Navy Cross.

Despite the Japanese heavily reinforcing the island with 1,000 men the following day, the nine managed to evade capture for nearly a month. After their capture, the nine were transported to Kwajalein. The initial plan had been to send them to Japan for incarceration.

But Vice Adm. Koso Abe, commander of all Marshall Island bases, claiming orders from Japanese central authorities, told navy Capt. Yoshio Obara, commander of Kwajalein, "From now on, it will not be necessary to transport prisoners to Japan. They will be disposed of locally [in Kwajalein]."

Obara stated at his subsequent trial that he refused to execute the nine Raiders until Abe threatened his life. The execution was set for mid-October as part of the Yasakuni Shrine Festival, a Japanese holiday honoring departed heroes.

Obara ordered his military-police chief, Cmdr. Hiusakichi Naiki, to carry out the executions. Naiki tried to persuade Obara not to carry out the executions but Obara would not yield, and on the morning of October 16, 1942, the nine prisoners were blindfolded and had their hands tied behind their backs. They were then taken to the southern edge of the island.

After Abe and Obara arrived, in full uniform, each Raider was led, one at a time, to an open pit and ordered to kneel. Each man was then beheaded by sword and dumped into the hole.

A war crimes commission in Guam later found the trio guilty of "violation of the law and custom of war and the moral standards of civilized society." Abe was hanged, while Obara and Naiki were sentenced to prison.

The first American to become aware of the fate of the nine Raiders was 1st Lt. Louis Zamparini, a downed B-24 bombardier and former Olympic athlete who was briefly detained on Kwajalein, nicknamed "Execution Island" by U.S. Army Air Force (AAF) airmen. Held in the same cell, he'd seen their names carved in the wall and reported it to military authorities after being liberated in September 1945.

Following the Makin raid, the Second Raiders returned to Pearl Harbor and rested until embarking on September 6, 1942, aboard the USS *Wharton* (AP-7) and arriving at Espiritu Santo Island, New Hebrides Islands, on September 12.

Roosevelt would not be with Carlson when the Raiders made their legendary "long march" on Guadalcanal in November. Ordered home in October and promoted to lieutenant colonel, Roosevelt took over command of the newly formed Fourth Raider Battalion on October 23.

The battalion trained through the remainder of 1942 and spent two weeks aboard navy vessels practicing amphibious landings January 10–25. On February 9, the Fourth Raiders embarked the USS *President Polk* (APA-103), at San Diego, and arrived at Espiritu Santo Island on March 1, 1943.

While training for the upcoming assault on New Georgia, Roosevelt was hospitalized with malaria and turned over command to his executive officer, Maj. James R. Clark, on April 28, before being evacuated stateside.

Recovering, Roosevelt was back in the Pacific by August, assigned as an intelligence officer on the staff of Vice Admiral R. K. Turner, commander amphibious forces, Pacific.

Roosevelt returned to Makin Island in November, going ashore as an observer attached to the 165th Regimental Combat Team, 27th Infantry Division, during the battle to capture the island, November 20–23. He was awarded a Silver Star for "accompanying the landing elements of the assault, exposing himself to constant danger" and "voluntarily (seeking) the scene of the heaviest fighting."

Promoted to colonel on April 13, 1944, Roosevelt was present for the campaign to retake the Philippines late in 1944 and at the invasion of Okinawa in April 1945. Roosevelt was discharged from active duty on August 13, 1945, after 26 months of combat duty, but he remained in the reserves until he retired on October 1, 1959, being advanced to brigadier general upon his retirement.

Returning to California after the war, Roosevelt was heavily involved in politics, running for governor in 1950 and losing to Republican Earl Warren by a 30 percent margin, but he was elected to Congress in 1954 from California's 26th District, serving six terms, during which he denounced the tactics of Senator Joseph McCarthy. He also unsuccessfully ran for mayor of Los Angeles in 1965.

He was a successful businessman and author in his later years and was the last surviving child of Franklin and Eleanor Roosevelt, dying from complications from a stroke on August 13, 1991, in Newport Beach, California at the age of 83.

But what became of the 18 dead and 12 missing Raiders? That nine of the missing Raiders later were executed by the Japanese on Kwajelein Island leaves 21 unaccounted for. The 18 killed in action and remaining three missing in action Marines were reportedly buried in a mass grave by island natives after the Japanese returned to the island. The Marines by tradition never abandon their dead.

No bodies of the raiding force were recovered when U.S. forces returned to capture the island in 1943. In 1949, an effort by a Marine Graves Registration team to locate and recover the bodies of the missing Marines proved equally unsuccessful. They remained missing, but not forgotten.

The families of the missing Marines, assisted by the U.S. Marine Raider Association kept the issue alive, putting pressure on Congress and the Pentagon.

In August 1998, a team from the army's Central Identification Laboratory, Hawaii, sent to Butaritari Island (formerly Makin Atoll), was unable to locate the burial site. Nor was a second attempt in May 1999 any more successful.

Whether from fate or good fortune, an identification team being sent to Vietnam was diverted to Butaritari Island in November 1999. They located a witness, Bureimora Tokarei, who as a 16-year-old youth had assisted with the burial of the dead Raiders. With his assistance, the site was located and excavated. The remains of 19 identified and one unidentified Marine were sent to the identification laboratory in Hawaii for confirmation and were returned to American soil on December 17, 1999.

The Hawaii lab began an exhaustive forensic identification process, including the use of mitochondrial DNA, to confirm the identities of 19 Marines.

The recovered remains were those of Capt. Gerald P. Holtom, Sgt. Clyde Thomason, Fireman 1st Class Vernon L. Castle, Cpl. I. B. Earles, Cpl. Daniel A. Gaston, Cpl. Harris J. Johnson, Cpl. Kenneth K. Kunkle, Cpl. Edward Maciejewski, Cpl. Robert B. Pearson, Cpl. Mason O. Yarbrough, PFC William A. Gallagher, PFC Ashley W. Hicks, PFC Kenneth M. Montgomery, PFC Norman W. Mortensen, PFC John E. Vandenberg, Pvt. Carlyle O. Larson, Pvt. Robert B. Maulding, Pvt. Franklin M. Nodland, and Pvt. Charles A. Selby. The identity of the 20th remains is unconfirmed.

On August 16, 2001, the remains of 13 of the Raiders arrived at Andrews Air Force Base, Maryland, for transport to Arlington National Cemetery.

Evans C. Carlson was present to welcome 13 of the Raiders home, and he was helped up from his wheelchair by a female Marine sergeant and his daughter, Karen Carlson Loving, to come to attention as an honor guard unloaded the caskets.

The following day, August 17, 2001, the 59th anniversary of the Makin raid, the 13 Raiders were finally laid to rest at Arlington. A horse-drawn caisson carried a casket containing the remains of the Raider whom forensic experts were unable to identify. Six others would be buried by their families in private ceremonies.

The Marine Band led the procession, playing "Onward Christian Soldiers." Earlier, at the Fort Myer Chapel, Gen. James L. Jones, commandant of the Marine Corps, had delivered a eulogy and the chaplain of the U.S. Marine Raider Association offered a prayer. Taps was played as the caskets were lowered into the ground, the flags folded and presented to family members, and a 21-gun salute was fired. The flag from the casket of the unknown was folded and given to Jones.

Perhaps the best summary of the Raiders was provided by 81-year-old Capt. Joe Griffith, the battalion's only living officer, who stated, "They were good men, and volunteers who did something over and above the call of duty."

Sources

Arlington National Cemetery. "World War II Marine Raiders Home at Last." http://arlingtoncemetery.net/raiders-1942.htm.
Haughey, David W. "Carlson's Raid on Makin Island." *Marine Corps Gazette*, August 2001.
Houseknecht, Stephen Mark. "The Elite of the Elites: The U.S. Marine Raider Battalions, 1942–1944: A Case Study in Elite Military Organizations." Missouri State University, Summer 2015. https://bearworks.missouristate.edu/cgi/viewcontent.cgi?article=2174&context=theses.
Karig, Walter, and Eric Purdon. "The Makin Island Raid at 70." U.S. Naval Institute. http://news.usni.org/2012/08/16/makin-island-raid-70.
Mortimer, Gavin. *The Daring Dozen: 12 Special Forces Legends of World War II*. London: Bloomsbury Publishing, 2012.
Perlman, Jeffrey. "Obituary: James Roosevelt, Son of F.D.R. Dies at 83." *Los Angeles Times*, August 14, 1991.
Persico, Joseph E. *Roosevelt's Secret War: FDR and World War II Espionage*. New York: Random House, 2002.
Schultz, Duane. "The Maverick Marine: Evans Carlson Led America's First Special Operations Force." *WW II History Magazine*, February 2015.
Shirer, Patrick. "The Makin Raid of 1942 and the Recovery of the Marines Lost After the Battle." https://www.military-history.us/2014/02/the-makin-raid-of-1942-and-the-recovery-of-the-marines-lost-after-the-battle/.
Wukovics, John F. *American Commando: Evans Carlson, His WW II Marine Raiders, and America's First Special Forces Mission*. New York: NAL Caliber Pub., 2009.

Douglas Munro
Only Coast Guard Medal of Honor

On Sunday, September 27, 1942, Coast Guard Signalman First Class Douglas Munro was returning to the Lunga Point Base, the former Lever Brothers coconut plantation now being used as a staging area for troops and supplies for operations on Guadalcanal and home to a pool of landing craft.

Munro, weeks short of his 23rd birthday, was leading a group of LCPs (Landing Craft Personnel) and LCTs (Landing Craft Tanks) when he learned that Marines he had just dropped off were being attacked by an overwhelming force of Japanese troops and needed to be withdrawn. Without hesitation, Munro volunteered to lead the rescue effort.

It is altogether appropriate to Coast Guard tradition that the only Medal of Honor awarded to a member of the Coast Guard should be awarded to Munro for his actions involved in an amphibious rescue operation. Saving lives was why he'd joined the Coast Guard.

Douglas Albert Munro was born in Vancouver, British Columbia, Canada, on October 11, 1919. The family moved to Cle Elum, Washington, where Munro grew up. He graduated from Cle Elum High School in 1937 and briefly attended Central Washington University before enlisting in the U.S. Coast Guard on September 18, 1939.

Seaman Recruit Munro (serial no. 217739) was trained as a signalman and first served on the Coast Guard vessel USCGC *Spencer*, a treasury-class cutter, which was involved primarily in search and rescue operations off the coast of Alaska.

Primarily tasked with rescue and revenue enforcement (anti-smuggling) operations before the war, the Coast Guard mission underwent a transformation after America's entry into the war.

In June 1941, with war on the horizon, President Roosevelt ordered the Coast Guard to man four large transports and serve as part of the crew aboard 22 naval ships. By the end of World War II, Coast Guardsmen would serve on 350 ships including transports, tankers, and cargo and attack cargo ships and frigates. Additionally, they manned over 800 cutters and 300 army ships, but perhaps the most vital Coast Guard contribution was in the area of amphibious operations, serving as crew aboard hundreds of amphibious craft.

Critical to the success of any amphibious assault is the operation of the numerous small crafts used to transport the assault troops, and later supplies and reinforcements, into the combat area and evacuate the wounded. A variety of small crafts were used including LCVPs (landing craft, vehicle, personnel), LVTs (landing vehicle, tracked), and LSTs.

Signalman First Class Douglas Munro (U.S. Coast Guard photograph).

Operating these small craft in the surf was a specialized skill not common in the navy. On the other hand, the Coast Guard coxswains were experienced in handling small craft from duty at lifesaving stations, skilled in maneuvering through heavy surf, reefs, sandbars and strong currents. They initially served as instructors for navy coxswains and operated small craft in combat.

In June of 1941, Munro had volunteered for service with the fleet and was assigned to the USS *Hunter Liggett* (APA-14) a 535-foot, 13,712-ton troop transport with a crew of 700 and a complement of 35 landing craft. In April of 1942, the Lucky Liggett sailed for Wellington, New Zealand, in preparation for operations in the Solomon Islands.

On August 7, 1942, the Marines landed and began the battle for Guadalcanal, a battle that would last until the island was secured on February 9, 1943. The action was necessary to counter Japanese advances in the Solomon Islands. It was the first major American amphibious assault, and the first major participation by the Coast Guard in the Pacific theater.

In August, Munro, now a signalman first class was attached to the staff of Rear Admiral Richmond Kelly Turner aboard the USS *McCawley* (APA-4) and saw action landing on Tulagi.

On September 27, Munro found himself petty officer in charge of ten LCVPs, which were known as Higgins boats. They landed three companies of the First Battalion of Lt. Col. Lewis "Chesty" Puller's Seventh Marine Regiment, unopposed, west of Point Cruz, hoping to expand the defensive perimeter, and cross the Matanikau River. The plan was to drive off the Japanese and establish a base on the west side of the Matanikau.

The USS *Monssen* (DD-436), a Gleaves-class destroyer supporting the landing, laid down a covering barrage with its five-inch guns at about noon, and Maj. Ortho L. Rodgers, in command, landed his Marines in two waves at 1:00 p.m. By 1:50, they had advanced to a ridge, Hill 84, about 600 yards from the beach.

From that point on, things turned bad. Col. Akinosuke Oka, recognizing the significance of this landing, ordered his forces to close on Rodgers's Marines from both the west and east. The Marines found themselves isolated in an area west of the Matanikau River, when they were attacked by overwhelming numbers of Japanese troops, even as a Japanese bombing raid forced the *Monssen* to withdraw, depriving them of their naval support.

Things got worse after Rodgers was killed by a mortar shell and one of the company commanders was wounded. Capt. Charles Kelley took over command and deployed the Marines in a perimeter defense around the ridge. The Marines on Hill 84 were without radio communication and thus could not call for help.

Improvising, the Marines used their white undershirts to spell out the word "H-E-L-P" on the ridge. A Cactus Air Force pilot, 2nd Lt. Dale Leslie, flying support in a Douglas SBD Dauntless dive bomber from Henderson Field, spotted the undershirt message and relayed the message to commanders by radio. A rescue mission to extract the trapped Marines was hastily put together, and Munro, just returning from delivering the Marines, volunteered to lead the rescue effort. He took charge of a group of two dozen Higgins landing craft attempting to evacuate the trapped Marines.

The Higgins boat, at just over 36 feet long and just under 11 feet wide, was not a large craft. Powered by a 225-horsepower diesel engine for a top speed of 12 knots, it would sway in choppy seas, causing seasickness, and its plywood sides and rear offered limited protection from enemy fire. The Higgins boat could hold either a 36-man platoon, or a jeep and a 12-man squad, or 8,000 pounds of cargo. Its shallow draft enabled it to run up onto the shore

Munro, supported by the *Monssen*, now with Puller aboard and laying down supporting fire, initially closed on the beach with five boats, under constant enemy fire, and then signaled the other boats to land while he placed his boat between the enemy and the evacuating, heavily laden boats, drawing enemy fire. Under intense enemy fire, Munro directed the evacuation while he and Petty Officer Raymond Evans, supported by the *Monssen* and Lieutenant Leslie's Dauntless, provided covering fire from the boats' .30-caliber Lewis machine guns. The boats' position provided physical cover but at great risk.

Although some accounts have Munro surviving until the last Marine was evacuated, with his dying words being, "Did they get off?" his Medal of Honor citation indicates that Munro was instantly killed by enemy fire just prior to completion of the evacuation, with his wounded crew carrying on until the last man was cleared from the beach.

Munro was posthumously awarded the Medal of Honor, becoming the first and only Coast Guardsman to receive the award. The navy named a destroyer escort in his honor, the USS *Douglas A. Munro* (DE-422), commissioned July 11, 1944, and it served with distinction for the remainder of World War II and during the Korean War before being decommissioned on June 24, 1960.

After his death, Munro's mother, Edith Fairey Munro, enlisted in the U.S. Coast Guard Women's Reserve as a lieutenant (junior grade, or jg) on May 27, 1943, and served two years on active duty before being discharged as a lieutenant on November 1, 1945.

On September 27, 1971, the U.S. Coast Guard commissioned the USCGC *Munro*, a 378-foot-high endurance cutter, the first named after a Coast Guard hero. But perhaps his Medal of Honor citation sums it up best:

"By his outstanding leadership, expert planning, and dauntless devotion to duty, he and his courageous comrades undoubtedly saved the lives of many who otherwise would have perished. He gallantly gave his life for his country."

Sources

Browning, Robert M., Jr. "Douglas Munro at Guadalcanal." U.S. Coast Guard. https://media.defense.gov/2018/Jun/04/2001926472/-1/-1/0/MUNRO_RBROWNING.PDF.

Bunch, John C. *Coast Guard Combat Veterans: Semper Paratus*. New York: Turner Publishing, 1994.
"Official U.S. Coast Guard Biography: SM1c Douglas A. Munro, USCG." https://www.uscg.mil/history/people/munrodouglasindex.asp.
Williams, Gary. *Guardian of Guadalcanal: The World War II Story of Coast Guard Medal of Honor Recipient Douglas Munro*. West Chester, OH: Lakota Press, 2014.

Demas T. Craw and Pierpont M. Hamilton
Operation Torch

During the predawn hours of November 8, 1942, Americans aboard hundreds of ships prepared for what would be the most ambitious combined-arms operation in history, the invasion of French North Africa, codenamed Operation Torch.

The operation would be the first American ground offensive of World War II against the Axis forces and would honor President Roosevelt's pledge to Churchill and Stalin to commit American ground forces before the end of 1942. The hope was that opening a second front would relieve pressure on the Soviet Union, whose fall to the Germans would have had disastrous consequences for the Allies.

Moreover, securing North Africa would facilitate the capture of the port of Tunis, which could be used as a staging area for an assault across the Mediterranean to Sicily and up into the "soft underbelly" of Southern Europe.

The proposed invasion had many variables that needed to be considered. From where would the invasion be launched? Gibraltar, the closest land mass under Allied control was too small to use as a staging area and was riddled with Axis spies, making secrecy impossible.

If the besieged Soviet Union fell, Hitler would be free to commit his forces to repelling the Allied invasion. Additionally, the response of Spain, officially neutral but friendly to the Axis powers, was unknown.

But the question foremost in every mind was, would the French resist and, if so, to what degree? Would the Americans be seen as liberators or invaders?

Ultimately, the decision was made to go forward, and overall command was given to an untried and newly promoted lieutenant general, Dwight D. Eisenhower, who with his diplomatic skills was the right choice to lead a multi-national alliance. The final plan involved three invasion forces. The Eastern and Central Task Forces would depart from England and land in Algeria at Algiers and Oran.

A third task force, the Western Task Force, Task Force 34, would sail from the United States and land in French Morocco. In total, the combined invasion force comprised 107,453 troops, 107 transports with accompanying naval escorts, and 9,911 vehicles and 96,089 tons of supplies.

Under the command of Rear Admiral H. K. Hewitt and Maj. Gen. George S. Patton Jr., Task Force 34 would further divide the landing into three task groups. Task Group 34.10, the Southern Attack Group, comprised 6,423 men, 54 M-4 Sherman medium tanks, and 54 M-3 Stuart light tanks and would land at Safi. Task Group 34.09, the Center Task Group, comprised 18,789 troops and 79 M-3 Stuart light tanks and would land at Fedala, 16 miles north of the fortified city of Casablanca. Task Group 34.08, the Northern Task Group, comprised 9,099 and 65 M-3 Stuart light tanks, was tasked with taking Mehdia and Port Lyautey.

The task forces set sail between October 22 and 26, with D-Day scheduled for the morning of November 8, 1942.

The Northern Task Group, Sub Task Force Goalpost, arrived off Mehdia, Morocco, just before midnight, November 7, 1942. During the voyage, the task force commander, Brig. Gen. Lucian Truscott, commanding elements of the 60th Infantry Regiment, Ninth Infantry Division, met with his G-2 (intelligence chief) Maj. Pierpont M. Hamilton aboard his flagship, the USS *Henry T. Allen* (APA-15).

Hamilton volunteered to carry a personal message to the commander of the Vichy French forces, Col. Charles Petit, transcribed into French, requesting a cease-fire and armistice to avoid unnecessary loss of French and American troops. Hamilton, an international investment banker before the war, was fluent in French and familiar with the French people. It was hoped he could broker the deal.

As the details were being worked out, another of Truscott's staff officers, his air chief Col. Demas "Nick" Craw, pressured his commander to allow him to accompany Hamilton on the mission. Initially reluctant, Truscott relented, agreeing that the professional soldier would enhance the mission, and he knew that Craw was quick thinking, capable and reliable.

Thus, it was that two AAF officers waded ashore on Green Beach with the first wave of the Second Battalion, 60th Infantry Regiment. For their actions that day, they would both be awarded the Medal of Honor, the only airmen to be awarded the medal during World War II for actions not involving air combat. Each man brought an interesting background to the mission.

Pierpont Morgan Hamilton was born in Tuxedo Park, New York, on August 3, 1898, the second of five children born to William Pierson and Juliet Pierpont (née Morgan) Hamilton, both members of prominent American families. His father was the great-grandson of Alexander Hamilton, the nation's first secretary of the Treasury. His mother was the daughter of John Pierpont (J. P.) Morgan, one of the wealthiest and most powerful men of his time.

He attended the Groton School, then Harvard University, earning a bachelor's degree in 1920 and a master's degree in 1946. His time at Harvard was interrupted by America's entry into World War I, and he enlisted as an aviation cadet on August 7, 1917.

Sent to the School of Military Aeronautics at Cornell University, he completed his initial training on October 17, and was sent to the Concentration Barracks at Hazelhurst Field, New Jersey, to process for shipment overseas and where he would complete his flight training. Illness over a period of six weeks

Maj. Pierpont Hamilton (top) and Col. Demas Craw (bottom) (U.S. Air Force Historical Division).

prevented him from sailing overseas with his detachment. In the meantime, the policy of giving primary flying training to cadets overseas had been discontinued.

Hamilton reported to Ellington Field in Texas on February 6, 1918, to complete his flight training. He passed the required tests for the rating of reserve military aviator on May 9, 1918, and was awarded his aviator wings and a commission as a first lieutenant in the Signal Officers Reserve Corps.

He remained at Ellington Field as an instructor, teaching aerial navigation, aerial bombardment and astronomy. Promoted to captain on September 21, 1918, he was honorably discharged after the end of the war, on December 31, 1918.

Between the wars, Hamilton worked as an international investment banker, living in France, where he became fluent in French. During this time, he was married and divorced twice and made significant contributions to the commercial development of color photography.

Following the Japanese attack on the American fleet at Pearl Harbor, Hawaii, on December 7, 1941, Hamilton requested reactivation of his commission in the army. He was commissioned a major in the air corps on March 2, 1942.

His first assignment was at Air Force Headquarters in Washington, D.C., as an A-2 (intelligence) staff officer assigned as liaison to Great Britain's Royal Air Force (RAF), and he was sent to London in June, serving as an operations/intelligence officer with the Office of Combined Operations under Lord Louis Mountbatten.

Hamilton was involved in formulating various plans for amphibious assaults on occupied Europe, including the disastrous Dieppe Raid. The amphibious assault on the French port city of Dieppe along the west coast by 5,100 Canadian troops, 1,000 British commandos and American Rangers, supported by 252 ships and 69 squadrons of aircraft was an unqualified failure, resulting in the loss of three-quarters of the Canadian force within six hours. But hard lessons were learned.

Hamilton was recalled to Washington in September to brief the commanding general of the Western Task Force, Maj. Gen. George S. Patton Jr., about a proposed plan to invade French North Africa.

By October 1942, Hamilton was at sea aboard the transport USS *George Clymer* (AP-47), assigned as the assistant S-2 and then the S-2 on the staff of Major General Truscott.

Unlike Hamilton, Demas Craw's upbringing was more modest. Demas Thurlow Craw and his twin brother, Theron, were born in Long

Lake Township, Michigan, on April 9, 1900, to Mark Craw, a Michigan game warden and conservation officer, and his wife Clara. Later, a sister, Jane, joined the family.

When America entered World War I, both boys dropped out of Traverse City Central High School to enlist in the army on April 18, 1918, shortly after turning 18. Demas Craw was assigned to the 12th Cavalry and was sent to Camp Stanley, Texas, and, later, Columbus, New Mexico, where he patrolled the Mexican border.

Promoted to private first class in November 1918, Craw was sent to the machine-gun school at Camp Hancock, Georgia, where he applied and was accepted for officer training. But the armistice and the resulting demobilization caused a downsizing, and Craw was discharged on February 15, 1919.

Craw reenlisted in the infantry three months later, in May, and was sent to Grand Rapids, Michigan, as a recruiter. He was promoted to corporal on June 1, but he continued to relentlessly pursue his desire for a commission. He was transferred to the Second Field Artillery at Camp Zachery Taylor, Kentucky, for a two-month preparatory course. Upon completion he returned to Grand Rapids on April 2, 1920.

Discharged on May 14, he reported to the U.S. Military Academy at West Point, New York, on July 1, 1920, a plebe in the Class of 1924. It was at West Point where his nickname of Nicodemas was shortened to Nick. He was captain and manager of the polo team, but an eye injury in a game temporarily derailed his plans to become an aviator.

Craw graduated West Point on June 12, 1924, 371st in a class of 401, and was commissioned a second lieutenant in the Coast Artillery Corps of the Regular Army.

On March 16, 1926, Craw applied for aviation training, and upon approval, he reported to Brooks Field, Texas, for primary flight training. Graduating on February 28, 1927, he went on to advanced training at Kelly Field, which he completed on August 12. Transferred to Selfridge Field, Michigan, he was officially transferred to the air corps on March 8, 1928, and was sent to Duncan Field, Texas, as a flight instructor. He was sent to teach advanced students at Kelly Field in January 1929. He was promoted to first lieutenant the following January 1930.

On June 30, Craw reported to Mitchel Field, New York, to prepare for an assignment overseas to the 19th Pursuit Squadron, at Wheeler Field, Hawaii Territory. While at Mitchel Field, he met, and eventually married, Mary Victor Wesson, daughter of Frank Wesson, president of the Smith & Wesson Arms, with whom he had one son, Nicolas.

Craw commanded the 19th Pursuit Squadron from August 4, 1932, until September 15, 1934, and then returned stateside to attend the Air Corps Tactical School from September 1937 until graduating on June 20, 1938.

Now a captain, Craw reported to Air Force Headquarters, Langley Field, Virginia, as inspector general and assistant intelligence officer, where he was promoted to major on March 11, 1940.

A good part of the world was already at war, but America remained neutral. Craw was sent overseas, temporarily assigned to the War Department as an "air observer," visiting the East Indies, China, the Philippines, and Bulgaria and giving on-the-ground assessments of conditions.

In October 1940, Craw was sent to Cairo, Egypt, as an observer with the British RAF, and he flew along on missions against the Italians in Libya. Almost continuously under fire, he was slightly wounded and was sent to Athens once the Italians invaded.

Serving as the assistant military attaché in Athens, he had a front-row seat for the Greco-Italian War and, according to official records, came under fire 136 times and participated in 21 RAF bombing sorties.

As one friend described him, "He didn't bother to just observe. He was in there, fighting with the rest of them. Sometimes he had trouble getting to the front, but he got there, walk, drive, or fly."

Craw was present with Greek forces in Albania during the battle of Himara in December 1940, during the counteroffensive of the Greek Army that followed the failed Italian invasion of Greece. During hand-to-hand combat, he was wounded by the blast of a hand grenade.

Captured by the Germans when they invaded Greece in April 1941, Craw was interned for six weeks before being released in a prisoner exchange. He was awarded the Order of George I, Fourth Class, by the king of Greece.

Craw was in Bucharest, Romania, when the Germans invaded Russia on June 22, 1941, during Operation Barbarossa, the Axis powers' invasion of the Soviet Union. He made his way through Turkey, Russia, Iran, Iraq, Syria and Palestine, eventually ending back in Egypt in time to observe the English campaign against Gen. Erwin Rommel's Afrika Korps.

Craw was recalled to Washington and reported on his observations. He was promoted to lieutenant colonel on November 15, and colonel on March 1, 1942. By the time he was assigned as air chief on General Truscott's staff, he had seen as much combat as anyone in the military, a fact that must have played a part in Truscott's decision to allow him to accompany Hamilton.

Now, on the morning of November 8, 1942, the two AAF officers, one from Harvard, one from West Point, both fluent in French, waited to go ashore with the first wave at Mehdia.

The plan was to land at the jetty on the Sebou River near French headquarters and make their way to the French commander at Port Lyautey. The taking of the airfield at Port Lyautey was critical to the success of Operation Torch, and the hope was the French would agree to a truce.

As the invasion began, a shortwave broadcast by President Roosevelt, speaking in French, was heard: "Mes Amis, we come among you to repulse the cruel invaders. Have faith in our words, help us where you are able. All men who hate tyranny, join with the liberators who at this moment are about to land on your shores. Vive La France eternelle."

The Central and Eastern Task Forces landed on schedule and thus were unaffected by the announcement. Unfortunately, the forces landing at Mehdia were delayed in reaching their objective, which resulted in the French defenders being alerted to the landing, a fact confirmed by the French steamer *Lorraine*, which sailing past the armada at 4:30 a.m. signaled "Be warned. They are alert on shore. Alert for 0500."

As the landing craft carrying Hamilton and Craw, and others carrying troops of the Second Battalion, 60th Regimental Combat Team, neared the channel of the Sebou River, they came under intense fire from shore batteries intent on denying the Americans access to the river.

Withdrawing, they landed on Green Beach, wading safely ashore at dawn, into a morass of confusion, as two French Dewoitine D.520 fighters flew overhead, strafing the beach and landing craft.

They commandeered a small truck, but it became mired in a muddy marsh and had to be extricated by combat engineers. They then found further progress inland hindered by both French and American naval barrages, and they were forced to return to the jetty where they'd started.

They radioed Truscott, "At mouth of river. Being shelled by enemy and our own Navy.... On Green Beach.... Troops landed and moving inland. Proceeding on mission." Truscott considered canceling their mission, but Craw persuaded him to allow them to continue.

Appropriating a jeep and its driver, PFC Orris V. Correy, they mounted American, French and a white flag of truce on the jeep and proceeded through the gunfire, directly toward the French defenses.

Driving up, literally under the guns of the Kasbah fortress, they were greeted warmly by a French officer, who regretfully declined their request for a guide, as he had no men to spare, but he offered directions.

They proceeded cautiously, passing through the French forces as they drove another six miles, making contact with French units, all refusing to provide a guide. They were approaching the outskirts of Port Lyautey, when, coming around a bend, they surprised a French machine-gun position, and the gunners, unprepared for the sudden appearance of the American jeep, opened fire from 30 yards away.

Bullets tore through the windshield, striking Craw in the chest, killing him instantly and causing the jeep to crash into a tree. Hamilton and Correy were uninjured, but Hamilton, livid, angrily upbraided the soldiers in French, outraged that they would fire on a flag of truce, and he demanded to be taken to the French commander.

Hamilton and Correy were taken prisoner, disarmed, and taken to French headquarters, where the local commander, Col. Charles Petit, apologized but regretfully stated that he could not order a cease-fire without authority from a higher command. Hamilton presented the letter from General Truscott, and Petit agreed to pass on the letter to his superior, Maj. Gen. Maurice Mathenet, but absent orders, he was obliged to continue resisting the invasion.

Petit refused Hamilton's request that he and Correy be allowed to return to their own lines, no doubt fearing the repercussions should it become known that the French had fired on, and killed, an American officer under a flag of truce. Instead, they were issued quarters, placed under guard, and denied communication with their own forces, segregated from other American prisoners.

Over the next two days, as the French struggled to define their loyalties, the American advance continued, with casualties on both sides. The French Navy put up the fiercest resistance, but no landing went uncontested.

In Oran, the French sank the U.S. Coast Guard cutter USS *Hartland*, sinking the ship and killing 189 of the 393 troopers of Third Battalion, Sixth Armored Infantry, including its commander, Lt. Col. George F. Marshall, the first American officer killed in the Mediterranean theater.

There were also political battles being fought, as French general in retirement Henri Giraud finally agreed to cooperate with Eisenhower, even as French Admiral Jean François Darlan, the highest-ranking Vichy officer in North Africa, indicated a willingness to engage in talks. The two men detested each other.

On D-Day plus one, November 9, with beachheads established, the Americans began moving inland, meeting surprisingly stiff resistance from the fortress at Kasbah. Negotiations continued but then stalled as Darlan refused to meet with American diplomat Robert Murphy, demanding instead a flag officer of equal rank.

Expressing his frustration, Eisenhower, in Gibraltar, wrote, "It isn't the operation that is wearing me down, it's the petty intrigue and the necessity of dealing with the little, conceited worms that call themselves men."

In the early hours of November 10, Colonel Petit and his orderly were inspecting positions in the rear when they were captured by troops of the 60th Infantry, advancing on Port Lyautey from the south. It was 4:30 a.m., and Petit surrendered himself and his regiment, the First Moroccan Tirailleurs (light infantry).

The Americans were moving north in support of the destroyer USS *Dallas* (DD-199), which was forcing its way up the Sebou River, piloted by a Frenchman, Rene Malavergne. The *Dallas* successfully landed a force of 75 U.S. Army Rangers and captured the airfield at Port Lyautey. Malavergne was later awarded the Navy Cross, the first civilian of World War II to be so honored.

The officer in charge, not wanting to be hindered with a high-ranking French prisoner, learned from Petit that he had Major Hamilton as a prisoner. Seeing a way out of his dilemma, the officer paroled Petit and ordered him to return to French headquarters and surrender himself to Hamilton, and within hours he and his staff did so, becoming Hamilton's prisoners. As Hamilton recalled, "This put me in command of Port Lyautey, but with no means of communicating that fact to the American forces."

Hamilton put in a telephone call to the French commander, General Mathenet in Meekness, asking him to issue a cease-fire order, but it wasn't until 10:30 p.m. that Mathenet returned the call, expressing a willingness to meet with General Truscott in Port Lyautey to discuss the terms. Marshal Henri Petain had already authorized the cease-fire.

"No way," Hamilton replied.

> I brought my colonel here three days ago and your men killed him beneath a flag of truce. I'll not risk my general to the same kind of treachery. All you need to do right now is to give the order for your men to quit fighting. When they quit, our soldiers will quit, and men from both sides will be spared. Then we can set up a meeting with General Truscott.

Resigned, Mathenet asked for Petit and issued an official cease-fire. The challenge now was how to transmit the order to both sides along a still active six-mile wide battlefield between Port Lyautey and the coast.

Hamilton, hoping to avoid additional casualties, requested a vehicle. Driven by PFC Correy, and accompanied by the deputy commander, Col.

Leon LeBeau, and a French bugler sounding "cease-fire," they drove through Port Lyautey to the airfield to make contact with six tanks of Company C, 70th Tank Battalion.

Disaster was narrowly averted. The French bugle call "cease-fire" is similar to the U.S. Cavalry "charge," and they were almost fired on, mistaken for attacking French forces.

Hamilton made radio contact with Lt. Col. Henry H. Semmes, commander of the Third Armored Landing Team and informed him of the French surrender. Semmes then drove his tank along the beachhead to General Truscott's command post to relay the news. Truscott, saddened by news of Craw's death, but relieved to discover Hamilton was alive after three days, arranged for a meeting for 8 a.m. the next morning, November 11, at the gates of the Kasbah fortress. Hamilton also contacted the *Dallas*, and hostilities officially ceased at 4 a.m., although some sniper fire continued until daylight.

Hamilton accompanied Mathenet and his staff to the Kasbah and was present at the surrender ceremony, while Admiral Darlan ordered the end of all resistance in Algeria. That same afternoon, the remains of Colonel Craw were interred in the American cemetery, outside the Kasbah's walls. His remains were later disinterred and cremated, and on June 24, 1949, the ashes were scattered over Wiesbaden, Germany.

Hamilton was awarded the Medal of Honor by President Roosevelt for "conspicuous gallantry and intrepidity" in a White House ceremony on February 19, 1943, and a similar ceremony to present the medal to Craw's widow Mary and his ten-year-old son, Nicolas, was held on March 4, 1943. In addition, the U.S. Navy named its air base at Port Lyautey as Craw Field.

In December 1942, Hamilton was appointed air and intelligence officer at headquarters for Allied forces in Constantine, Algiers, and was promoted to lieutenant colonel. He then served at headquarters for the African Tactical Air Force before being recalled to Washington, D.C., in March 1943, assigned as assistant chief of air staff planning, with a promotion to colonel on October 27, 1943. He finished the war serving on the staff of AAF, the Joint Chiefs of Staff and the assistant secretary of War before being discharged from active duty in December 1945.

Hamilton returned to active duty in February 1947 and was promoted to brigadier general on December 21, 1948. He served in various high-level planning and policy positions until leaving active duty on March 31, 1952, and retiring to Montecito, California, while remaining in the reserves.

Promoted to major general on June 20, 1955, he completed the

Reserve and National Guard General Officer Orientation Course at the Air War College in 1957 before retiring in 1959.

Hamilton enjoyed success as a businessman and bank executive until failing health caused another retirement in 1979, and he passed away at the Wadsworth Veteran's Administration hospital in Los Angeles on March 4, 1982.

Perhaps the greatest tribute to Craw and Hamilton is that the defining moment for these two warriors was achieved on a mission of peace.

Sources

Air Force Historical Support Division. "Craw Biography." http://www.afhistory.af.mil/FAQs/Fact-Sheets/Article/639621/craw-col-demas-t-craw/.

Bowman, Joseph P. "Demas T. Craw and Pierpont M. Hamilton." Hamilton National Genealogical Society. http://www.hamiltongensociety.org/index2.php?option=com_content&do_pdf=1&id=126-title=Demas.

Herder, Brian Lane. *Operation Torch—1942*. Oxford: Osprey Publishing, 2017.

Howe, George F. "U.S. Army in WW II: Mediterranean Theater of Operations, Northwest Africa—Seizing the Initiative in the West." Chap. 8, "Mehdia to Port-Lyautey." http://www.ibiblio.org/hyperwar/USA/USA-MTO-NWA/USA-MTO-NWA-8.html.

"Major General Pierpont M. Hamilton." USAF Biography. http://www.af.mil/About-Us/Biographies/Display/Article/106865/major-general-pierpoint-m-hamilton/.

Nelson, Wes. "Colonel Demus T. Craw Medal of Honor Memorial." Military History of the Upper Great Lakes. http://ss.sites.mtu.edu/mhugl/2017/10/22/colonel-demus-t-craw-medal-of-honor-memorial/.

Smith, Brad. "Order of Battle: Casablanca / North Africa Invasion." November 8, 1942. http://www.navweaps.com/index_oob/OOB_World War II_Mediterranean/OOB_World War II_Casablanca.phpNav.

Sterner, Doug. Home of Heroes. http://www.homeofheroes.com/.

U.S. Senate Committee on Veterans' Affairs. "Medal of Honor Recipients: 1863–1978." Washington, D.C.: Government Printing Office, 1979. http://www.cmohs.org/recipient-detail/2694/craw-demas-t.php.

Waggoner, Walter H. "P.M. Hamilton, 83, Dies on the Coast." *New York Times*, March 16, 1982.

The Niland Brothers
Inspiration for Saving Private Ryan

In circumstances that parallel those of the fictional hero in Steven Spielberg's film *Saving Private Ryan* (1998), Sgt. Frederick Niland was ordered home from the war by presidential order after his three brothers were reported dead or missing in action after D-Day in June 1944.

Michael and Augusta Niland of Tonawanda, New York, had six children: Clarissa, Edward, Preston (Pete), Margaret, Robert (Bob) and Frederick (Fritz). The children grew up together, graduated Tonawanda High School, and attended Canisius College, a Catholic institution in Buffalo.

With war clouds gathering in Europe, Preston was the first to enter the military, enlisting in the army as a private (serial no. 32036580) on March 31, 1941. He served as an enlisted man, rising to the rank of corporal before being accepted for officer candidate school. He graduated Christmas Day, 1942, and was commissioned a second lieutenant (serial no. 1305819) the next day.

He was assigned as a platoon leader with the 22nd Infantry Regiment, Fourth Infantry Division (Ivy Division), and he traveled with the regiment from Fort Dix, New Jersey (April 1943) to Camp Gordon Johnston, Florida (September 1943), to Fort Jackson, South Carolina (December 1943), as the unit prepared to be shipped overseas to Europe. On January 29, 1944, the regiment arrived in England to prepare for the cross-channel invasion.

The second Niland son to enter the service was Robert, who enlisted in the army as a private (serial no. 32200180) on November 7, 1941. After basic training, Robert volunteered for training as a paratrooper and earned his jump wings at Fort Bragg, North Carolina. He was assigned to the 505th Parachute Infantry Regiment, which was activated at Fort Benning, Georgia, on July 6, 1942.

Attached to the 82nd Airborne in February 1943, the division moved operations to Fort Bragg. The 82nd landed in Casablanca, North Africa, on May 10, 1943, to train for the invasion of Sicily, and the 505th, with the Third Battalion of the 504th, jumped into Gela, Sicily, on July 9, securing the airfield there, linking up with the First Infantry Division the following day.

On September 15, the 505th parachuted near Salerno to support the 504th, which had airdropped south of the Sele River the previous day. The division fought on to Naples, occupying it on October 2. After security duty, the division began preparing for the invasion of Europe, returning to Ireland late in October, and England by December.

Edward followed his brothers, entering the AAF as a private (serial no. 32251492) for training as a radio operator / mechanic / gunner. Niland took training at Harlington, Texas, and Scott Field, Illinois, and then flew across the country, serving at Will Rogers Field in Oklahoma (January 1943), Army Air Base, Tullahoma, Tennessee (March 1943), and Army Air Base, Greenfield, South Carolina (October 1943).

He was assigned to the 434th Bombardment Squadron at Foggia, Italy. The 434th was activated at McChord Field, Washington, on January 15, 1941, as the 94th Bombardment Squadron and saw combat in the Middle East before arriving in Italy in August 1943. Assigned to the 12th Bombardment Group, the 434th saw action in Italy (the campaigns for Naples and Rome) and later in the China-India- Burma theater of operations from Kurmitola, India. His B-25 Mitchell medium bomber was shot down over Burma and reported missing on May 20, 1944.

Frederick was the last to be inducted, entering the army as a private (serial no. 12051971) on November 27, 1942. Like Robert, Frederick volunteered for duty with the paratroopers and was assigned to the 501st Parachute Infantry Regiment, which was forming from the parachute test platoon, later the 501st Parachute Battalion, which had formed at Fort Benning, Georgia, on July 1, 1940.

On November 15, 1942, the newly redesignated 501st Parachute Infantry Regiment was formed at Camp Toccoa, Georgia. The unit was jump qualified at Fort Benning, Georgia, in March 1943 and then sent to Camp Mackall, North Carolina, where they participated in maneuvers for several months. The unit departed for England in January 1944 and was attached to the 101st Airborne Division (Screaming Eagles) in May 1944. The unit was selected to participate in Operation Overlord, the Normandy Invasion, on June 6, 1944.

On D-Day, the Fourth Infantry Division landed at Utah Beach, the first American troops to engage German forces at Normandy. Brig. Gen. Theodore Roosevelt Jr., the assistant division commander, led the first wave. Lt. Preston Niland led a platoon of the 22nd Infantry Regiment, involved with the mission to occupy the high ground surrounding Utah Beach. By dusk, the division had pushed 4–7 miles inland, sustaining only light casualties. Lieutenant Niland was killed by enemy fire the next day, June 7.

The 505th was given the task of jumping east of the Merderet River to capture the village of Sainte-Mère-Église and then secure the river crossings near La Fiere and Chef-du-Pont, eventually linking with elements of the 101st Airborne. The regiment jumped into the interior early in the morning on June 6. Sgt. Robert Niland was a mortar squad leader in D Company, but many units, including his, were unable to locate their heavy weapons or ammunition, which was dropped separately.

Cpl. Jim Kelley, a medic in D Company, was scrounging in the area throughout the day, looking for lost equipment. He located some heavy weapons and a trooper with a broken leg, before linking up with a lieutenant and eight soldiers, including Niland and more wounded. The men engaged in skirmishes with Germans throughout the day, before the lieutenant ordered a withdrawal because of a shortage of ammunition.

Kelley decided to remain with the wounded, hoping his status as a non-combatant would keep him safe. His buddy, Bob Niland, said, "If you're staying, I'm staying," and he remained when the others withdrew. As the German attack increased, the men decided to leave the wounded to be treated by the German medics and attempted to pull back. This was about 1500 hours. As they crossed a road under fire, Kelley dove into a ditch, with Niland falling on top of him. It took him a moment to realize that Niland had taken two hits in the head.

Unable to extract himself, Kelley was taken prisoner and held at a farmhouse at Neuville-au-Plain. The village was shelled by American artillery and naval fire throughout the rest of the day and night. Kelley and the wounded were liberated by forces of the Fourth Armored Division the following afternoon. (Kelley remained with the regiment for the remainder of the war, ending as a sergeant, and was recalled during the Korean War.)

Sgt. Fritz Niland departed with his unit from Merryfield Airport at 2245 hours on June 5 and jumped into France with the mission of securing the canal locks at La Barquette. The situation had stabilized by June 14, when Fritz heard rumors that his brother Robert had been killed in action.

With a buddy, Sgt. Norman Marshall, and the regimental chaplain,

Capt. Francis Sampson, Fritz went by jeep to search out his brothers. He traveled to the 82nd's area to learn that Robert had been killed on D-Day. He proceeded to the Fourth Infantry to learn that Preston had also been killed. He returned to the company area in the village of Carentan to find two pieces of news waiting.

Niland was told that his brother Edward was missing in action in Burma, and that the president had ordered him home as the last surviving son. According to his daughter, Fritz told the chaplain, "You tell my mother that I'm with all the brothers I have left," but Sampson told him, "You can argue with General Eisenhower or the president, but I think you're going home." He was put on a plane for London the next day.

Niland spent the remainder of the war assigned as a military policeman in Buffalo, New York, close to home. In May 1945, Fritz got the good news that his brother Edward, who was reported missing on May 20, 1944, had been captured by the Japanese and held as a POW in Calcutta, India, until he escaped in early May.

Eddie was among a group of POWs being moved ahead of the Allied advance. He took off into the jungle when the column was strafed by Allied fighters. He remained in hiding as the column was reformed, and he stayed in the brush until being rescued by British forces and was liberated on May 5, 1945. Edward was discharged as a technical sergeant on October 6, 1945, with a Purple Heart and POW medal. Fritz was discharged on December 11, 1945, as a sergeant with a Bronze Star.

Edward returned to the United States disabled from his time as a POW, suffering from malnutrition (he weighed 70 pounds at the time of release). He got a job after the war as a guard for Railway Mail in Buffalo, where he worked until he retired. He married and started a family. He passed away on February 28, 1984.

Fritz never really adjusted to civilian life after the war, and delayed stress syndrome was not recognized as an illness. Nonetheless, he returned to school at Georgetown University, earning a degree in oral surgery and another in anesthesiology. He practiced at Walter Reed Medical Center in Washington, D.C., and a private practice in New York, and he later worked for the public health service in Guam. He married, had children, and passed away on December 1, 1983.

The Niland brothers were mentioned in numerous books after the war, including *Look Out Below* by Father Sampson and *D-Day: June 6, 1944—The Climactic Battle of World War II* and *Band of Brothers*, both by historian Stephen Ambrose, who later served as a consultant on Spielberg's *Saving Private Ryan*. Although the writers insisted that Ryan was a fictional character, the parallels between the Nilands and the Ryans are numerous and striking, and many consider Fritz Niland to be the model for Private Ryan.

SOURCES

Ambrose, Stephen. *Band of Brothers: E Company, 506th Regiment, 101st Airborne from Normandy to Hitler's Eagle's Nest*. New York: Simon & Schuster, 2001.

Bando, Mark. *101st Airborne: The Screaming Eagles at Normandy*. Minneapolis, MN: Zenith Imprint, 2011.

Churchill, Ron. "*Saving Private Ryan*: A Real-Life Drama Steven Spielberg's World War II Film Loosely Based on the Family of UB's Pete Niland." *University of Buffalo Reporter* (NY) 30 (2) (1998).

"The Niland Boys." Buffalo, NY: Canisius College, Andrew L. Bouwhuis Library. https://web.archive.org/web/20120310220526/http://www.canisius.edu/archives/niland.asp.

Sixth Corps Combat Engineers. http://www.6thcorpscombatengineers.com/engforum/index.php?/topic/976-the-story-of-frederick-fritz-niland/.

Tillman, Barrett. *D-Day Encyclopedia*. Washington, D.C.: Regnery History, 2014.

The Borgstrom Brothers
Further Inspiration for Saving Private Ryan

Over a six-month period in 1944, Alben and Gunda Borgstrom, farmers in rural Garland, Utah, lost four sons killed in action, all in different theaters of battle.

Like the brothers in the fictional Spielberg film *Saving Private Ryan*, the Borgstrom brothers made the ultimate sacrifice in service to their country during World War II.

Alben and Gunda Borgstrom grew up in rural Utah, and as did many Mormons, desired a large family. Their prayers were answered with the birth of ten children beginning with a daughter, Aleda, followed by Veran Alban, Leroy Elmer, Clyde Eugene, Wilma, Boyd Carl, Rolan D. and Rulon J. (twins), Mildred and Eldon Kay.

The children worked the farm, went to church, and attended Bear River High School, although only Aleda graduated. Their childhood was poor but happy, and the family was close. During World War II, the Borgstrom family proudly displayed five blue stars, signifying five members serving in the military.

Boyd (serial no. 300809) and Clyde (serial no. 300810) enlisted together in the Marine Corps on October 14, 1940, more than a year before Pearl Harbor. They took basic training together with the First Recruit Battalion, Recruit Depot, San Diego, California.

Boyd was trained to operate heavy anti-aircraft guns, and Clyde was trained as a heavy equipment operator and assigned as an engineer with Marine Aviation.

Boyd left San Diego aboard the MS *Day Star* on August 23, 1942, and arrived at Pearl Harbor on September 1. The next day, he left for Johnston

Island in the South Pacific aboard the USS *Midway*, arriving on the sixth. He provided air defense, operating a 90 mm anti-aircraft gun as part of the Tenth Defense Battalion, later 16th Defense Battalion, Fleet Marine Force.

Clyde was assigned to Company A, Second Aviation Engineer Battalion, First Marine Amphibious Corps, and landed at Guadalcanal on August 7, 1942, fighting until the island was "secured" on February 7, 1943, when the Japanese evacuated 13,000 remaining troops.

Once the island was secured, it became essential to rapidly expand and improve airfields and roads, and engineers went to work clearing debris, trees and wrecked vehicles, often in torrential rains and always in the mud. Clyde was driving a bulldozer at Henderson Field when he was killed by a falling tree on March 17, 1944. The first to go to war, PFC Clyde Borgstrom was the first to be killed.

The next brother to enter the service was Leroy, or Roy, who entered the army as a private (serial no. 39901970) on November 7, 1942. After training at Camp Lewis, Washington, and training as a medic, Roy was assigned to the 361st Infantry Regiment, 91st Infantry Division.

The 91st was activated at Camp White on August 15, 1942, Maj. Gen. William Livesay commanding, with troops arriving in October and November. Training began on November 15 and continued through June 1943, when the division went on maneuvers that lasted until July 10. The division returned to Camp White, then moved to Camp Adair on November 4, 1943, and participated in maneuvers in the Bend, Oregon, area.

The 361st moved by train to Camp Patrick Henry, Virginia, on March 18, arriving on the 24th. On April 3 through 12, the 361st boarded Liberty ships for North Africa and arrived at the port of Oran in Algeria 19 days later. After amphibious training, the regiment boarded British ships and landed in Naples on May 27, 1944.

Shipped by boat to Anzio, the 361st landed well after the battle for Anzio had ended, on June 1, 1944, and advanced to Velletri by June 3. Victorious troops entered Rome on June 6, 1944, the day of the Normandy Invasion in Europe. The unit continued advancing north and was in the vicinity of Roccastrada on June 22 when PFC Roy Borgstrom was killed carrying a wounded soldier to safety while under enemy fire.

The twins, Rolan (serial no. 39917713) and Rulon (serial no. 39917677) enlisted in the army together on July 21, 1943, after they turned 18. They took basic training together at Camp Walters, Texas, after which Rolan went to the air corps and Rulon to the infantry.

Rolan was trained as a tail gunner aboard B-24 "Liberator" bombers.

He was shipped overseas to England on June 28, 1944, and was assigned to the 506th Bombardment Squadron, 44th Bomber Group of the Eighth Air Force at Shipdham, England.

Activated on February 1, 1942, the Eighth's mission was the long-range bomber offensive against German-occupied Europe, and the 44th flew missions over Germany, France, Belgium, Holland, Romania, Poland and Italy, including flying support against enemy transportation targets during the Normandy Invasion.

On August 7, 1944, Rolan received word that his brother Roy had been killed in action in Italy. The following day, August 8, Rolan was severely wounded on a mission over Germany, and he died of his wounds upon returning to England.

While Rolan had gone to the air corps, Rulon had been trained as an infantryman and assigned to the 38th Infantry Regiment, Second Infantry Division (Indianhead Division). In October of 1943, the 38th was moved to Camp Shanks, New York, and sent overseas to Newry, Ireland, for six months of further training in preparation for the invasion of the European mainland.

The 38th first saw combat when it landed at Omaha Beach on June 7, 1944, D-Day plus one, while under intense enemy fire. Hampered by lost equipment until June 10, the 38th advanced on Trévières, participating in the fighting through the hedgerows as the Allies consolidated their hold on Southern France.

On August 25, 1944, little more than two weeks after Rolan's death, PFC Rulon Borgstrom was reported missing in action at La Dreef, France, after an intense artillery barrage.

After becoming aware of Rolan's death, both of Utah's senators, Elbert Thomas and Abe Murdock, as well as Utah governor Herbert Maw, petitioned FDR to return Rulon and Boyd Borgstrom from combat. Rulon was killed in the interim.

On January 4, 1944, Boyd left Johnston Island aboard the USS *Panay* to Pearl Harbor, switching to the USS *Kasaan Bay* and arriving in San Diego on January 23. After a furlough home, Boyd was sent to Camp Lejeune, North Carolina, where he was stationed when efforts began to have him released from the service. President Roosevelt took a personal interest in the case, writing a personal letter of condolence to the parents.

On the order of Lt. Gen. Alexander Vandegrift, commandant of the Marine Corps, Boyd was honorably discharged as a private first class on October 7, 1944. In many ways, Boyd was the fifth casualty of the war in the Borgstrom family.

Boyd suffered depression after his discharge and never fully recovered, suffering delayed stress syndrome, although it was not recognized as such in 1945. He began drinking, leading to divorce and a life of wandering. He was beginning to get his life back together when he died of a heart attack in Ogden, Utah, in 1973.

All Americans were willing to sacrifice during World War II, but few families were asked to make the sacrifices that the Borgstroms made. Although devastated by their loss, the Borgstroms made speeches and sold bonds in support of victory in the war.

Following the end of the war, families began to request the remains of family members to be returned to the United States, and in 1947, Gen. Mark Clark was chosen to oversee that mission.

It was almost four years after the four brothers' deaths before their bodies were returned to Utah by the American Graves Registration Service.

On June 25, 1948, the Borgstrom brothers were returned to Tremonton, Utah, where they lay in state for a day. The following day, the boys were honored at a memorial service at the Garland LDS Tabernacle.

Clarence E. Smith, former principal of Bear River High School, Governor Herbert B. Maw, LDS church president George Albert Smith, and Gen. Mark W. Clark spoke at the funeral. Rear Admiral John R. Redman, Maj. Gen. LeRoy P. Hunt, and Brig. Gen. Ned Schramm were in attendance, and the brothers were posthumously awarded three Bronze Star medals, one Air Medal, and one Good Conduct Medal. The four brothers were then interred next to each other in the Riverview Cemetery in Tremonton, Utah.

During a break in the service, General Clark recalled being asked by Mrs. Borgstrom, "Will you take my young one?" Korea was on the horizon, and the youngest Borgstrom boy, Eldon, was 18.

He told her that with two surviving sons, Eldon would be eligible for service, but that so long as he, Clark, remained in the army, he would do his best to make sure that Eldon was assigned duty at home.

Mr. Borgstrom, overhearing the whispered conversation said, "Mother, I have overheard your conversation with the general about our youngest, and I will make no deals about his service. If his country needs him, he will go."

General Clark later called the Borgstroms the "personification of Americanism."

Perhaps influenced by the losses of families like the Borgstroms and Sullivans (five brothers went down together aboard the USS *Juneau* on

November 13, 1942), the Department of Defense in 1948 enacted the Sole Survivor Policy, or Department of Defense Directive 1315.15 Special Separation Policies for Survivorship, which was designed to protect members of a family from the draft or from combat duty if they had already lost family members in military service and did not allow brothers to serve together.

SOURCES

Bagley, Pat. "Living History: Utah Family Lost Four Sons to World War II; a Fifth Came Home." *Salt Lake Tribune*, May 29, 2011.
"Four Fallen Heroes Honored," *Deseret News* (UT), June 26, 1948.
"Military, State, LDS Heads Pay Tribute to Borgstroms." *Salt Lake Tribune*, June 27, 1948.
"The Parents Wait: Four Sons Killed in the War Are Brought Back to Utah." *Life*, July 19, 1948. "*Private Ryan* Reminds Family of Tragedy." *Augusta Chronicle*, July 23, 1998. http://chronicle.augusta.com/stories/1998/07/23/ent_234048.shtml#.WaxxK8iGPIU.

The Stokes Twins
Awarded the Silver Star for the Same Action

On November 13, 1942, while supporting the invasion of Guadalcanal Island, the USS *Juneau* (CL-52), a U.S. Navy Atlanta-class light cruiser, was torpedoed by the Japanese destroyer *Amatsukaze* at 0148 hours. The *Juneau* was severely damaged and forced to withdraw from the battle.

Accompanied by two other cruisers damaged in the battle, the USS *Helena* (CL-50) and USS *San Francisco* (CA-38), the *Juneau* was headed for repairs. Operating with only one screw, she had a severe list as she proceeded to Espiritu Santo. A few minutes after 1100, the *Juneau* was torpedoed a second time, in the same place struck earlier, and a tremendous explosion split the cruiser in two, and it sank in 20 seconds.

A second tragedy occurred when, assuming that all hands had been lost, unaware that over 100 men were in the water, and fearful of further attacks, the *Helena* and *San Francisco* departed without attempting to rescue any survivors.

Left in the water for eight days before being spotted by rescue aircraft, only ten men survived the ordeal of exposure to the elements and shark attacks.

A total of 687 men died in the tragedy, among them the five Sullivan brothers from Waterloo, Iowa; George Thomas, 27, gunner's mate second class (previously discharged in May 1941 as gunner's mate third class); Francis Henry, "Frank," coxswain (previously discharged in May 1941 as seaman first class); Joseph Eugene, 24; Madison Abel, "Matt," 23; and Albert Leo, 20.

As a direct result of the Sullivans' deaths, the U.S. Department of Defense adopted the Sole Survivor Policy. Although not enacted into law until 1948, the policy's intent was to prohibit brothers from serving together to prevent similar tragedies.

It would take a personal letter from President Roosevelt himself for identical twins Claude and Clyde Stokes to serve together on the same M-10 tank destroyer during World War II.

Claude and Clyde Stokes were born in rural Dierks, Arkansas, on November 17, 1923, the third and fourth surviving children of the five born to James Whitmore Stokes and Nancy Jane Bagley. They had an older brother and sister, Carl Emmit and La Vern, and a younger sister, Eupal Lee.

The family moved to Tishomingo, Oklahoma at the end of 1925. Their father worked as a cotton farmer, and life was tough in rural Oklahoma, more so once the Great Depression hit in 1929. But the family never thought of themselves as poor.

Mother Stokes was a stern disciplinarian, and the children attended church and were raised not to smoke, drink, or cuss. They attended a one-room schoolhouse while the family rented a 100-acre farm, growing corn, raising cattle and planting a vegetable garden.

The farmhouse was about seven miles northwest of McAlester, Oklahoma, but there was no electricity, and water had to be brought to the house from a nearby spring and then boiled before drinking.

Although raised to be scrupulously honest, the twins were not above "pranks," such as one brother buying a ticket for the movie house, then having his twin "come looking for him with a message from mom." Once in the theater, they would switch places, and the other brother would leave so that both got to see the movie on a single ticket.

The twins were just 18 when the Japanese attacked Pearl Harbor on December 7, 1941, and on the day after their 19th birthday, November 18, 1942, the twins went to the McAlester Draft Board and volunteered, although their enlistment was delayed until a sufficient number of men from Pittsburg County were recruited to justify transport to Tulsa for their induction physicals.

Rated 1A by army doctors, Claude and Clyde were issued serial numbers and sworn in on January 14, 1943. They were given seven days' leave to put their affairs in order and say goodbye. Their older brother, Carl, was already serving with the 45th Infantry Division.

Earlier, their father, concerned that the twins might be separated in the military, wrote a letter to President Roosevelt asking that his boys be allowed to serve together. Despite the skepticism of his neighbors, their father received a letter from FDR assuring them that the brothers could serve together and directing them to present the letter if the army tried to separate them.

They were transported by bus to Fort Sill, Oklahoma, for processing and were quartered in 20-man tents. As Clyde recalled, "Claude and I were familiar with farm living and we were tough."

At Fort Sill, recruits were evaluated with respect to preference for service, education, and work experiences. After three days of testing and paperwork it was decided that, with their experience with tractors and heavy equipment, the Stokes boys should serve in Army Armor—that is, tanks.

When the officer in charge advised them that they would be separated, they showed him the letter. It was the first of many times.

The Stokes boys were next sent to Fort Knox, Kentucky, for basic training, this time housed in wooden barracks, assigned to Third Platoon, Company B, 13th Armored Replacement Battalion, commanded by Lt. Col. B. R. Moore.

They trained in the use of pistols, rifles, and machine guns and learned to drive jeeps, motorcycles, trucks and tanks, including the M-4 with its 75 mm gun and the M-5 with a 37 mm gun and two .30-caliber machine guns. They learned the duties of all crew positions, including tank commander, driver, assistant driver, gunner and loader.

As Clyde later recounted, "We did not realize how important the training was until later when we stood in battle…. [It] saved our lives many times."

At the end of their training, they showed the letter to Lieutenant Colonel Moore, who took the letter and made it part of their permanent record. They never saw the letter again, but they remained together for the remainder of the war.

Following another short leave, the twins reported to Camp Campbell, Kentucky, for advanced training in tank maneuvers and operations. Once training was completed, they were shipped out to Newport News, Virginia, for embarkation overseas, and on June 18, 1943, the brothers and 7,000 other troops boarded a former luxury liner, now serving as a troopship, destination unknown.

Since they had been issued a large amount of wool uniforms, the scuttlebutt was that they were headed for a cold climate. Three days out, they learned they were headed for Africa. They spent a week zigzagging the Atlantic to avoid German submarines, and arrived at Casablanca, North Africa, without incident seven days later, on June 25.

Assigned to a replacement depot, and while awaiting assignment, they drove trucks delivering war supplies over 700 miles across the Sahara Desert, often being strafed by German aircraft.

The 36th Division had arrived in April, and the brothers were sent to the Second Platoon, Company C, 636th Tank Destroyer Battalion, assigned to the crew of an M-10 Wolverine tank destroyer, nicknamed "Jinx."

Sgt. Edward Yost was the tank commander, Cpl. Alvin Johnson the gunner and PFC Joseph O'Brian the driver. Clyde joined the crew as the assistant driver, and Claude as loader/assistant gunner.

The M-10 was a 32-ton, diesel-powered Sherman tank with an open turret and armed with a three-inch, 50 mm gun and was designed to be a "tank-killer."

On September 3, 1943, the 36th Division embarked from the Port of Oran aboard British ships, bound for the Port of Biserte, arriving three days later.

Crew of the M-10 tank, "Jinx" (left to right, S.Sgt. Raymond Murphy, Sgt. Edwin Yost, Cpl. Alvin Johnson, PFC Joseph O'Brian and Pvts. Claude and Clyde Stokes) (U.S. Army photograph).

Sicily had been invaded in early July, and the Italian Army surrendered to General Patton's Third Infantry Division at Palermo on July 22. Mussolini was arrested on July 25, replaced by Marshal Pietro Badoglio, who took over the government and ordered a withdrawal of all Italian forces from Sicily on August 3. The Germans evacuated Messina on August 17.

Fearing an Italian collapse, Hitler ordered German troops into Italy to disarm the Italian Army and prevent its defection to the Allies, but despite these efforts, a secret cease-fire agreement was signed on September 3, and the decision was made for Gen. Mark Clark to invade Salerno with his Fifth Army.

On September 9, elements of the 36th Division, under the command of Maj. Gen. Fred Walker, landed under fire at Salerno, the first American division to invade the European mainland. The 636th went ashore the following morning, on September 10. It was the twins' first experience with actual combat. It would not be their last.

The beachhead was under continuous fire from enemy mortars, artillery, machine guns, tanks and attacking aircraft. The battle went back and forth for three days, with the Americans gaining ground, only to lose it.

The actions of the 636th on the night of September 13–14 would make a significant difference in the battle and are credited with saving the Salerno beachhead. Second Platoon was given a section on the beachhead to protect, which turned out to be the center of the German attack.

As Claude Stokes recalled, "The enemy pounded us all night ... the following day, they made their attack with thirteen tanks headed our way," and he remembered a general saying, "If you can't swim to Sicily, or if you don't like sauerkraut and wieners, you had better stop those Germans now."

Their tank destroyer was dug in behind the infantry to provide close support.

The battle pitted German Mark-4 and Mark-5 Panzer tanks with their 88 mm guns against the American M-10s with their 50 mm guns. However, although the panzers had the greater firepower, the American tanks were faster and outmaneuvered the larger tanks, getting off the first shot. The advantage was decisive.

The entire crew would be awarded the Silver Star for that 25-minute action, when the Jinx's crew maneuvered the tank into the open, under direct fire from the enemy to engage their targets. As their Silver Star citation noted, "[They] moved with it to a position under direct fire of enemy artillery and small arms, in the face of five enemy tanks. From that position [they] assisted in the destruction of five enemy tanks and one ammunition vehicle, going about their duties in a clear, deliberate manner in spite of the heavy fire.... The destruction of these tanks removed a grave menace to our troops in that sector."

The crew of the Jinx was credited with knocking out five of the seven tanks destroyed by Company C that day. In addition, they destroyed an armored half-track, an ammunition truck, and a pillbox and captured a house, taking 180 German prisoners. They were credited with preventing a German breakthrough that would have put the entire beachhead at risk. As Claude recalled, "Everyone did his job with skill and accuracy." Their award of the Silver Star made the Stokes twins unique in American military history. The 636th was awarded a Presidential Unit Citation.

Following Salerno, the 636th worked its way north up the Italian boot, going into reserve, off the line, on September 20, and Company C was tasked with providing security for Fifth Army Headquarters.

Altavilla, Paestrum and Capaccio were all secured as the American's advanced north, and on October 1, 1943, the Americans captured Naples. At the end of the month, Second Platoon was detached to an anti-tank regiment of the British Seventh Armored Division to train them in the use and deployment of the M-10.

By November, they were back with the 636th, battling a new enemy; the rain and mud of the Italian winter was taking its toll, along with fighting the Germans as they advanced on Mt. Sombrero, San Pietro, San Viltore, Venefro, and on to capture Highway 6. At San Pietro, 16 tanks went into battle with only four coming out, one of them Jinx.

In mid-December, they were pulled off the line, fed hot meals, allowed to bathe, and issued new uniforms, and they caught up on sleep. It was memorable to the Stokes twins as their first Christmas away from the family.

On January 17, 1944, the twins came out of bivouac aboard an M-10 renamed "Oklahoma Wildcat," with Sgt. Claude Stokes as tank commander and Sgt. T/4 Clyde Stokes as driver.

They continued fighting snow, sleet, rain and mud throughout February as they advanced northward toward Cassino, a city of 19,000, located in a valley surrounded by high mountains, most prominent of those being Monte Cassino, atop which rested a 1,400-year-old Benedictine abbey founded by St. Benedict of Nursia around AD 529. The desired outcome was for a breakthrough to Rome.

The advance was hindered by difficult terrain, wet weather and an enemy fighting from prepared defensive positions. The enemy's strategy was one of inflicting heavy casualties, then withdrawing, buying time to construct new positions along the Gustav line, defensive positions that ran east to west across Italy, hoping to stop the Allied advance toward Rome.

Between January 17 and May 18, 1944, there would be four assaults on Monte Cassino and the Gustav defenses, involving American, British, Canadian, South African, Australian, Free French and Italian Royalist troops, as well as troops from New Zealand and Poland, resulting in 55,000 Allied casualties, compared with German losses of 20,000 killed or wounded.

During the assaults, the Allies became convinced that the Germans were using the abbey as an observation post for German artillery, and the severe casualties the Allies were suffering seemed to confirm that belief.

Controversy continues to this day as to whether or not the Germans were actually using it, but as Major General Kippenberger of the New Zealand Corps commented, from a military standpoint, it was immaterial. "If not occupied today, it might be tomorrow and it did not appear it would be difficult for the enemy to bring reserves into it during an attack or for troops to take shelter there if driven from positions outside."

On February 15, 1944, 142 Boeing B-17 "Flying Fortress" heavy bombers followed by 47 North American B-25 Mitchell and 40 Martin B-26 Marauder medium bombers dropped 1,150 tons of high explosives and incendiary bombs on the abbey, reducing the entire top of Monte Cassino to a smoking mass of rubble, while between the bombing, Polish II Corps artillery pounded the hilltop and fighter bombers attacked.

The Vatican's secretary of state, Cardinal Luigi Maglione, bluntly stated that the bombing was "a piece of a gross stupidity" and subsequent investigations found that the only people killed in the monastery by the bombing were 230 Italian civilians seeking refuge in the abbey.

Following its destruction, paratroopers of the German First Parachute Division occupied the ruins of the abbey and turned it into a fortress and observation post, which became a serious problem for the subsequent Allied attacks.

Finally, on May 17, Polish II Corps launched their second, and what was to become the final, attack on Monte Cassino, taking the ruins of the mountaintop monastery the following day after the Germans evacuated their positions overnight, leaving behind only thirty seriously wounded men as they withdrew to new defensive positions along the Hitler Line.

During this period, the 636th was assigned in support of various elements, and the Stokes brothers, and the Oklahoma Wildcat, served with French Moroccan Goumiers and Indian Punjab Gurkhas, and they wrote letters home, amused by the Scottish troops who wore "skirts" into battle.

On May 11, the 36th Division, with the 636th Tank Destroyers, joined the 45th and Third Divisions in an effort to end the stalemate at Anzio and break out, and several days of heavy combat followed as they pushed the Germans north to Velletri, as both the 36th Division and 45th Division raced to be the first to enter Rome.

With the capture of Velletri, the way was open to Rome. The Oklahoma Wildcat entered Rome on June 4, 1944, knocking out two German tanks, and the twins believe they were the first tank into Rome, an honor also claimed by, among others, the tank commanded by Capt. William H. Darby, C Company of the 752nd Tank Battalion.

The brothers often regretted that, as combat troops, they would fight through the city and press on, while the trailing support troops would be greeted as the liberators and get the flowers and kisses.

After almost a year in combat, across North Africa and Italy, despite some close calls, the brother's luck had held, but that streak ended for Clyde on June 14, 1944, in the outskirts of Citaveccia, Italy.

Supporting infantry pinned down by an enemy machine gun, Clyde exited the tank to confer with a machine-gun crew. As he ran back to the tank, a mortar shell struck the tank, scattering shrapnel in all directions, and he was wounded, but he was luckier than the five-man crew, all of whom were killed.

Patched up at an aid station, Clyde refused evacuation to a field hospital, fearing that he would be separated from his brother, and instead returned to duty, driving the Oklahoma Wildcat to destroy the enemy position.

Late in June, the 36th Division was ordered back to Rome, then to the Port of Civitavecchia where tanks and crews were loaded aboard LSTs and carried to Naples, enduring a severe storm at sea along the way.

As one of the most "seasoned" divisions, the 36th Division had been selected to spearhead the impending invasion of Southern France. Although the invasion of Northern and Southern France had originally been planned to be simultaneous, delays in Italy had disrupted the timetable.

On June 6, 1944, American, Canadian and British forces landed on the Normandy Peninsula in Northern France, invading "Fortress Europe."

During July, the 636th trained for the upcoming invasion in the

Salerno area, and the 36th Division was transferred from Fifth Army to Maj. Gen. Alexander Patch's Seventh Army.

On August 7, the twins and the Oklahoma Wildcat were loaded aboard LSTs, and the brothers learned that Second Platoon of C Company, along with First Platoon of B Company, would be supporting the 141st Regimental Combat Team during the landing, the 141st comprising primarily Texans.

By August 11, 400,000 troops, aboard 1,000 ships, sailed toward Southern France. Fortunately, the breakout at St. Lo had caused the Germans to reduce their forces in Southern France from 13 to nine divisions, those troops being withdrawn to reinforce the north.

August 15 was D-Day for Operation Dragoon, the invasion of Southern France, and the 36th Division landed at Camel Beach, near the coastal town of San Raphael on the French Riviera, with the 636th landing at Camel Green.

Green Beach was a difficult objective, flanked by an abrupt cliff and stone retaining wall on the left, a jutting barren rock formation on the right. There was only a single narrow dirt road leading to the main coastal road, which ran under a railroad bridge. Blowing up the bridge would jam all vehicular traffic. Behind the beach rose an irregular slope, broken by an easily defended granite quarry. The most serious fighting would be centered there, as the landing was contested by well-emplaced coastal guns and flak batteries.

Despite a pounding by 90 Allied B-24s and naval gunfire, the resistance was so stiff that landings at Camel Red were abandoned, the troops redirected to Camel Blue and Camel Green.

At 0800 hours, the first and third battalions of the 141st Regimental Combat Team went ashore, with Second Platoon, Company C, not far behind. The Stokes twins fought their way through the town and, on August 17, they were assigned as part of a task force racing through Southern France, pursuing the German 19th Army and 11th Panzer Division. "We advanced some days thirty, forty, fifty, sometimes as much as 100 miles in a day," Claude recalled.

By August 22, the Americans captured Grenoble in the French Alps, and three days later, on August 25, Claude and several others were wounded when an artillery shell exploded, disabling their tank. Claude spent three days in a field hospital, where they removed 53 pieces of shrapnel from his back and legs. He was far from the only casualty.

Between August 15 and 30, the 636th suffered seven killed, 76 wounded and the loss of 13 tank destroyers, two jeeps and a half-track. On September

2, the Oklahoma Wildcat was ordered on a combat patrol to scout the city of Lyons and determine if the Germans had destroyed the bridges over the Rhone River, which ran through the city. They entered the town to find the Germans gone, and they were greeted as liberators by celebrating French.

The 636th continued north, liberating towns throughout October in fighting the Stokes described as "house to house, block by block." They advanced into the Vosges Mountains to find the Germans heavily entrenched and the fighting more costly as they drew closer to the German border.

On October 23, 1944, infantrymen of the First Battalion, 141st Infantry Regiment, the famous Lost Battalion were cut off and surrounded by the Germans. For seven days, the 275 men held out with little food, ammo, or supplies, and efforts to breakthrough or supply them were unsuccessful.

On October 30, Second and Third Platoons, Company C, 636th Tank Destroyers, providing support to the 442nd Infantry Regiment, the Go for Broke Japanese American regiment, broke through German lines to relieve the 441st.

On November 28, parked by a house in support of nearby infantry, their tank took a direct hit from a *panzerfaust*, the German version of a bazooka, and their tank caught fire.

Forced to leave the burning tank, they sought refuge in the cellar of the house, only to discover six wounded infantrymen, left behind when the infantry withdrew. Worse, enemy artillery had set the house on fire.

Aware that abandoning the wounded men would result in their capture or being burned to death, the Stokes brothers, along with their platoon sergeant, Staff Sergeant Glenn McGuire, in what their award citations would describe as "great personal risk," made two trips to evacuate the wounded soldiers, carrying them under fire across 125 yards of exposed terrain to cover, successfully saving all six.

For their actions, the Stokes twins were awarded the Bronze Star with a "V" device, denoting valor, and McGuire was awarded the Distinguished Service Cross, although his award would be posthumous, as he was subsequently killed in action.

On December 13, Company C took the French village of Mittlewihr, near the German border, but a shell from the artillery barrage during the counter-attack set the tank on fire, and Claude was wounded in the face and neck from shrapnel.

The crew safely escaped and took shelter in a nearby cellar with about

30 other tankers and infantrymen. Trapped and surrounded, backlit by burning vehicles, they discussed surrender but instead chose to fight their way out.

With Sergeant McGuire in the lead, they charged from the cellar into enemy gunfire. McGuire was killed, but the others escaped into the dark woods, although losing two killed and six wounded.

By December 20, they were in Strasbourg, France, and on the 24th, the 636th got what Claude called a "Christmas present"; they were pulled from the line and sent to a rest area at Harbouey following a record 133 continuous days in combat. Their rest was short-lived.

On January 2, 1945, the 636th was put on alert and ordered to stand by, but the following day were back in combat, and the Second Platoon was mentioned in a *Stars and Stripes* story calling them the "Armored Devils": when outnumbered 12–3, they destroyed seven enemy tanks.

In February, Companies A and B of the 636th received the new M-36 tank destroyers with 90 mm guns, while C Company continued using the M-10. By March, things were slowing down, but resistance continued as it took three days to capture Oberhoffen.

On March 11, the Stokes twins were informed that they'd been selected for a 45-day furlough back to the States, their selection determined by their length of time with the unit. Of the 128 men who had landed at Salerno, only less than a dozen remained. That night, an artillery barrage almost ended their furlough prematurely.

The following day, they were trucked to Le Havre, France, then put on a ship to England. They were informed that their award of the Silver Star entitled them to transport by air, but it was unknown when the next flight would depart. Or they could travel by ship; the *Queen Elizabeth* was preparing to depart. For the Stokes twins, the choice was easy.

They boarded the *Queen Elizabeth* on March 19 and arrived in New York harbor four days later, the absence of German submarines reducing the time necessary for the crossing.

From New York City, they traveled by train to Fort Dix, New Jersey, and then to Camp Chaffee, near Fort Smith, Arkansas, where they were put on a bus to McAlester, Oklahoma, to begin their 45-day furlough.

Two days later, on March 27, both brothers married their hometown sweethearts, and they spent their leave visiting family. On April 12, President Roosevelt died, and following the German surrender at Reims, France, on May 7, their furlough was extended 15 days.

They returned to Camp Chaffee to process out of the army under the new point system for discharges, and peace accomplished what war was never able to; it separated the brothers.

Although both Claude and Clyde had been awarded the Silver Star and Bronze Star Medals, Claude's two Purple Hearts to Clyde's single award meant that Claude had 89 points versus Clyde's 84 points, which qualified Claude for discharge but not Clyde.

Sgt. Claude Stokes was honorably discharged on June 7, 1945, after two years, four months, and 28 days of service. Sgt. Clyde Stokes was eventually sent to Camp Bowie, Texas, assigned as platoon sergeant with the 781st Chemical Mortar Battalion.

When his service records finally caught up with him, it was discovered that the brothers had been awarded a second Bronze Star, making Clyde eligible for discharge, and he mustered out on September 19, 1945, with two years, six months, and 19 days of service. The brothers had fought in five major campaigns across Africa, Italy, France, and Germany. Along the way, they were credited with destroying 17 enemy tanks.

Both brothers spent a good portion of their post-war career working at the Naval Ammunition Depot in McAlester, with Claude retiring in 1979 and Clyde in 1985.

Over the years, the twins have been honored numerous times; a school was named in their honor and a street, but early in 2017, a letter from the French consul general of France, Sujiro Seam, informed the Stokes brothers they were to be honored:

> I am pleased to inform you that by decree of the President of the French Republic you have been appointed a Chevalier of the Legion of Honor.
>
> This award testifies to the President's high esteem for your merits and accomplishments. In particular, it is a sign of France's infinite gratitude and appreciation for your personal and precious contribution to the United States' decisive role in the liberation of our country during World War II.
>
> The French people will never forget your courage and your devotion to the great cause of freedom.

On August 13, 2017, in a ceremony held at the First Baptist Church in McAlester, Oklahoma, before a crowd of 350, the 93-year-old brothers were presented the medal by the French consul engraved with the words "In the name of the president of the Republic of France, we bestow upon you the medal of Chevalier in the National Order of the Legion of Honor."

Claude credited their success as tankers with his brother Clyde's ability to drive the tank. Success in tank warfare came from being a moving target. As Claude would often remark about his twin, "He made the right turns at the right times."

Sources

Beaty, James. "McAlester Brothers Reflect on WWII Heroics." *McAlester News* (Oklahoma), November 16, 2004.

Beaty, James. "The Stokes Brothers: Grateful Nation Remembers." *McAlester News* (Oklahoma), August 20, 2017.

Sterner, Doug. Home of Heroes. http://www.homeofheroes.com.

Stokes, Madlyn V. *The Stokes Twins Ride the Oklahoma Wildcat*. North Charleston, SC: Booksurge, 2003.

Zaloga, Steven J. *US Armored Units in the North African and Italian Campaigns, 1942–1945*. Oxford: Osprey Publishing, 2013.

Guy "Gabby" Gabaldon
The "Pied Piper of Saipan," from Hell to Eternity

By early 1944, American forces in the Pacific theater of war had vastly improved their ability in making amphibious landings; however, the Japanese had simultaneously improved their ability to defend their islands, resulting in greater and greater number of casualties.

Saipan, in the Mariana Islands, would put the Marines' ability to the test, as its capture was considered essential to victory in the Pacific.

The eventual full-scale invasion of the Japanese mainland, which could result in an estimated one million American casualties, would require airfields within range of the mainland from which to launch B-29 "Superfortress" bombers, with an operational range of 1,500 miles, to support the invasion, and Saipan fit the bill.

The invasion of Saipan would involve 535 ships and 127,570 personnel, primarily troops of the Second and Fourth Marine Divisions. Two days prior to the invasion, on June 13, 1944, the guns aboard seven battleships and 11 destroyers shelled Saipan and a sister island, Tinian, expending 15,000 16-inch and 5-inch shells and 165,000 other shells.

The following day, eight older battleships and 11 cruisers replaced the more modern "fast" battleships and continued bombarding the island.

At 0700 hours on June 15, 1944, 300 LVTs began landing Marines of the Second and Fourth Marine Divisions on the west coast of Saipan, taking the Japanese high command by surprise. They had expected the landings further south.

By 0900 hours, 800 Marines were ashore. A naval force of 11 ships—two battleships (USS *Tennessee* and USS *California*), two cruisers (USS *Indianapolis* and USS *Birmingham*), and seven destroyers—provided fire support for the invasion. By nightfall, the Marines had established a beachhead, six miles long by a half mile deep. That night, a Japanese counter-attack failed, with heavy casualties.

On June 16 the army's 27th Infantry Division landed and advanced to the airfield at As Lito, and a nighttime counter-attack again failed, with the Japanese abandoning the field on June 18.

On June 19–20, the Battle of the Philippine Sea, nicknamed the Great Marianas Turkey Shoot, took place, the largest, and last, carrier-to-carrier battle of World War II. The disastrous loss by the Japanese of three fleet aircraft carriers and between 550 and 645 aircraft eliminated any possibility of resupply or reinforcement of the Japanese garrison on Saipan, sealing their fate.

Thus began a twenty-four-day battle (June 15–July 9) that would pit Marine Lt. Gen. Holland "Howling Mad" Smith and approximately 71,000 troops landed on the island against approximately 31,000 troops of the Japanese 31st Army under the command of Lt. Gen. Saito Yoshitsuga.

Surrounded and cut off, the Japanese refused to surrender, choosing to fight to the last man from caves and in the mountainous terrain. In desperation, at dawn on July 7, the Japanese launched a "Banzai charge," which was "for the honor of the Emperor," hoping to drive the invaders back into the sea. They sustained a loss of over 4,000 soldiers and civilians who had joined the charge.

In the close-quarters combat that made up most of the fighting for the island, Americans suffered 2,949 killed or missing and another 10,364 wounded, compared to Japanese losses of 29,000 killed (of which 5,000 were suicides) and only 2,100 prisoners taken. Figures vary depending on source.

The battle for Saipan includes many legendary stories of courage and valor, among them, the Navajo Code Talkers, who used their native language to direct naval gunfire onto targets and frustrated Japanese attempts at eavesdropping on sensitive communications, and 800 African American Marines who unloaded food and ammunition on the beach under fire, the first Black Marines to see combat in World War II.

Four Marines would be awarded the Medal of Honor for their actions on the island, all of them posthumously.

On June 16, Gunnery Sergeant Robert H. McCard, Fourth Tank Battalion, Fourth Marine Division, courageously exposed himself to enemy guns when his tank was put out of action, bringing all the tank's weapons to bear on the enemy, until the severity of hostile fire caused him to order his crew out the escape hatch while he covered them, killing sixteen of the enemy but sacrificing himself to ensure the safety of his tank crew.

On June 25, PFC Harold G. Epperson, First Battalion, Sixth Marines, Second Marine Division, was fighting in the defense of his battalion's position and maintaining a steady stream of devastating fire against rapidly infiltrating enemy. A Japanese soldier, assumed to be dead, sprang up and hurled a powerful hand grenade into Epperson's emplacement. Determined to save his comrades, PFC Epperson unhesitatingly threw himself on a grenade to contain the blast, saving the other members of his squad.

On July 7, PFC Harold C. Agerholm, Fourth Battalion, Tenth Marines, Second Marine Division, disregarded heavy enemy fire and, as his citation recounted, "appropriating an abandoned ambulance jeep, repeatedly made extremely perilous trips under heavy rifle and mortar fire and single-handedly loaded and evacuated approximately forty-five casualties." He was killed by a sniper as he tried to help two other wounded men.

On July 8, Sergeant Grant F. Timmerman, Second Tank Battalion, Sixth Marines, Second Marine Division, fearlessly covered an open tank hatch with his own body to prevent an enemy grenade from killing his crew and the grenade exploded on his chest, killing him instantly. Although two members of the crew received slight wounds from the grenade, none were killed.

An estimated 22,000 civilians died on the island, the majority of them by suicide, jumping from cliffs later named Suicide Cliff and Banzai Cliff, many holding babies and small children. Civilians were encouraged to commit suicide rather than be captured by the Americans, who they were told were committing atrocities.

Operating by himself, to prevent this useless waste of life by Japanese soldiers and civilians, was a streetwise, Japanese-speaking 18-year-old Mexican American private first class from the barrios of East Los Angeles who would become famous as the "Pied Piper of Saipan."

Credited with capturing over 1,000 Japanese soldiers and 500 civilians on Saipan, Guy Louis Gabaldon holds the distinction of capturing more enemy soldiers than anyone else in American military history.

Born one of seven children in a Mexican American family in East Los Angeles on March 22, 1926, Guy Louis Gabaldon, trying to escape the gangs, made friends with twins Lane and Lyle Nakano. Impressed with their self-discipline and honesty, he was taken in by their Japanese American family when he was 12, and he attended Japanese language and culture classes with the family's children, where he learned to speak what he called "backstreet" Japanese.

Japanese prisoners on Saipan, 1944 (U.S. Marine Corps photograph).

After Pearl Harbor was attacked on December 7, 1941, his adopted family, along with all Japanese Americans on the West Coast, was ordered to relocate. His brothers enlisted in the 442nd Regimental Combat Team, an all-Nisei unit of the U.S. Army for service in Europe, and his parents and sister were interned at the Heart Mountain "relocation camp" in Wyoming.

"I wanted to go with them," he later recounted, "but they wouldn't let me." At age 15, he moved to Alaska and found work in a cannery. Gabaldon wanted to enlist in the navy and serve aboard submarines, but the navy wasn't interested in a man who was five foot three and had a perforated eardrum. He enlisted in the Marines upon turning 17, on March 22, 1943. The recruiter, aware of the corps' need for Japanese speakers, overlooked his size and eardrum.

After basic training at Camp Pendleton, at San Diego, California, Private Gabaldon (serial no. 517054) was trained in heavy weapons (mortars) and sent to Enlisted Marine Japanese Language School at Camp Elliott, also at San Diego, where he qualified as a scout/observer and Japanese translator.

After training in amphibious landings, Gabaldon was assigned to the Headquarters and Service Company, Second Marine Regiment, Second Marine Division, and sailed for Hawaii from San Diego on December 23, 1943, aboard the SS *Young America*, arriving at Pearl Harbor on December 30.

After more amphibious training in Hawaii, the Second Marines embarked aboard the USS *Feland* on May 30, landing on Saipan on June 15, 1944, the first day of battle. He was 18 years old.

During the early days of the campaign, Gabaldon found his small size an advantage in the close-in fighting required in jungle warfare and earned respect as a fighter.

But from almost his first night on the island, Gabaldon began going on unauthorized, solo patrols, leaving his position to scout out the enemy lines. With his knowledge of the language, he decided to try to talk some Japanese soldiers into surrendering. Gabaldon's method was to approach a Japanese cave, shoot the guard, and yell to the Japanese inside that they were surrounded.

The first night, Gabaldon returned with two prisoners, but instead of praise, his commanding officer threatened him with a court-martial for leaving his lines and ordered him not to do it again. Disobeying his orders, Gabaldon made another trip the next night and came back with 50 prisoners. Acknowledging his success, his commanders granted Gabaldon authority to come and go as he pleased, or as he put it, become a "lone-wolf" operator.

Gabaldon entered caves, pillboxes and the jungle, often under direct fire, to persuade the Japanese troops and residents to surrender. Working alone, at great personal risk, he would speak to them in Japanese, working to convince them that the island was secured and that fighting "to the last man" as the code of Bushido required would be a senseless loss of life.

As he recounted in a September 5, 2006, interview on National Public Radio's *All Things Considered*,

> My ability to speak Japanese [was] very limited, but it wasn't difficult to say raise your hands and come on out. At night, I'd usually go over to the caves. Saipan is just full of caves, and I'd get to one side of the mouth of a cave, and I'd say you are completely surrounded. I've got a bunch of Marines here with me behind the trees. If you don't surrender, I'll have to kill you, and usually it worked—not always. I'd have to throw grenades in and kill, and I'd get maybe 10, 15, 20 at a time, and one day I got 800.

That day was July 8, 1944. Cut off behind enemy lines a day earlier, Gabaldon had witnessed Japanese troops and civilians massing for a Banzai charge, a suicidal assault on July 7, the largest of the war, with over 4,000 Japanese killed. Following the charge, Gabaldon found himself trapped behind the lines. In a 1998 interview with *War Times Journal*, he remembered,

> It was in the morning of 8 July that I took two prisoners on top of the Banzai Cliffs. I talked with them at length trying to convince them that to continue fighting would amount to sure death for them. I told them that if they continued fighting, our flame throwers would roast them alive.
> I pointed to the many ships we had lying off shore waiting to blast them in their

caves. "Why die when you have a chance to surrender under honorable conditions? You are taking civilians to their death which is not part of your Bushido military code."

The big job was going to be in convincing them that we would not torture and kill them, that they would be well treated and would be returned to Japan after the war. I understood that their Bushido Code called for death before surrender, and that to surrender was to be considered a coward. This was going to be a tough nut to crack.

It was either convincing them that I was a good guy or I would be a dead Marine within a few minutes.

Gabaldon sent one of his prisoners back to try to convince the other survivors to surrender, keeping the other soldier with him.

I knew that there were hundreds of die-hard enemy at the bottom of the cliffs and if they rushed me I would probably kill two or three before they ate me alive…. I finally talked one of my two prisoners to return to the bottom of the cliffs and to try to convince his fellow survivors that they would be treated with dignity if they surrendered.

I kept the other one with me, not as a hostage, but because he said that if he went to the caves with my message and they did not buy it, off with the head. I couldn't help agreeing with him. The one that descended the cliff either had lots of guts or he was going to double-cross me and come back with his troops firing away. Who was the prisoner, me or the Japs?

The soldier returned with about a dozen men, including an officer, all armed. "They [weren't] pointing their weapons at me, but on the other hand, they didn't have to. If I go to fire they would have the drop on me. They'd chop me down before I fire a round."

Once the officer was convinced that his men would receive medical care and be well-treated, he went back to the caves and then returned with a group of 50 men, explaining that there were hundreds of people down below, some wounded, some civilians. Then, as Gabaldon remembered, "They start coming up. The lines up the trails seem endless."

Fortunately, to Gabaldon's relief, others had seen the large number of Japanese, and he was soon joined by "hundreds of Marines." He would be credited with capturing over 800 prisoners in a single day.

Overall, Gabaldon would be credited with capturing 1,500 Japanese soldiers and civilians over the course of the campaigns on Saipan and Tinian. He also witnessed the suicides of dozens of Japanese civilians.

In the course of his mission, he was forced to kill 33 enemy soldiers and was twice wounded. He also landed on Tinian, where he saw combat and captured additional soldiers and civilians, and then returned to Saipan where he was ambushed and wounded by machine-gun fire while engaged in fighting Japanese guerrillas on the island.

He returned to San Francisco aboard the USS *Tryon* (APH-1), arriving on March 11, 1945. Hospitalized in Oceanside, California, while recovering from his wounds, he was honorably discharged from the Marines as a private first class on November 10, 1945.

His company commander, Capt. John Schwabe, stated that Gabaldon's actions resulted in obtaining vital intelligence that shortened the period of combat, resulting in the significant saving of life. He recommended Gabaldon for the Medal of Honor. He was awarded the Silver Star. In comparison, during World War I, army Sergeant Alvin C. York was awarded the Medal of Honor for single-handedly capturing 132 prisoners.

In June of 1957, Gabaldon appeared as a guest on the NBC television show *This Is Your Life*, and in 1960 a movie, *From Hell to Eternity*, was made about his actions at Saipan. He was played by Jeffery Hunter, a blue-eyed, tall Caucasian. The resulting publicity resulted in Gabaldon being awarded the Navy Cross, the second-highest award for valor, on December 20, 1960.

The citation was

> for extraordinary heroism while serving with Headquarters and Service Company, Second Marines, Second Marine Division, in action against enemy Japanese forces on Saipan and Tinian, Mariana Islands, South Pacific Area, from 15 June to 1 August 1944. Acting as a Japanese Interpreter for the Second Marines, Private First Class GABALDON displayed extreme courage and initiative in single-handedly capturing enemy civilian and military personnel during the Saipan and Tinian operations. Working alone in front of the lines, he daringly entered enemy caves, pillboxes, buildings, and jungle brush, frequently in the face of hostile fire, and succeeded in not only obtaining vital military information, but in capturing well over one thousand enemy civilians and troops. Through his valiant and distinguished exploits, Private First Class GABALDON made an important contribution to the successful prosecution of the Campaign and, through his efforts, a definite humane treatment of civilian prisoners was assured. His courageous and inspiring devotion to duty throughout reflects the highest credit upon himself and the United States Naval Service.

Many felt that Gabaldon's actions justified the award of the Medal of Honor, and that he was passed over because he was Hispanic. Efforts were made to have the government acknowledge Gabaldon's actions with the award of the Medal of Honor but as of 2016 were unsuccessful.

Following his honorable discharge, Gabaldon returned to Boyle Heights and married June, a girl from the neighborhood, with whom he had six children before divorce ended the marriage. He moved to Mexico and tried his hand at fishing, learned to fly and started a successful import-export business. He also met and married Ohana Suzuki, with whom he had five more children.

In the mid-1970s, Gabaldon and Ohana moved to Saipan, where he worked as police chief, gave tours, and was a drug-abuse counselor. He also wrote his autobiography, *Saipan: Suicide Island*, published in 1990.

After two decades on Saipan, Gabaldon returned to California in 1995 and then moved to Florida in 2003. In 2000, Marine Corps Gen. James L. Jones upgraded Gabaldon's rank from private first class to corporal. "He told me to keep my nose clean and maybe in another 50 years, I'd be a sergeant," Gabaldon said.

Gabaldon passed away in Old Town, Florida, of heart disease on August 31, 2006, at the age of 80. He was buried with full military honors at Arlington National Cemetery, Section 8AA, Row 19, Site 1. Gabaldon was survived by his wife, Ohana, and nine of his eleven children.

Sources

Burbeck, James. "Interview with Guy Gabaldon." *War Times Journal*, September 19, 1998. http://www.wtj.com/articles/gabaldon/.

Goldstein, Richard. "Guy Gabaldon, 80, Hero of Battle of Saipan, Dies." *New York Times*, September 4, 2006.

"Guy Gabaldon, from East Los Angeles Kid to Pied Piper of Saipan." World War II History Archives, June 2016. http://ww2awartobewon.com/wwii-articles/guy-gabaldon-pied-piper-saipan/.

Hoeferlin, Collin. "Guy Gabaldon." Marineparents.com, September 2016. https://marineparents.com/marinecorps/guy-gabaldon.asp.

Kakesako, Gregg. "'Pied Piper' Returning to Saipan: The Chicano Recipient of the Navy Cross Will Revisit the Site of a Historic World War II Battle." *Honolulu Star Bulletin*, June 6, 2004.

Rasmussen, Cecilia. "The 'Pied Piper of Saipan' Stood Tall during World War II." *Los Angeles Times*, November 13, 2005.

Eugene B. Fluckey
Only Sub Commander to "Torpedo" a Train

Late on the evening of July 22, 1945, the captain of the submarine USS *Barb* (SS-220) watched the sky anxiously. For four days, they had been waiting for favorable weather to put a landing party ashore. Their mission was to plant a 55-pound scuttling charge to destroy a coastal railway line. It was near the end of the *Barb*'s 12th war patrol, and time was running out.

The captain ordered the landing party be made up of volunteers from every division of the boat, giving preference to former Boy Scouts, believing them better at finding their way in uncharted territory, and he excluded married men.

Although he would have preferred to lead the mission himself, the captain gave command of the mission to Lt. William M. Walker. Also selected were Chief Gunners Mate Paul G. "Swish" Saunders, Electrician's Mate Third Class Billy R. Hatfield, Signalman Second Class Francis Neal Sever, Ship's Cook First Class Lawrence W. Newland, Torpedoman's Mate Third Class Edward W. Klingesmith, Motor Machinist's Mate Second Class James E. Richard, and Motor Machinist's Mate First Class John Markuson.

It was midnight when the eight men launched two rubber rafts and paddled to shore as the *Barb* waited 950 yards offshore Karafuto, Japan, in shallow waters, the landing having been delayed while they'd waited for two small vessels to pass.

The previous evening, the captain had given Walker the following instructions:

Bill, avoid trouble. If the spot isn't good or the odds poor, bring the squad back.... Keep your men together and quiet going and returning ... don't get cocky and try something else. I want neither prisoners nor injuries to the Japanese except those positively required. Slip in and slip out without being detected.... You have one mission only: booby-trap the train and bring the men back safely. The latter is more important.

Throughout his long career, the captain, Eugene B. Fluckey, could claim many achievements and distinctions. Leading his sub on war patrols, he was the first and only American submarine skipper to fire rockets at Japanese targets on shore, is officially credited with sinking 17 enemy vessels and one train, and initiated the only ground combat in the Japanese home islands. Being awarded the Medal of Honor and four Navy Crosses, the navy's highest award for valor, he rose to the rank of rear admiral, and served as the Director of Naval Intelligence. But Fluckey considered his greatest achievement to be that not a single member of his crew was killed or seriously wounded during the war.

Rear Adm. Eugene Fluckey (U.S. Naval Historical Center).

Eugene Bennett "Lucky" Fluckey was born in Washington, D.C., on October 5, 1913, one of three children of Issac Newton and Luella Fluckey. An early achiever, with ambitions to attend Annapolis, he graduated Western High School in 1928 at age 15 and earned the rank of Eagle Scout in the Boy Scouts.

Fluckey took classes at Mercerburg Academy in Pennsylvania and the Columbian Preparatory School in Washington, D.C., until he was old enough to apply for the U.S. Naval Academy, where he entered as a midshipman on June 13, 1931.

At the academy, Fluckey excelled in athletics and is remembered in the Lucky Bag, the academy yearbook, as someone who could be counted on for "good books and great conversations."

He graduated as a member of the Class of 1935 and was commissioned an ensign in the U.S. Navy on June 6, 1935. His first assignment was to the USS *Nevada* (BB-36), first of two Nevada-class battleships assigned as part of the Pacific Fleet. He reported aboard in July 1935. On December 7, 1941, during the Japanese attack on Pearl Harbor, the *Nevada* would be the only battleship to get under way during the attack.

In May of 1936, Fluckey transferred to the USS *McCormick* (DD-223), a Clemson-class destroyer launched in 1920. She was homeported in San Diego, California, awaiting decommissioning, which occurred in October 1938.

In the interim, Fluckey reported for instruction at the Submarine School at New London, Connecticut, and reported aboard the USS *S-42* (SS-153) in December 1938. The USS *S-42* was the first member in the third group of S-class submarines, launched on April 30, 1923.

Homeported at the Coco Solo Naval Reservation in the Canal Zone of Panama, Fluckey lived ashore with his wife, Marjorie, and a daughter, Barbara. In June 1941, with World War II already in progress but America still official neutral, Fluckey was transferred aboard the USS *Bonita* (SS-165), an older Barracuda-class submarine.

The *Bonita* had been taken out of commission and put in reserve at Philadelphia, Pennsylvania, on June 4, 1937, but was recommissioned on September 5, 1940, and departed New London, Connecticut, on November 17 for Coco Solo.

Following the United States' entry into the war on December 7, 1941, the USS *Bonita* patrolled in the Pacific, off Panama, until she returned to Philadelphia for an overhaul in October 1942.

However, in June of 1942, Fluckey was detached from the *Bonita* and returned to Annapolis to earn a graduate degree in naval engineering in November 1943. He then returned to New London to attend the Prospective Commanding Officers School.

In January 1944, Fluckey was assigned as executive officer aboard the USS *Barb* (SS-220) under the command of Lt. Cmdr. John Randolph Waterman. The *Barb*, a Gato-class submarine commissioned July 8, 1942, was state of the art and already a veteran of five war patrols in the Atlantic. Newly overhauled in September 1943, she sailed to Pearl Harbor for service in the Pacific.

With a speed of 21 knots on the surface and nine knots submerged, and with a range of 11,000 nautical miles on the surface, along with the ability to remain on patrol for up to 75 days, the *Barb* was a formidable warship, armed with 10 torpedo tubes (six forward, four aft), as well as 40 mm and

20 mm guns. Fluckey, and his crew of five officers and 54 enlisted sailors would put the *Barb* to good use.

Fluckey was one of a new generation of submarine commanders who aggressively hunted their targets on the surface, where their boats could travel faster and keep a better lookout for enemy ships. It was more dangerous, but these new tactics decimated the Japanese merchant fleet. In essence, the former role of reconnaissance was changed to using submarines as offensive weapons.

Assuming command on April 27, 1944, Commander Fluckey and the *Barb* set off on the ship's eighth war patrol on May 21, departing Midway island for the Sea of Okhotsk, north of Japan, and the Kuril Islands. His success the first time out as captain resulted in his first award of the Navy Cross, the citation recording that Fluckey "launched torpedo attacks to sink five enemy ships totaling more than 37,000 tons and account for two more in aggressive gun battles. Despite persistent hostile countermeasures, he employed skillful evasive tactics to bring his ship to port without damage." The *Barb* returned to Midway on July 5, with seven enemy scalps in its belt.

On August 4, 1944, the *Barb* set out from Midway on its ninth war patrol, headed to the South China Sea, off Formosa. Fluckey's second outing in command of the *Barb* was every bit as eventful and successful.

On August 31, while patrolling the Luzon Strait, the *Barb* torpedoed the Japanese transport *Okuni Maru* (5,633 tons) and the auxiliary minesweeper *Hinode Maru* No. 20 (281 tons), sinking both, and damaged a tanker, the *Rikko Maru*.

On September 11, the *Barb*, as well as the submarines *Growler, Sea Lion, Pampanito* and *Queenfish*, were alerted by SubForce Pacific that a Japanese convoy was headed from Singapore to the Formosa Strait, and they were directed to intercept. Unknown to the Americans, the convoy of five ships and four escorts was transporting, among other cargo, 2,100 British and Australian POWs.

Just after midnight, on September 12, the *Growler* made contact, followed by the *Sea Lion* and *Pampanito*. The *Growler* sank the frigate *Hirado* at 0057 hours. At 0425, the *Sea Lion* put two torpedoes into the *Nankai Maru* and two more into the *Rakuyo Maru*, which carried 1,350 POWs. At 0553, the *Growler* sank the destroyer *Shikinami*. At 0700, the *Nankai Maru* sank. Later that evening, at 2140 hours, the *Pampanito* sank the *Zuiho Maru* and the *Kachidoki Maru*, which carried 750 POWs.

On the afternoon of September 15, the *Pampanito*, passing west of the *Rakuyo Maru* sinking, encountered a number of rafts loaded with men.

They suspected them of being Japanese until one called up, "First you bloody Yanks sink us, and now you're bloody well going to shoot us?" They pulled aboard the first of the surviving British and Australian POWs. Along with the *Sea Lion*, the *Pampanito* searched the area until dark, reaching capacity, then departed for Saipan with 73 survivors aboard the *Pampanito* and 54 aboard the *Sea Lion*.

On September 16, the *Barb* and the *Queenfish* were ordered to the area to continue the search. That same day, Japanese convoy HI-74 was in the area, having departed the Seletar-Singapore area at dawn on September 11.

HI-74 comprised five tankers: the *Azusa Maru*, the pride of Japan's tanker fleet, carrying 100,600 barrels of oil; the *Harima Maru*, *Otowayama Maru*, *Omuroyama Maru* and *Hakko Maru*. The tankers were protected by the carrier *Unyo*, the light cruiser *Kashii*, four frigates and two destroyers.

At 2231 hours, the *Queenfish* made contact and attacked, firing four torpedoes. One hit the *Omuroyama Maru*, but the others passed the *Kashii* to starboard. Her torpedoes expended, the *Queenfish* withdrew as the *Barb* attacked.

At 2332 hours, the *Barb* fired a volley and struck the oil tanker *Atsusa Maru*, possibly twice. It exploded in a fireball and sank. At 0037 on the morning of the 17th, two of *Barb*'s torpedoes found the *Unyo*, hitting the starboard side. All while evading a frigate intent on ramming them.

The first struck the *Unyo*'s stern at the steering compartment, and the second detonated in the engine room. She settled aft immediately. Damage-control crews made heroic efforts, but the rough seas flooded in at an accelerated pace, and soon she was listing heavily starboard. The order to abandon ship was given. The *Unyo* sank at 0650 hours. The two kills earned the *Barb* another 32,500 tons sunk.

The *Barb* and *Queenfish* spent the day and evening searching for survivors from the *Rakuyo Maru*, with *Queenfish* recovering 18 POWs and *Barb* 24, none in good shape. The additional "passengers" would put a strain on the remaining food, fresh water, medicine and space as the subs made speed for Saipan, arriving on September 25 and departing for Majuro in the Marshall Islands the following day.

Fluckey would receive a second Navy Cross for that and other acts:

> Effecting the rescue of fourteen British and Australian prisoners of war who were survivors of a torpedoed enemy transport, he provided care and treatment for the sick and wounded and, although heavy enemy counterattacks caused minor damage to his ship, employed evasive tactics and returned to port without further damage.

Promoted to full commander, Fluckey took the *Barb* out on her tenth war patrol on October 27, departing Majuro for the East China Sea. On November 10, the *Barb* sank the *Gokoku Maru* (10,500 tons) off Koshiki Jima, Kyushu, Japan.

On November 11, the *Queenfish* made contact with MoMa-07 (Moji to Manila), a Japanese convoy of 12 merchant ships, under-protected by five escorts. The original convoy of six freighters and five escorts had been joined by additional vessels, increasing the convoy's vulnerability to attack. The *Queenfish* attacked and damaged the *Miho Maru*.

Early the following morning, at 0120 hours on the 12th, the *Barb* spotted a convoy of 11 ships and five escorts. Approaching on the surface, the *Barb*'s attack was hindered by bad weather, rough seas and high winds. Despite these limitations, the *Barb* launched six torpedoes at 0142 hours, sinking the transport *Naruo Maro* (4,823 tons), which exploded in a fireball, and damaging the cargo ship *Kokuyo Maru* and the *Gyokuyo Maru* (5,396 tons), which was sunk by the USS S*padefish* (SS-411) two days later.

Close to midnight on November 15, the *Barb* spotted a large ship accompanied by four escorts and identified the large ship as the Shokaku-Class carrier *Katsuragi*, although Japanese records after the war indicate it might have been the carrier *Junyo*.

In any event, at 2323 hours, with seven torpedoes remaining, the *Barb* launched five, delivering one hit, before being forced to take evasive action from numerous depth charges. Fluckey and other subs trailed the damaged carrier, hoping for another opportunity, but none presented itself.

After unsuccessfully firing her last two remaining torpedoes, the *Barb* finished her tenth war patrol, returning to Midway on November 25. Fluckey was awarded his third Navy Cross, the citation reading,

> Maneuvering his ship in extremely shallow water and with skill and aggressiveness, Commander Fluckey braved intense hostile countermeasures to penetrate strong enemy escort screens and launch smashing torpedo attacks against Japanese shipping, sinking five enemy ships for a total of more than 28,000 tons and damaging three other vessels, including a large aircraft carrier.

Between patrols, the crew was constantly drilling and practicing, honing their skills, aware that every crew member was essential and that a single mistake by anyone could sink the boat.

On December 19, 1944, the *Barb* departed Midway for the Formosa Strait for her 11th war patrol, arriving in the waters off Wenzchou on January 6, 1945.

The following morning, at 0545 hours, the *Barb* made contact with a large group of ships. Raising the periscope, Fluckey saw a tanker, a freighter, and five destroyers, but rough seas and bad weather hid their quarry, making it difficult to acquire a target. Finally, they launched four torpedoes, with two hits heavily damaging the *Munakata Maru*, a 10,045-ton tanker.

On January 8, the MoTa-30 (Moji to Takeo) convoy departed Fuzhou, China, at 0800 hours. The convoy comprised the *Anyo Maru* (9,256 tons), carrying supplies and troops; *Hisagawa Maru* (6,886 tons), a converted passenger liner carrying troops and vehicles; *Shinyo Maru* (6,892), carrying troops on her maiden voyage; *Manju Maru* (6,515 tons), a tanker; *Rashin Maru* (5,454 tons), a freighter carrying 1,042 troops; *Hikoshima Maru* (2,854 tons), a tanker; and *Meiho Maru* (2,857 tons), a freighter. The escort was four frigates and four patrol craft. Later, they were joined by the tanker *Sanyo Maru* (2,854 tons), carrying aviation fuel.

Sighting the convoy at 1300 hours, the *Barb*, joined by the *Queenfish* and USS *Picuda* (SS-382), tracked the convoy, awaiting an opportunity.

At 1724, the *Barb* fired three torpedoes from the forward tubes, followed by three more from the aft tubes a minute later. This was followed by two hits, then an explosion that rocked the submarine, and she withdrew to reload.

The *Queenfish* made a pass, firing six misses, followed by the *Picuda* with two hits, and then, reloaded, it was the *Barb*'s turn again. She attacked from the rear, firing three torpedoes at the rearmost ship at 2012 hours and then three more at 2033, resulting in another explosion.

The *Barb* is credited with sinking the *Anyo Maru*, *Shinyo Maru* (carrying explosives), and *Hisawgawa Maru* and the tankers *Hikoshima Maru* and *Sanyo Maru* and damaging the *Meiho Maru*.

On January 23, 1945, Commander Fluckey and the crew of the *Barb* would pull off an extraordinary attack so remarkable that it would make them legends in U.S. naval history and earn their captain the Medal of Honor.

Deducing that a large number of enemy vessels were anchored at Mamkwan Harbor, 250 miles south of Shanghai, Fluckey resolved to attack, aware that a safe retirement would necessitate an hour's run at full speed through the uncharted, mined, and rock-obstructed waters. Advised by his officers that success would require a lot of luck, Fluckey stated, "Luck is where you find it. But to find it, you have to look for it."

In the predawn hours, evading detection and cruising on the surface in dangerously shallow waters, the *Barb* entered Mamkwan Harbor. Radar indicated at least 30 ships present, as well as escorts.

At 0402 hours, *Barb* launched her last four forward torpedoes. Quickly coming about, she launched four torpedoes from her stern tubes and then, as the Medal of Honor citation states, "clearing the treacherous area at high speed, [Fluckey] brought the *Barb* through to safety."

The eight torpedoes resulted in eight hits, the Medal of Honor citation credits him with six vessels hit, and Fluckey, in his book *Thunder Below*, credits himself with only four ships. The citation also gives the date as January 25.

One ship, the *Taikyo Maru*, a 5,244-ton cargo freighter carrying explosives, exploded in a fireball that rained down shrapnel and debris, setting fires and causing extensive secondary damage.

The fires lit up the smoke-filled harbor as the *Barb* proceeded at full speed into uncharted and mined waters. Evading rocks and shore battery fire, reloading her aft tubes as she ran at an astonishing 23.5 knots, a record for a submarine, and risking the danger of blowing the engines as the pursuing frigates closed the distance, the *Barb* maneuvered among several anchored fishing junks, causing the frigate's radar to lose the target as the sub raced for deeper water, reaching it and diving just as Japanese aircraft arrived on the scene.

On January 29, at 0540 hours, the *Barb* fired her last two torpedoes at the 1,735-ton cargo-passenger ship *Katsuura Maru* sinking it, even as the *Picuda* sent the *Clyde Maru* (5,467 tons), a cargo-troop ship, previously used as a POW ship, to the bottom.

Their supply of torpedoes exhausted, the *Barb* and her crew headed for Midway, arriving on February 10, departing the following day for Pearl Harbor, and ultimately arriving at the Mare Island Navy Yard outside San Francisco on February 27 to begin a major overhaul, including the installation of 5-inch (130 mm) rocket launchers at Fluckey's request.

On March 23, 1945, Secretary of the Navy James Forrestal presented the Medal of Honor to Fluckey in a ceremony, in the secretary's office in Washington, D.C., with Fleet Admiral Ernest King and Fluckey's wife, Marjorie, observing. FDR had hoped to personally award the medal but was too ill to do so. The crew was awarded the Presidential Unit Citation, the highest award to the crew of a warship.

Although submarine captains were usually restricted to four war patrols, Fluckey persuaded his superior, Admiral Charles Lockwood, commander, Submarine Force Pacific, to allow him a fifth war patrol.

Her overhaul complete, the *Barb*, now known as "the Galloping Ghost of the China Coast," departed Pearl Harbor on June 8, 1945, on her 12th war patrol with orders from Lockwood to "raise a rumpus." Fluckey, as always, was true to his orders and began a series of hit-and-run raids, and they headed toward the northern end of the Japanese home islands.

On June 21, just after midnight off the northwest coast of Hokkaido, the *Barb* made radar contact with two small craft. Following them until they were silhouetted against the dawn at 0318 hours, the *Barb* sank to two Japanese tugboats with her 5-inch and 40 mm guns.

On June 22, the *Barb* made naval history when, at 0105 hours, the command "Man battle stations—rocket" went over the ship's intercom. The "rocketeers" came on deck to load 12 five-inch, spin-stabilized, high-capacity rockets, each with 9.6 pounds of explosives, into the launcher. At 0234 hours, Fluckey ordered, "Rockets away," and for the first time, rockets were launched by a submarine at targets on shore, doing extensive damage to the factories at Shari.

On June 23, the *Barb* sank a fishing vessel in the La Perouse Strait using her guns.

At dawn on July 2, the *Barb* attacked Kaihyo To Island near Shikuka, Japan, and using her guns laid down a 33-minute barrage. Her 40 mm gun destroyed a pillbox, an observation post, three sampans and an oil dump. The five-inch gun destroyed a radar and radio station, shelled barracks, warehouses and shops, and set buildings afire. Fluckey later reported, "The island is out of commission. No communications, no radar, no power, no buildings, no boats exist." He would later refer to the action as "Little Iwo Jima." The Japanese claimed the attack had been carried out by "six warships and a submarine."

On July 3, *Barb* launched rockets at Shikuka Air Base and sank an unnamed cargo ship (1,000 tons) and two days later sank the *Sapporo Maru* (2,820 tons), a cargo ship, outside Odomon Harbor, near Sakhalin. On July 10, she sank the cargo ship *Toyu Maru* (1,256 tons) and a coastal defense frigate, no. 112, on July 18, all while searching for an appropriate site to go ashore and destroy a coastal railroad line.

On July 22 the eight-man sabotage team in their rubber rafts headed to Karafuto, Japan. Fluckey had wanted to destroy the railroad and blow up a train, but decided that for the men to wait until a train approached would put his men in danger, an unacceptable risk. Engineman Third-Class Billy Hatfield came up with a solution, devising a pressure switch that would detonate the explosives by the weight of the passing train.

As the *Barb* waited offshore, the boats landed unopposed, and the team made their way to the tracks and began placing the explosives but were forced to scramble for cover when a train passed through at 0047 hours.

By 0132, with the scuttling charge and battery buried, the shore party departed the beach and rowed toward the sub, but they were only halfway back to the ship when, at 0147, another train crossed the tracks. The explosion sent 16 rail cars into the air and wreckage flying in all directions. Cheers went up from all hands as the shore party was taken aboard and they hastily departed the area.

The *Barb* earned the distinction of carrying out the only ground combat operation in the Japanese home islands during World War II, for which Lieutenant Walker was awarded the Navy Cross, and the seven sailors received the Silver Star. For the remainder of the patrol, the *Barb* attacked targets up and down the Japanese coast, making rocket attacks at Shiritori on July 24 and the factories at Kashiho the following day and gun attacks on small vessels, before completing the patrol and returning to Midway on August 2. This last patrol would earn Fluckey his fourth Navy Cross.

Between the dropping of two atomic bombs on the cities of Hiroshima and Nagasaki on August 6 and August 9 and Japan's formal surrender on September 2, Fluckey turned over command of the *Barb* to Cmdr. Cornelius Patrick Callahan, Jr., on August 17.

Fluckey was scheduled to take command of the submarine USS *Dogfish* (SS-350), then under construction; however, this assignment ended after a few months when he was assigned duty in Washington, D.C., first in the Office of the Secretary of the Navy, then at the War Plans Division, and beginning in December 1945, as personal aide and flag secretary to the chief of naval operations, Fleet Admiral Chester W. Nimitz.

In June 1947, he assumed command of the modernized submarine USS *Halfbeak* (SS-352). In 1949 he was assigned to the staff of commander, Submarine Force, Atlantic Fleet, and from August 1950 until July 1953, Fluckey was the U.S. naval attaché at Lisbon, Portugal.

In August 1953, Fluckey took command of Submarine Division 52, Squadron Five and then, following his promotion to the rank of captain, command of the submarine tender USS *Sperry* (AS-12) in June 1954. From October 1955 until January 1956, he commanded Submarine Flotilla Seven.

In January 1956, Fluckey was assigned to the U.S. Naval Academy, as head of the Department of Electrical Engineering. During that tour he also spearheaded the campaign to raise $2.2 million to build the Navy Marine Corps Memorial Stadium. He attended the National War College and served with the National Security Council before his selection for promotion to rear admiral in July 1960, and in October, he was appointed commander, Amphibious Group Four.

Back in Washington, Fluckey served as president of the Board of Inspections and Survey from November 1961 until June 1964, followed by a tour as commander, Submarine Force, Pacific.

In July 1966 he reported as director of Naval Intelligence. Two years later, he became chief of the Military Assistance Advisory Group, Portugal. Rear Admiral Fluckey retired from active duty at the beginning of August 1972.

After retiring, Fluckey continued to live in Portugal until 1979, when he moved to Annapolis to seek medical treatment for his wife, Marjorie. She died in August 1979 after 42 years of marriage. For several years, he and his second wife, Margaret, maintained a home in Portugal, where they ran an orphanage.

His memoir of World War II, *Thunder Below*, published in 1992, won the Samuel Eliot Morison Award for Naval Literature in 1993.

Admiral Fluckey passed away at 11:45 p.m. on June 28, 2007, in hospice, suffering from advanced Alzheimer's disease, and was buried in the cemetery at the U.S. Naval Academy at Annapolis.

Along with the Medal of Honor and four Navy Crosses, he received two Navy Distinguished Service Medals and two Legion of Merit awards.

On January 24, 2008, the nuclear submarine USS *Pasadena* (SSN-752), while on a deployment to the South China Sea, buried part of the admiral's cremains at sea, at the exact location Fluckey and the crew of USS *Barb* saved 14 prisoners of war during World War II.

He summarized the key to success as "[putting] more into life than you expect to get out of it. Drive yourself and lead others. Make others feel good about themselves. They will outperform your expectations, and you will never lack for friends."

Sources

"Eugene Bennet Fluckey." *Encyclopedia Britannica*, 2017. https://www.britannica.com/biography/Eugene-Bennett-Fluckey.

Fluckey, Eugene B. *Thunder Below! The USS Barb Revolutionizes Submarine Warfare in World War II*. Chicago: University of Illinois Press, 1992.

Goldstein, Richard. "Eugene B. Fluckey, 93, a Top Sub Commander, Is Dead." *New York Times*, July 2, 2007.

Hernandez, Nelson. "A Salute to Officers of the USS *Barb*." *Washington Post*, November 22, 2003.

Sorlie, Devon Hubbard. "Flag Friday: Why a Train Is on the Battle Flag of USS *Barb*." Naval History and Heritage Command. http://usnhistory.navylive.dodlive.mil/2015/12/22/flag-friday-why-a-train-is-on-the-battle-flag-of-uss-barb/.

Sterner, Doug. Home of Heroes. http://www.homeofheroes.com.

Stewart, William. *Admirals of the World: A Biographical Dictionary, 1500 to the Present*. Jefferson, NC: McFarland, 2009.

UBoat.net. "USS *Barb*." https://uboat.net/allies/warships/ship/2966.html.

USS *Barb* website. https://www.ussbarb.com/.

John C. "Jack" Lee, Jr.
Joint German American Force at the End of World War II

By May 1945, the war in Europe was on its last legs, with Germany's surrender imminent. American, English, Canadian and French troops had crossed the Rhine River on March 22, 1945, pressing into Germany from the west, while on April 20, Soviet troops began a siege of Berlin, the German capitol, from the east. On April 30, Adolf Hitler committed suicide in his underground bunker, and Berlin fell to the Soviets two days later, on May 2.

With the Third Reich in ruins, many soldiers of the German Wehrmacht were anxious for the war to end so they could return home, a sentiment shared by their Allied counterparts.

On May 4, 1945, Capt. John "Jack" Lee was thinking much the same, not wanting to be the last American killed in the war. As a platoon leader in Company B, 23rd Tank Battalion, he had been in the savage fighting in the Alsace-Lorraine region in the winter of 1944–1945, earning a Bronze Star for valor.

That morning, Company B had cleared the Austrian town of Kufstein, just across the border from Germany, of all German troops. Now, as he sat atop his M-4 Sherman tank, nicknamed "Besotten Jenny," hoping they'd fought their last fight, Lee saw a *Kübelwagen*, a German jeep, carrying a driver and officer, approach bearing a white flag.

The officer, Wehrmacht Maj. Josef "Sepp" Gangl carried a letter in English from Christiane Mabire, a prisoner at nearby Schloss Itter, near the village of the same name, pleading to be liberated.

Schloss (Castle) Itter, a 13th-century medieval fortress, stands on a hill in the rustic Brixental Valley in the Austrian Tyrol. Rebuilt in 1532 and renovated in 1878, it was transformed into a hotel in the early 20th century.

Austria became part of Germany following its annexation by Nazi Germany on March 12, 1938, and the castle was rented to the German government.

On February 7, 1943, the German Schutzstaffel, the infamous SS, took control of Schloss Itter, and it came under the administrative control of the Dachau concentration camp, one of nearly 200 sub-camps and satellite facilities across Germany and Austria, located about 90 miles away.

Surrounded by steep ravines and a deep, dry moat, the Germans made additional renovations, transforming the castle into a special SS detention facility for high-profile political prisoners who had potential value as hostages. The prison became operational on April 25, 1943, under the command of SS Hauptsturmfuhrer (Captain) Sebastian Wimmer.

Wimmer, a former Munich police officer, in 1923–1935, had a reputation for brutality when he joined the SS in March 1935. He was assigned to the Dachau concentration camp, where he remained until the autumn of 1939 when he transferred to the Third Waffen SS Panzer Division "Totenkopf," then to the Second SS Panzer Division "Das Reich" at the end of January 1942 and back to the Third Panzer in September 1942. Both divisions, and others, were found guilty of war crimes after the war, and it is likely Wimmer participated.

Returning to his work in concentration camps, Wimmer worked at the Majdanek concentration and extermination camp until he returned to Dachau, eventually to command Schloss Itter.

Most of the prisoners were French and included two former prime ministers (Edouard Daladier and Paul Reynaud), two former commander in chiefs of the French Army (Gen. Maurice Gamelin and Gen. Maxime Weygand), and Michel Clemenceau, son of Georges Clemenceau, the noted French statesman.

Politically, the prisoners were as diverse as right-wing political leader François de La Rocque, trade union leader Leon Jouhaux, Marie-Agnes Cailliau (the sister of Charles de Gaulle) and legendary tennis star Jean Borotra. Eastern European prisoners, on loan from Dachau, served as servants and laborers.

The prisoners were housed in converted hotel guest rooms and had adequate food and were free to roam freely within the compound. But the prisoners followed the war on a secret radio, and it became clearer that Germany was losing the war. The prisoners began to fear for their safety. There were rumors of rampaging SS troops carrying out executions, trying to cover up their crimes. Daladier and Reynaud even met with Wimmer, who assured them he would do what he could to protect them.

On April 30, Dachau's commandant, Obersturmbannführer (Lieutenant Colonel) Eduard Weiter arrived at Castle Itter, taking flight as Dachau was being liberated by U.S. troops. On the morning of May 2, shots were heard, and Weiter was found dead of an apparent suicide.

Two days later, on May 4, Castle Itter's commandant, Wimmer, and camp guards abandoned their posts, leaving the prisoners in charge as resistance crumbled before the American advance. Arming themselves with the abandoned German weapons but unable to leave because many hostile Germans remained in the area, they decided to wait to be liberated by the American, but there were still concerns about the marauding SS troops.

On May 3, the prisoners had sent out Zvonimir "Andre" Čučković, their Yugoslavian handyman. He left the castle under the pretext of being on an errand for Captain Wimmer and carried a letter in English seeking help from the advancing Americans. Čučković made contact with an advance party of U.S. troops of the 409th Infantry Regiment, 103rd Infantry Division in Innsbruck. The castle was outside their division's area of operations. In defiance of orders, Maj. John T. Kramers dispatched a small rescue group.

Not knowing the fate of Čučković, on May 4, the Itter prisoners sent out a second messenger, the Czech cook, Andreas Krobot. He bicycled to the village of Wörgl, where he succeeded in contacting members of the Austrian resistance, even as SS troops searched for and executed deserters and fired into houses displaying white flags or Austrian flags.

They introduced him to a covert ally of the underground, a decorated German Wehrmacht officer, Maj. Josef Gangl who, with the remains of his unit, had defied orders to retreat and had taken sides with the Austrian anti-Nazi partisans to protect local residents from SS reprisals.

Made aware by Krobot of the dire situation at Schloss Itter, Gangl wanted to rescue the French VIPs but also wanted to keep his men alive until the war ended, and he still needed to protect the town from the plundering, out-of-control SS troops. He saw the solution to all three problems in surrendering the town to the Americans.

Major Gangl and his driver, Corporal Keblitsch, set out toward the village of Kufstein in a *Kübelwagen*, braving both Wehrmacht and SS roadblocks as they neared the front and displaying a white flag as they rode into the town, where they encountered Captain Lee and his tanks.

Now, the two men, the German major and the American captain, both of whom passionately wanted to survive the war, planned to put themselves one last time in harm's way to rescue the French dignitaries. Fortune smiled that day, and fate would have it that the first American that Gangl should come into contact with was Captain Lee.

By all accounts a natural tank commander, John C. "Jack" Lee was almost a caricature of the hard-driving, cigar-chewing, whiskey-drinking, pistol-packing American tanker, beloved by his men, who called him "Captain Jack."

Born in Nebraska, on March 12, 1918, Lee was the oldest of four children born to Dr. John C. Lee and his wife, Mary. In the 1920s, following the completion of his internship, John Sr. moved the family back to New York, and in 1926, Lee graduated from Norwich High School where he performed well academically but excelled as an athlete.

In part because of his skills on the football field, he was accepted to the Class of 1942 at Norwich University in Vermont, the oldest private military college in the country.

Lee was a student at Norwich when the war started, and the student body enlisted to a man. Lee was a superior horseman and a star on the football field, and he was quick to adapt cavalry maneuvers to the concept of mechanized warfare. He had a reputation as someone willing to seize the initiative and take action, a natural leader.

Lee graduated Norwich on May 11, 1942, and was commissioned as a second lieutenant, armored branch, and was sent to the Armored Warfare School at Fort Knox, Kentucky, where he practiced tank gunnery and armor tactics.

After the three-month Basic Armor Officer Course, Lee managed a quick pass home to marry his fiancée, Virginia, before reporting to Camp Barkley, outside Abilene, Texas, assigned to the 12th Armored Division (Hellcats).

Lee was placed in command of the First Platoon, B Company, 23rd Tank Battalion. Each tank company comprised 18 tanks, divided into three platoons, each consisting of three M-4 Sherman medium tanks and two M-5 Stuart light tanks, and a headquarters platoon with two M-4s and one M-4 105 mm tank destroyer.

Each tank had a five-man crew of driver and assistant driver in the hull and loader, gunner and tank commander in the turret.

The battalion trained stateside in tank warfare and then was alerted for shipment overseas in July 1944. By this time, Lee was a first lieutenant and the company's executive officer.

After traveling by train to Camp Shanks, New York, in August, the division was processed, and on September 18 and 19, the 23rd Tank Battalion was shipped to the Brooklyn Navy Yard and loaded aboard the Canadian steamship *Empress of Australia*. After an uneventful 11-day voyage, they landed at Southampton, England.

The 12th Armored Division was refitted with new jeeps, tracks, trucks and the upgraded M4A3 Sherman tanks. After some refresher training, the division was transported across the English Channel aboard navy LSTs, arriving at La Havre, France, on November 11, 1944, the 26th anniversary of Armistice Day.

The 12th Armored Division was attached to the Seventh Army and saw vicious fighting in the Alsace-Lorraine region near the French-German border. On December 9, 1944, Lee took command of B Company when the company commander, Capt. Donald Cowan, was killed when his jeep ran over a land mine.

On January 18, 1945, Company B of the 23rd Tank Battalion, along with Company B, 66th Armored Infantry Battalion, attempted to reach survivors of the 17th Armored Infantry Battalion, still trapped in the town of Herrlisheim, but were unsuccessful. They were pulled from the line for a brief rest in Strasbourg. Company B lost half its tanks in that action with the 23rd Tank Battalion losing 72 killed in action.

After Strasbourg, the 23rd returned to combat with the French First Army, reaching the Rhine River, north of Mannheim, on March 20, 1945, and fighting across Germany and into Austria, with Company B the tip of the spearhead into Austria, crossing the border on May 3, and liberating Kufstein the following afternoon.

Now, with the war almost over, Lee was being asked to put his men at risk to liberate a castle. Radioing back to battalion headquarters, Lt. Col. Kelso Clow advised Lee to use his own judgment. Before leading an attack on the castle, Lee wanted to explore the area. Lee and his gunner, Cpl. Edward Szymczyk, got into the rear of Gangl's *Kübelwagen*, with Gangl in front beside his driver, and they set off for Wörgl and Itter.

At 34, Gangl had seen his share of combat. Born in Obertraubling, Bavaria, on September 12, 1910, the oldest son of a minor official of the Royal Bavarian State Railroad and his shopkeeper wife, Gangl had enlisted into the Reichwehr, the post–World War I German army limited to 100,000 men by the Treaty of Versailles, shortly after his 18th birthday, on November 1, 1928.

It proved to be a good place to weather the Great Depression, and Gangl had regular meals, a clean bed, and a small paycheck. Gangl served with various artillery regiments during the 1930s, and in November 1938, with war on the horizon, Gangl was promoted to master sergeant and was scheduled to attend an officer training course in October.

Following the outbreak of war following Germany's invasion of Poland on September 1, 1939, Gangl was sent with the 25th Artillery Regiment to the Saarplatz region, near the border with France, to fortify the border for an anticipated French invasion.

Eleven French Divisions crossed the border on September 7, penetrated five miles, accomplished nothing and withdrew two weeks later. Gangl fought and was wounded, spending six months recovering in the hospital before returning to duty March 14, 1940, commanding a reconnaissance unit of the 25th Motorized Artillery Battalion, 25th Infantry Division.

Promoted to second lieutenant in May, the regiment was transferred to the eastern front in June 1941, and Gangl fought in the Battle of Kiev. He was awarded the Iron Cross Second Class after Kiev and later the Iron Cross First Class, as well as earning a promotion to first lieutenant in January 1942.

Gangl returned to the west, assigned to Volks-Werfer Brigade Seven, utilizing the *Nebelwerfer* (smoke mortar), essentially an early version of a rocket launcher used in almost every campaign of the German Army. The loud, shrill howling noise of incoming rockets earned them the nickname of "Screaming Meemies."

Gangl's unit fought during the Normandy campaign, in the Ardennes during the Battle of the Bulge, and in the long retreat east into Germany. The unit was sent south to defend the German town of Saarbrucken, near the French border, and they fought fiercely but were overwhelmed by the advancing U.S. Seventh Army.

Promoted to major, he was given command of the Second Battalion, but by April, with his unit at half strength, few vehicles, and fewer artillery pieces and no chance of reinforcement or re-supply, Gangl was ordered to retreat into Austria where defensive positions were being organized. When Major Gangl crossed into Austria, his command consisted of 30 exhausted soldiers.

At some point, Gangl made contact with members of the Austrian resistance, providing weapons and sharing intelligence, and perhaps motivated by his own anti-Nazi sentiments, he became trusted to the point of being placed in command of the resistance in the Wörgl sector.

Thus, when Krobot arrived in Wörgl, he was taken to Major Gangl, who in turn sought the Americans in Kufstein, with whom he was now returning to Wörgl in his *Kübelwagen*.

They arrived at Wörgl in the late afternoon to find the town under the control of Gangl's soldiers and Austrian partisans, the Waffen SS having recently withdrawn, and the Germans formally surrendered the town to Lee. Given the proximity of SS troops, Lee decided to allow his German "allies" to remain armed.

Accompanied now by a squad of Wehrmacht soldiers in a truck, Lee, Gangl, Corporal Szymczyk and Rupert Hagleitner, a local resistance leader, proceeded to the village of Itter, avoiding SS roadblocks to reach Itter and make contact with a friendly former SS captain, Kurt-Siegfried Schrader, who was returning from having met with the French in the castle and who had agreed to assist in defending them. Schrader updated Lee and Gangl on the situation.

Continuing on, they arrived at the castle to be greeted by two armed former prisoners acting as sentries, who were astonished to see their American liberator arriving in a German *Kübelwagen*.

Former prime ministers Daladier and Reynaud met with Lee and were dismayed by how small his force was and even more dismayed that it was mainly German soldiers. After the meeting, Lee departed, promising to return with more men, and he rushed back to Kufstein, leaving the defense of the castle to Gangl's men, under the command of Captain Schrader.

As Lee rushed away from the castle, elsewhere another force was organizing to come to the castle's relief.

After being contacted by Čučković, Major John Kramers, a German-speaking officer in the 103rd's military government section, along with a French liaison officer, Lt. Eric Lutten, had formulated a rescue plan, pulling together a small task force of four M-10 tank destroyers, three jeeps, and a truck bearing a platoon of infantrymen from the 409th Infantry Regiment.

Along with the task force was an American war correspondent, Meyer Levin, and a French photographer, Eric Schwab. The relief column set out for Itter along the same clogged roads Čučković had earlier negotiated on his way to Innsbruck, now even more choked with refugees.

Several miles out of Wörgl, Kramers's column was halted by a group of Austrian anti-Nazi partisans who had been fighting SS units further along the road. As the Americans were pondering their next move, they began taking enemy artillery rounds, some landing less than 100 yards away.

Kramers and the senior M10 officer decided to pull under the cover of the nearby trees and wait for the barrage to lift before continuing toward Itter.

Unaware of Major Kramers's efforts, Lee returned to Kufstein and asked for eight volunteers to man the patrol's two Sherman tanks. Lee's crew in his tank, Besotten Jenny, included Sgt. William T. Rushford, Cpl. Edward J. Szymczyk, Cpl. Edward J. Seiner, and PFC Herbert G. McHaley.

Lt. Harry Basse, B Company's motor officer, took command of Lt. Wallace S. Holbrook's tank Boche Buster, whose crew included Tech. Sgt. William E. Elliot and Sgt. Glenn E. Sherman.

At the last moment, Lee dragooned five M-4 Sherman tanks and crews from 753rd Tank Battalion, assigned to the 36th Infantry Division. He also brought three infantry squads of Second Platoon, Company E, Second Battalion, 142nd Infantry Regiment, to provide extra firepower. Bringing up the rear of the column were the Wehrmacht troops, Gangl in his *Kübelwagen* and a truckload of ten German soldiers who tied a dark cloth around their left arm to identify them.

The improvised task force set off toward Wörgl, well aware that Waffen SS units were still putting up fierce rearguard resistance throughout their sector of northern Austria.

At Brixentaler Ache, a tributary of the River Inn, a bridge began to collapse as a fifth tank was crossing, and Lee was forced to send three Shermans and their infantry back to Kufstein. Now reduced to four tanks, 14 GIs and their Wehrmacht allies, the task forced continued to Wörgl.

Fortunately for Lee and his men, by the time they arrived, the SS regiment that had been fighting in Wörgl had withdrawn and pulled out of the town. Austrian partisans welcomed the Americans, and Lee, giving in to their pleas, reluctantly agreed to leave the two 753rd tanks and some infantry on the northern edge of Wörgl, to defend the main road leading into the city from the SS returning.

Now commanding two tanks, 14 Americans, and Gangl's 10 Wehrmacht troops, Lee set off through the center of town and toward Schloss Itter.

A bridge across a river bisecting the valley had been wired, but not blown, by retreating Germans, and after removing the explosives, Lee left Boche Buster and more of the infantry to secure the crossing, but Lieutenant Basse accompanied Lee, leaving Sergeant Elliot in command of the tank, and they proceeded on toward the castle, routing out some SS troops attempting to set up a roadblock before finally arriving at the castle as night was falling.

The sight of the approaching American tank set the French POWs to cheering wildly, holding up wine bottles and celebrating, which turned to consternation when they saw the size of the meager force of their rescuers. Rather than more Americans, Lee had brought more Germans.

Captain Schrader advised Lee that some of Gangl's men had observed SS troops maneuvering near the castle, and concerned that they might be attacked at any moment, Lee ordered the French VIPs to seek shelter in the basement for their safety. They resisted the idea of "cowering in the cellar" until Lee persuaded them that they were vital to the future of France, and they reluctantly complied.

The American and German officers surveyed their situation and considered their options. Since they lacked sufficient vehicles to evacuate the VIPs, Americans and Germans to Kufstein, they opted to shelter in place until relieved by the approaching American forces.

Lee reasoned that they held a fortified position, on high ground, and the thick castle walls provided protection from small arms fire. Attacks from the north, south or west would require attackers to scale sheer walls under fire. If they attacked from the east, they'd be exposed on the main road. If the outer ramparts were breached, they could retreat into the keep and force the enemy into a costly siege.

Leaving Besotten Jenny at the castle gate to command the road, Lee placed his remaining Americans at the gatehouse; Cpl. Willie Sutton and Privates Alex Petrukovich, Arthur Pollock and Alfred Worsham. He placed his "allied" troops into defensive positions and arranged for his men to be fed and quartered.

Just after 11 p.m., SS troops began probing the castle's defenses, opening fire with rifles and machine guns, and looking for weaknesses, continuing off and on throughout the night, until dawn the next morning.

The attack began early, at 4 a.m. on May 5, as 100–150 troopers of the 17th Waffen SS Panzer Grenadier Division began an assault on the castle. Machine-gun fire raked the castle keep, blowing out windows, and 88 mm anti-tank guns destroyed the upper floor of the main building and struck Besotten Jenny, igniting its gas tank, giving Corporal Szymczyk barely enough time to escape before the tank exploded into a fiery inferno, signaling a general assault.

Lee was concerned that the large number of SS troops in the area could pose a risk to the advancing American 36th Infantry, and he wanted to send out a warning, but he wasn't in communication with higher headquarters, his radio having been destroyed with the tank.

Learning the telephone lines were still intact, Gangl called Wörgl, asking for a messenger to the advancing Americans to advise them of the situation at the castle and request reinforcements. Wehrmacht lieutenant

Wegschneider and corporal Linsen, Wehrmacht soldiers loyal to Gangl, and a 17-year-old partisan, Hans Waltl, snuck in through the SS lines, the only reinforcements available.

SS troops swarmed out of the tree line to the east toward the main gate and scrambled up the hill from the west, but the accuracy of the American and German small-arms fire, from the castle's fortifications, took a heavy toll on the attackers. But they were rapidly exhausting their limited ammunition.

Even some of the French VIPs, disobeying Lee's orders, fired at the enemy with captured weapons, among them Reynaud, Clemenceau, La Rocque and Borotra, who manned defensive positions.

The elderly Reynaud advanced to the gatehouse eager for a fight. Gangl rushed to move the former prime minister to a safer position but was killed by a sniper's shot to his head, the only fatality the defenders would suffer.

Meanwhile, Major Kramers and his halted rescue force received orders via radio from Col. Guy Meloy, the 103rd Infantry Division's chief of staff, to return to Innsbruck, as Castle Itter was within the 36th Division's area of operations, and despite Kramers explaining the dire circumstances of the French VIPs, the order stood.

Disgusted, Kramers ordered the M-10 tank destroyers and infantry back to Innsbruck, then stubbornly proceeded on to Itter in a jeep, accompanied by Lieutenant Lutten, Čučković, and Sergeant Gris, his driver. The two war correspondents, Levin and Schwab, followed in a second jeep. Despite the danger of entering an enemy-controlled area along roads seeded with land mines, they sensed an amazing story unfolding.

As the situation became more desperate inside the castle, Lee remembered that when he'd set out on this mission, he'd been assured by Col. George Lynch, the 142nd Regimental commander, that the rest of the regiment would be "right behind him."

Lynch ordered Lt. Col. Marvin Coyle's Second Battalion to move southwest from Kufstein to Wörgl and then proceed up the Brixental Valley to Hofgarten, putting them in the vicinity of Schloss Itter, and Lynch was confident that Coyle would be able to relieve Lee.

Four companies of the 142nd Infantry (E, F, G, and H) set out in half-tracks, supported by M-4 Shermans of the 753rd Tank Battalion, but their progress was delayed by having to break through roadblocks.

Meanwhile, Major Kramers's two-jeep convoy had proceeded the 20 miles to Wörgl without incident, linking up with Sergeant Elliot and the M-4 Boche Buster along with ten partisans on the edge of town. They could hear the sounds of small-arms fire coming from the castle and could see a plume of dark smoke they assumed was Besotten Jenny.

When Kramers asked if they were in communication with Lee, Elliot shook his head, but one of the partisans suggested the telephone line might still be open.

The two jeeps drove into the center of town, and Kramers was able to telephone up to the castle and speak with Lee, who advised him that they were running low on ammunition. As Lee said, "They're shelling the bejabbers out of us," there was an explosion and the line went dead.

Almost simultaneously, Schwab ducked in from outside to announce the arrival of American tanks, as six M-4s of the 753rd and half-tracks carrying Company E rolled to a stop, and Kramers conferred with Capt. Joe Gill, who told him his orders were to link up with elements of the 103rd Division, not attack a castle.

After contact was made with the battalion commander, Gill was directed to leave a platoon behind in Wörgl and proceed to relieve the castle.

The task force was further delayed when, despite assurances from the Austrian partisans that the Germans had withdrawn, the Americans had to clear the town block by block until the town was secured.

At 1 p.m., with Boche Buster in the lead, followed by three M-4s of First Platoon, D Company, 753rd Tank, three platoons of E Company aboard half-tracks, and Kramers's two jeeps bringing up the rear, they set out for the castle.

They were delayed both by surrendering Germans, mainly old men and young boys, and Germans who refused to surrender, primarily the Waffen SS. Along the way, they were met by Jean Borotra, the tennis champion, who had escaped the castle to seek out the Americans and guide them back. After donning an American uniform and taking a weapon, Borotra led the relief force back to the castle.

As E and G Companies advanced through the woods, Gill, with Boche Buster in the lead, led the armored column up the main road, fighting their way through several roadblocks.

In the castle, the defenders were down to their last few rounds of ammunition, and Lee was preparing to order the defenders to withdraw into the keep. He was determined to fight to the last to protect the French civilians.

Outside, a squad of Waffen SS was massing for an assault on the front gate with a panzerfaust when, just as in the movies, the cavalry arrived at the last moment to save the day.

But instead of horses, these horse soldiers rode tanks, and instead of bugles, there was the sound of cannon and machine-gun fire as Boche Buster, leading the relief column, came to a halt at the village end of the *Schlossweg*, and the Germans retreated into the woods.

The relieved, ecstatic defenders came out, celebrating their liberators, as Lee and Basse, after greeting and thanking Captain Gill, strode out to Sergeant Elliot and in mock irritation asked, "What kept you?"

As Gill's E Company set up a defensive perimeter around the castle, Colonel Lynch had Major Kramers gather the French VIPs together in the courtyard, even as correspondents recorded statements and took photos, and Captain Schrader, still in his SS uniform approached Lynch, saluted, and formally turned over custody of the French prisoners.

What was perhaps the last battle of the European war was over. Two days later, on May 7, 1945, Gen. Alfred Jodl, representing the German High Command, signed the unconditional surrender of both east and west forces in Reims, France.

For their actions in rescuing the French from almost certain execution by the SS, Lee was awarded the Distinguished Service Cross and Basse the Silver Star. Gill would also be awarded the Distinguished Service Cross but for actions that occurred two weeks earlier during an assault on an enemy position.

Lee's citation describes the events of that day:

> Captain Lee, with a small group of soldiers infiltrated into hostile territory, demoralized enemy forces, prevented the destruction of two key bridges and caused 200 German soldiers to surrender. He found many prominent French prisoners at Itter Castle and immediately organized a defense with both American and German troops. Despite a fanatical SS attack and heavy artillery barrage, Captain Lee's men held until friendly troops arrived.

The citation acknowledged his "initiative, boldness, courage, resourcefulness and outstanding qualities of leadership."

As for Sepp Gangl, he is recognized as a leader of the Austrian resistance, and a street is named in his honor in the city of Wörgl.

Sources

Benz, Wolfgang, and Barbara Distel, eds. *The Place of Terror: History of National Socialist Concentration Camps*. Vol. 7, CH Beck, Nördlingen, 2005.

Harding, Stephen. *The Last Battle*. Boston: First De Capo Press, 2013.

Ramos, Daniel. "Castle Itter: The Strangest Battle of WWII." 2013. http://militarywiz.tumblr.com/post/116582883769/castle-itter-the-strangest-battle-of-ww-ii.

Operation Ginny II
Execution of 15 American Commandos

It was a cold and foggy Saturday morning on December 1, 1945, as a mist hugged the ground of the firing range at the Peninsula Base Section Garrison Stockade No. 1, a military prison just outside Aversa, Italy.

At one end of the yard, in front of a dirt embankment, a post had been set into the dirt. At the opposite end, members of the 803rd Military Police Battalion stood in formation. To one side, officer witnesses and a large number of reporters, photographers and cameramen stamped their feet and tried to stay warm.

At a little before 8 a.m., former Wehrmacht Gen. Anton Dostler marched into the yard, escorted by three MPs and two Catholic priests, one an American chaplain, the other a German POW.

Dostler, the former commander of the 75th Army Group, had been a prisoner of the Americans since May 8, 1945, being held at the 85th Division POW camp until evidence of war crimes, a mass grave uncovered on May 23, led to his arrest.

Transported to Rome, Dostler was later taken to the Royal Palace at Caserta in southern Italy. From 1923 to 1943 the palace had the location of the Accademia Aeronautica, the Italian Air Force Academy. From October 1943 the royal palace served as the Allied Force Headquarters in the Mediterranean area. In April 1945 the palace was the site of the signing of terms of the unconditional German surrender of forces in Italy.

Then, on October 8, the palace was the site of the first War Crimes Military Tribunal and Dostler was brought before a military commission of five senior officers. Dostler was found guilty of ordering the execution of fifteen American soldiers, and he was sentenced on October 12 to execution by a firing squad.

The murdered soldiers, two officers and thirteen enlisted, were all Italian Americans assigned to the 2677th Headquarters Company, Detachment C (Unit A, First Contingent), one of the special Office of Strategic Services (OSS) units activated in April 1943, under the command of Col. Edward J. Glavin.

The OSS was a wartime intelligence agency formed on June 13, 1942, with Col. William J. "Wild Bill" Donovan, a World War I Medal of Honor recipient, as its first, and only, director and reporting directly to President Roosevelt.

There was no coordination between the intelligence services of the Army, Navy, Treasury and Justice Departments, and Roosevelt was aware of these intelligence deficiencies by late 1940. Roosevelt appointed Donovan to draft a plan to create an intelligence agency similar to the British Secret Intelligence Service and Special Operations Executive and in July 1941, Donovan was named as coordinator of information. His plan led to the formation of the OSS, following America's entry into World War II, tasked with collecting and evaluating strategic information and conducting special operations.

In February 1943, Gen. Dwight D. Eisenhower agreed to allow OSS Operational Groups to conduct operations in Italy and Southern France, and once the German troops on the island of Corsica withdrew to the mainland following Italy's surrender in September 1943, the 2677th set up a forward base at Ile Rosse on Corsica, only 35 miles from the Italian mainland.

The OSS Operational Groups were given four tasks;

- Instigate the Italian population to carry out acts of resistance to the Germans
- Direct attacks on transportation and transportation targets
- Destroy enemy aircraft on the ground
- Destroy enemy supply depots and drops

Considered most vital was cutting German supply lines to deny food, munitions and petrol to German forces fighting at Cassino and Anzio. Targeted was the Genoa–La Spezia rail line running along the western coast of Italy. Attempts by the U.S. AAF to bomb the line by air (Operation Strangle) proved unsuccessful, so the Allied G-3 Special Operations branch suggested sending in a sabotage team, landing by boat along the coast, to blow up one of the tunnels with explosives.

On January 9, 1944, the OSS proposed the destruction of tunnels between Levanto and Bonassola along the Genoa–La Spezia line, and numerous targets were considered before settling on a tunnel 15 miles northwest of La Spezia, between a small station, Stazione di Framura, and the small fishing village of Bonassola, targeting the northern end, 500 yards southeast of the station.

The mission, codenamed Operation Ginny, was assigned to the 2677th, and the unit's operations officer, 1st Lt. Albert R. Materazzi, developed a plan for 15 men, a 9-man demolitions team and a 6-man security team, to be inserted by two PT (patrol torpedo) boats under cover of darkness.

The team, dressed in U.S. Army field uniforms, would make their way up a natural ravine to the tunnel entrance, neutralize the signal house, blow the tunnel, return to the rubber boats and paddle out to the waiting PT boats.

The OSS had recruited Italian American soldiers into the Operational Group, and they were a diverse group from varied backgrounds. Sgt. Al de Flumeri, married, and one of the oldest at 33, was called Pop and was a bulldozer operator from Philadelphia. T/5 (technician fifth class) Santoro Calcara built cars in Detroit. T/5 Sal di Sclafani, was a 28-year-old construction worker from Brooklyn, as were T/5s Angelo Sirico and Thomas Savino, and T/5 Liberty Tremonte was a 24-year-old metal worker from Westport, Connecticut.

Some were born in Italy and immigrated with their families, and some were native born. What they all had in common was an Italian American heritage, some degree of fluency in the Italian language, and that all were volunteers, willing to risk going on hazardous missions behind enemy lines.

Fifteen soldiers were selected for the Ginny mission. In command of the shore party was 1st Lt. Vincent Russo. The members of his demolition team included T/5 Salvatore di Sclafani; T/5 John J. Leone, T/5 Angelo Sirico, T/5 John Lepore, T/5 Vittorio Amoruso, T/5 Thomas Savino, T/5 Sorbello and T/5 Joseph Noia.

The security team, headed by 1st Lt. Paul J. Traficante, was made up of Tech. Sgt. Livio Vieceli, Sgt. Carmine Armando, Sgt. Dominick Mauro, T/5 Joseph Libardi, and T/5 Rosario Squatrito.

First Lieutenant Materazzi, in command of the mission itself, would remain with the boats, as would Capt. Donald Wentzel and Master Gunnery Sgt. W. B. Crossen, both observers, and S.Sgt. Joseph di Carli, a medic.

The mission had a tight timetable, with the teams leaving the boats at 11 p.m. to reach the target no later than 12:30 a.m., setting charges, and being picked up at 3:30 a.m. The contingency plan was that if the commanding officer determined the mission could not be accomplished that night, he could notify the PT boats by 2 a.m. and hide until the following night, with pickup scheduled for the same time. If contact couldn't be made with the boats after blowing the tunnel, they were to proceed to a safe house, 40 miles inland.

The night of the mission, February 27–28, 1944, the OSS commandos boarded two PT boats of Motor Torpedo Boat Squadron 15 with their explosives and weapons for the 120-mile trip across the Ligurian Sea to a point off La Spezia.

PT boats were the fastest U.S. naval warships at the time and the smallest craft to be equipped with radar. Manufactured by Higgins Industries of New Orleans, the 78-foot craft had three 1,500 hp Packard W-14 M2500 gasoline engines capable of speeds up to 41 knots (47 mph).

The boats were armed with two depth charges and four 21-inch Mark XIII torpedoes. In addition, two turrets, port and starboard, mounted twin .50-caliber machine guns, with a 20 mm Oerlikon anti-aircraft gun forward and a 40 mm Bofors cannon aft. Its speed, mobility and armament made it a formidable opponent.

PT 203 *"Shark's Head,"* commanded by Lieutenant (jg) Wittibort, carried 1st Lt. Traficante's security party and PT 204 *"Aggie Maru,"* skippered by Lt. (jg) Eugene Clifford, carried First Lieutenant Russo and the demolition team.

The boats got under way on schedule at 6 p.m., February 27, 1944, but they hadn't cleared Bastia Harbor before they discovered that the radar aboard PT 204 wasn't working, and they had to return and transfer personnel and equipment onto the standby boat, PT 210, creating a delay of 45 minutes. The skipper of PT 210, Lt. Harold Nugent, had no knowledge of the mission.

They were further delayed by detours to avoid radar contacts, although no enemy ships or aircraft were sighted, and it wasn't until 1:25 a.m. that they disembarked onto rubber boats, with Russo radioing they were safely on shore at 2 a.m. They soon discovered that they'd landed at the wrong point when they heard the train to the northeast and realized they were south of the target. At 2:45 a.m., Russo radioed they were still at least an hour and a half away from the target.

Deciding that by the time they destroyed the target and returned to the boats it would be daylight, exposing them to discovery and attack by enemy boats and aircraft, Materazzi ordered the team back to the boats.

All personnel and equipment were back on board by 3:30 a.m., and they arrived back in Bastia, without incident, at 7:30 a.m.

A second attempt, Operation Ginny II, was scheduled for the end of March, and the unit did a more complete target study, using intelligence gathered from the Italian Railways Maintenance Section and photographs from a reconnaissance mission flown by the 52nd Fighter Group on March 10, 1944.

For Operation Ginny II, most members from the previous mission were the same except that four members—Armando, Lepore, Amoruso, and Savino—were replaced by T/5 Joseph M. Farrell, T/5 Liberty J. Tremonte, T/5 Santoro Calcara, and Sgt. Alfred L. de Flumeri for this mission. The team completed a dry run of the mission on March 20–21, and the mission was set for March 22–23.

The evening of March 22, the teams departed Bastia at 5:55 p.m. aboard PT 214, commanded by Lt. R. T. Boehel, and PT 219, commanded by Lt. Harold Nugent, and arrived at the disembarkation point at 10:45 p.m.

As they paddled the rubber boats closer to shore, they were confronted by sheer cliffs, so they paddled further up the coast. Fighting rough seas, and losing some of their explosives, they made landfall west of Stazione di Framura a little before midnight, only to discover they had again missed their target point.

Lieutenant Russo took one or two men and went on a reconnaissance to try to locate the target, while Lieutenant Traficante tried unsuccessfully to contact the PT boats by radio. Russo returned to report the tunnel was a mile and a half to the northwest, but he decided not to blow the tunnel until contact was reestablished with the boats.

Unknown to the men on shore, the boats had sighted a convoy of German torpedo boats at 11:45 and PT 219 diverted them away, exchanging fire, while PT 214 idled offshore and attempted to make radio contact.

At 2 a.m., the boats rendezvoused five miles out, but their radar detected numerous targets, and they remained quiet until 3 a.m., when they moved closer to shore and tried to raise the shore party by radio without result.

At 4 a.m., PT 214 reported a malfunction in the main steering mechanism, which was repaired by 4:15. Unable to make contact and with dawn approaching, the boats returned to base, to return that night per the contingency plan.

Russo figured the boats had returned to base, and he knew that they would return later that night, so he ordered the boats and explosives dragged off the beach and concealed among some trees. The men moved inland over steep terrain until they located an abandoned barn to hide in.

Later that morning, Russo and Sergeant Mauro went out searching for food and information and approached a farmhouse near the village of Bonassola. They identified themselves to 16-year-old Franco Lagaxo, a fisherman, and his mother as Americans and persuaded Lagaxo to guide them to the railroad tracks.

Following a path through the trees, they arrived after ten minutes, only to realize they were at the southern exit of the tunnel at Bonassola rather than the northern entrance at Framura. After giving Lagaxo money and sending him to buy food in the village, they waited hidden, then met him at the farmhouse at noon.

After eating, Lagaxo agreed to lead the Americans, and at 3 p.m. he led them to the northern end, about an hour's distance, overlooking Stazione di Framura. Lagaxo departed, and Russo and Mauro returned to the barn.

On the evening of March 23–24, two PT boats departed Bastia for the pickup after making radio contact at the prearranged time, but one had engine trouble and turned back, and the other detected too many targets in the area and was unable to get close enough to shore. The decision was made to abandon the attempt and try again the following night. The shore party would have to remain hidden another day.

That evening, a returning local fisherman, Gaetano Oneto, spotted the rubber boats hidden in the trees, which although not visible from the hills, were visible from the sea, and reported their sighting to the local Fascist militia in Bonassola.

The following morning, two militiamen, Vittorio Bertone and Giobatta Bianchi, were guided to the site by the fisherman and they uncovered the boats and explosives.

The Germans were alerted, and Italian Fascists and German troops began searching the area. On his way to fish, Lagaxo saw the Fascists by the boats. He returned home to find two of the Americans, most likely Russo and Mauro, and told them about the Fascists finding their boat.

Lagaxo was going down into town when he saw a group of Fascists and Germans coming up the path, and he hurriedly went to the barn to warn the Americans, learning for the first time that there were several more of them.

Taking another path home, Lagaxo came across Bertone and another Fascist who asked if he'd seen anyone. Replying in the negative, he continued home to find Fascists and Germans conducting a search of the area.

Two Americans were captured near Lagaxo's mother's house. They claimed they were alone, but the presence of three boats proved they were lying. Having found a whistle in one of the boats, one of the captors blew it, and the Americans emerged from hiding and opened fire. After a short firefight, in which Russo was wounded, the Americans surrendered and were disarmed.

After a search of the area for others, the Americans were taken to Fascist headquarters in Bonassola, where they were questioned by a Fascist commissar named Guglielmini, who discovered they were Italian-speaking Americans who had come to blow up the Framura–Bonassola tunnel. At 2:30 in the afternoon, a German truck transported the prisoners to a castle in Carozzo, a small town overlooking La Spezia, headquarters of Col. Kurt Almers, commander of the 135th Fortress Brigade. Almers reported the capture of 15 Americans to his superior, Gen. Anton Dostler at 75th Army Corps headquarters.

To understand subsequent events, it must be understood that on October 18, 1942, Hitler issued the Commando Order, or *Kommandobefehl*, through the High Command of the German armed forces, which stated that all Allied commandos encountered in Europe and Africa should be killed immediately without trial, even if in proper uniforms or if they attempted to surrender. The order, issued in secret, made it clear that failure to carry out these orders by any commander or officer would be punishable by court-martial.

At some point, General Dostler sent word of the capture up the chain of command to the headquarters of Field Marshal Albert Kesselring, commander of all German forces in Italy.

At Carozzo, Oberleutnant Wolfgang Koerbitz, a staff officer, was put in charge of the interrogation, and the men were searched for identification, papers, weapons and personal effects and then confined in four rooms, the two officers segregated from the others.

Assisting in the interrogation was Corvette Kapitan Friedrich Klaps, a *Kriegsmarine* (naval) intelligence officer, who brought another officer fluent in English, Lt. Georg Sessler, who conducted most of the interrogations.

At 8 p.m., they interrogated Lieutenant Traficante, followed by two of the enlisted men, all of whom revealed only their name, rank and serial number, as required by the Geneva Convention. Taking a break at 10 p.m., the interrogators briefed Anders on their lack of progress.

Anders showed them a teletype from 75th Corps inquiring as to the results of the interrogation and expressing worries that the men might be a vanguard for an invasion force from Corsica. The men decided to change tactics with the next man, Lieutenant Russo.

Advising Russo they had orders to shoot him and his fellows if they didn't cooperate, and using one of the oldest tricks in the interrogator arsenal, they told Russo they only needed him to confirm what Traficante had already told them. Fatigued and demoralized, Russo gave an outline of the mission.

At 12:30 a.m., the morning of March 25, Koerbitz composed his first report, detailing that the 15 men had been captured in uniform on a military mission to blow up the tunnel at Bonassola, and sent the report to 75th Corps at 2:30 a.m.

They interrogated two more enlisted men, who only gave name, rank and serial number, and finished up at 4:00 a.m., planning to resume later that morning. When they resumed questioning at 10:30 a.m. on March 25, they were joined by an officer of the SD (Sicherheitsdienst) the intelligence branch of the SS.

Anders was already in possession of a telegram from 75th Corps, "The captured Americans are to be shot immediately," but he took a broad interpretation of "immediately" and allowed the interrogations to continue.

They questioned the remainder of the Americans, but all gave only their name, rank and serial number, and Sessler suspected they knew they were going to be shot.

In an unusual coincidence, it turned out that one American, Joe Farrell, knew Sessler from before the war, having delivered ice to ships in New York Harbor in 1936–1937, including ships of the Hamburg-American line for which Sessler had been an officer.

Farrell confirmed that the Americans knew that they were going to be shot and not treated as POWs, and Sessler assured him, "[We are] doing everything we can to get you evacuated as prisoners of war."

Sessler finished with Farrell and continued questioning the remaining Americans until 8 p.m., when the officers reported their conclusions to Anders that the 15 men were not commandos and were on a military mission, again stressing that they were captured in uniform.

Throughout the 25th, Dostler and his staff debated the options of sending the Americans to a POW camp, executing them as saboteurs, or turning them over to the SD.

Anders called 75th Corps to request that the execution be postponed or delayed, and spoke with Colonel Krache, Almers's chief of staff, and expressed the opinion that since they were in uniform, it would be impossible to execute them. Dostler came on the line and said, "Almers, we cannot change anything. You know the Fuhrerbefehl [Hitler's order]. The execution is to be carried out." Dostler reminded him of the consequences of ignoring the Fuhrer's orders. Unable the persuade Dostler, Almers ended the call.

A call by Klaps to Dostler at 7 p.m. was no more successful in obtaining a delay. He spoke with Krache, who said the execution was to be carried out by midnight, then later agreed to a delay until 7 a.m. on March 26. Again, Dostler came on the line and told Klaps to conclude the interrogations by 7 a.m.

Klaps sent Dostler a report, explaining his reasons for requesting the delay, including the fear of repercussions against German POWs, and he sent a copy to Kesselring's headquarters. Aware of the consequences of failing to obey an order from Hitler, Anders had earlier ordered Koerbitz to make the necessary preparations to carry out the execution should the order stand.

When Sessler found out the Americans were to be executed, he had Farrell brought back into the interrogation room. He told Farrell that they'd done everything they could, but the decision had been made, and he offered Farrell a chance to escape by taking a pistol from the holster hanging on the door, but he had to promise not to shoot anyone. He advised him to head into the mountains and join up with Italian partisans.

Initially reluctant, Farrell pocketed the gun while Sessler distracted a sergeant taking notes. Farrell returned to the holding area and passed the gun to Lieutenant Traficante, who must have decided to delay the escape attempt until they were transported.

The trucks arrived at dawn on the morning of March 26, and as they were led to the trucks, Traficante attempted to draw the gun from his pocket, but an alert guard pointed his rifle and a scuffle ensued, with Farrell, de Flumeri and Traficant attacking the guard, but the Germans overpowered them.

After searching the remainder of the group, their hands were behind their back with wire, and they were loaded aboard the trucks and driven to the execution site, Punta Bianca. A burial site was prepared near an ammunition dump called La Ferrara, using Italian laborers from the Todt Organization.

The sedan carrying Captain Rehfeld, commander of the 906th Fortress Battalion, was followed by two four-ton trucks. Twenty-five German soldiers guarded the prisoners as they dismounted the trucks, and it was decided they would be executed in two groups. The men were placed with their backs to the sea and executed in two volleys. The bodies were loaded on the trucks and driven to the burial site.

The medical officer of the 905th Fortress Battalion, who was present at the execution, later recalled, "The executed men died quietly and calmly and bravely."

The 15 Americans were placed in a mass grave and buried, the site covered with fresh sod and branches to conceal it, and the soldiers on the burial detail admonished not to talk about it. No markers were placed at the site, and two weeks later, both the Abwehr (Intelligence) and 135th Fortress Brigade (commanded by Almers) headquarters in La Spezia received orders from Kesselring's headquarters to destroy all documents relating to the fifteen Americans and report upon completion. A cover-up was already under way.

When the PT boats had failed to make contact on March 23, they returned on the 24th and 25th without contact, and an aerial reconnaissance mission showed no damage to the tunnel. Initially listed as "captured by the enemy," the status of the 15 men was updated on May 9, 1944, to "missing in action."

On January 23, 1945, the Military Personnel Casualty Branch of the War Department began a review of their status to see whether they could issue a "finding of death," which was necessary to terminate the deposits of pay and allowances and issue death benefits to next of kin.

Colonel Livermore and Captain Materazzi of the OSS provided all available information, which included conflicting radio broadcasts that claimed that 15 Americans were "wiped out" in combat and that commended Fascists for capturing 15 American Rangers. The first hint of their fate came with the interrogation of an Italian civilian from La Spazia on February 2, 1945, who told of the execution of 11 Americans captured near Framura in March and subsequently executed and buried near Ferrara.

Bit by bit, the cover-up unraveled, and on April 26, as the battle lines moved north, Capt. Nevio Manzani and Capt. Albert Lanier were sent to La Spazia to find out what happened to the Ginny team, and they began interrogating Italian and German POWs, learning that soldiers of the 135th Fortress Brigade had captured, questioned and executed their team on the morning of March 26 and had dumped their bodies into an unmarked grave near La Ferrara.

An interview with Franco Lagazo yielded more information, as did the Fascist files, and once the site was located, excavation by Graves

Registration personnel, assisted by Italian laborers, began on May 20, 1945.

Fifteen badly decomposed bodies were unearthed. Medical officers from the 103rd Station Hospital examined the bodies, and the physical evidence suggested that, rather than being shot, it was possible that they had been bludgeoned to death.

Following the end of the war in May, the OSS created a special unit to investigate war crimes, and largely with the assistance of Sessler, now in Allied custody, they were able to piece together the chain of events.

By the end of May, it was determined that Anton Dostler, commander of the 75th Army Corps, had issued the order to execute the Americans. Located in a British POW camp in Taranto, he was transferred to the custody of the Americans. Dostler freely admitted giving the order to Colonel Almers to execute the Americans, in compliance with his orders from higher headquarters. Unable to document orders from a higher command, and under a time constraint of officers being rotated stateside, authorities decided to put Dostler on trial for the murder of the 15 Americans, and he was formally charged on September 10.

On September 26, 1945, Lt. Gen. Joseph T. McNarney, the Mediterranean theater commander, issued Special Order 269, creating a military commission to try Dostler's case.

He appointed Maj. Gen. L. C. Jaynes as president of the commission and included Brig. Gen. Thoburn K. Brown, Col. Harrison Shaler, Col. James Notestein, and Col. Franklin T. Hammond.

Maj. F. W. Roche would serve as trial judge advocate (prosecutor), assisted by 1st Lt. William Andress. The defense was headed by Col. Claudius O. Wolfe and Maj. Cecil K. Emery. Gen. Fridolin von Senger und Etterlin was appointed as special German counsel and interpreter.

In Circular 114, "Regulations for the Trial of War Crimes," issued September 23, McNarney had set out the rules and procedures for the commission. Most significant, it included instructions that "the fact that accused acted pursuant to an order of his government or a superior shall not free him from responsibility, but may be considered in mitigation of punishment."

Dostler had already admitted to ordering the execution of the 15 Americans in compliance with the *Fuhrerbefehl*. The only question for the commission was what punishment to order.

The trial began on October 8, 1945, the commission was sworn in and the charges and specifications read, charging Dostler with violating the law of war by issuing the order that led to the execution of 15 American soldiers.

The defense entered several procedural objections, including challenging the jurisdiction of the commission to hear the case, all of which were overruled. A series of witnesses, including Klaps and Sessler, established that the Americans had been in uniform and related Almers's attempt to postpone the execution and Dostler's response, "The execution is to be carried out." The last prosecution witness, German general Gustav von Zangen, Dostler's superior, denied any knowledge of the execution.

The defense presented witnesses who testified to the severe consequences of disobeying Hitler's orders and to Dostler's reputation and character. Then Dostler agreed to take the stand and be sworn in. His defense, to nobody's surprise, was obedience to higher orders. On cross examination he declared he tried to turn the men over to the SD, but they had refused to take custody. The prosecution pointed out that the execution order was issued prior to his contacts with the SD.

Closing arguments were presented on October 11. The prosecution argued that the Americans had been on a military mission, in uniform, and had been denied their rights as prisoners or war. Dostler had admitted to ordering the summary execution in violation of The Hague and Geneva Conventions and the law of war.

The defense admitted the Americans had been unlawfully executed but questioned whether Dostler was ultimately "the criminal responsible for the crime." Defense stated that he had attempted to pass the matter to higher authority. They also pointed out that General Kesselring's order to destroy all records raised questions that couldn't be answered.

The commission convened at 9 a.m. the following morning, October 12, to announce a verdict of guilty on all counts and a sentence of death by firing squad.

On October 23, 1945, Lt. Gen. Matthew Ridgeway succeeded McNarney as acting theater commander, and it fell upon him to review the trial record and consider pleas for clemency or confirm the sentence.

On November 6, the theater judge advocate, Col. Tom Barrett, reviewed the trial record and found no errors and nothing to merit further hearings. On November 27, Ridgeway issued General Order 301, which approved and confirmed the sentence of death, to be carried out on or before December 1, at or in the vicinity of Aversa, Italy. On November 28, Dostler was told the sentence.

In a last-ditch effort, Colonel Wolfe attempted to gain a three-month delay of sentence accorded to condemned prisoners of war, citing Paragraph 139 of Army Field Manual 27–10.

On November 30, Barrett met with Ridgeway and gave his legal opinion that Dostler was not a POW but a war criminal who had committed an "unlawful belligerent act." Ridgeway let the order stand.

On the morning of December 1, Lt. Walter Willie and Cpls. Gordon Wilkerson and James W. Murray escorted Dostler, dressed in a general's uniform, with all insignia removed, to the execution site. The four were followed by two priests, Franz Gruber, a German chaplain, and Capt. H. B. Crummins, a U.S. Army chaplain.

Twelve enlisted men of Company B, 803rd Military Police Battalion, stood in two ranks at one end of the firing pit. At the other end, Dostler was secured to a post as the priests prayed and the officer in charge, Lt. John Magnocavallo, read the charges, finding, sentence and execution order.

Earlier, Magnocavallo had inspected, tested, and then loaded the dozen rifles with at least one, and no more than four, blank rounds of

Gen. Anton Dostler stares into the camera moments before his execution by firing squad on December 1, 1945 (U.S. Army photograph).

ammunition, as per army regulations. Now the firing squad, a sergeant and 11 enlisted men, filed in and retrieved their rifles and formed into two ranks.

Dostler was asked if he had any last words. "No," he replied. "Es Lebe Deutschland [long live Germany]," and then more softly, "My soul in God's keeping, my life for the Fatherland."

One guard then removed Dostler's hat, and the other placed a black hood over his head, while the medical officer, Capt. Arthur Lieberman, pinned a four-inch oval patch over his heart.

Sightless, Dostler didn't see the second row of the firing party take one step to the right to stand between the men in the front row, who went down on one knee. Using hand signals, Magnocavallo had the men come to the ready position and aim their rifles. The last sound Dostler heard was Magnocavallo calling, "Fire," at 9:09 a.m.

The chaplains came forward to administer last rites as the medical officer inspected the body, and Dostler was pronounced dead at 9:11 a.m. The body was wrapped in a white mattress cover, placed on a stretcher and lifted into the back of a truck for eventual burial in the German War Cemetery in Pomezia, near Rome.

The 15 men were buried at the U.S. Military Cemetery in Florence, Italy, with eight eventually returning home for burial by the families. In 1946, Headquarters, U.S. Army Forces, Mediterranean Theater of Operations, issued General Order 21 posthumously awarding all 15 men of the Ginny II operation the Silver Star. The citation reads, for each man,

> [He] was a member of an operational group consisting of two officers and 13 enlisted men, whose mission it was to land behind the enemy's lines and demolish or block an important railway tunnel. Despite the announcement by the Germans that all Allied saboteurs captured behind the lines would be executed, [he] volunteered for this hazardous duty. To avoid detection, landing boats had returned to Corsica after putting the raiders ashore. Plans were to pick up the saboteurs the subsequent night, upon completion of the mission. Two attempts were made by pursuit torpedo boats to retrieve the party, both of them unsuccessful. Later, information was received that the party had been captured and no precise accounts were received until 1946 when it was learned that the group had been brutally executed four days after it had landed. The soldier's graves were located and all 15 men were found buried together with their hands bound behind them. His gallant actions and dedicated devotion to duty, without regard for his own life, were in keeping with the highest traditions of military service and reflect great credit upon himself, his unit, and the United States Army.

The real significance of Operation Ginny II was that their murder and Dostler's trial and execution for those murders set a precedent for future war crimes trials that "obedience to orders" would not be accepted as a defense for carrying out unlawful orders, as the subsequent Nuremberg war trials would confirm.

SOURCES

Lulushi, Albert. *Donovan's Devils: OSS Commandos Behind Enemy Lines, Europe WWII.* New York: Arcade Publishing, 2016.
"Nazi General Executed for Ordering Deaths of G.I.'s." *San Bernardino (CA) Sun*, December 2, 1945.
Office of Strategic Services Operational Groups. "Ginny I." http://www.oss-og.org/italy/gimmy_01.html.
Showalter, Dennis E., ed. *Anatomy of Perjury.* Newark: University of Delaware Press, 2008.
Smart, Don. "Top Secret OSS Operation Ginny." *WWII History Magazine*, September 2005.

Matt Urban
Most Decorated Soldier in American History

Everyone knows that Audie Murphy was the most decorated soldier of World War II; however, when Matt Urban was awarded the Medal of Honor at a White House ceremony in 1980, 35 years after earning it, he became, according to the Guinness World Records, the most decorated soldier in U.S. military history.

In addition to his Medal of Honor, Urban would be awarded two Silver Stars, three Bronze Stars, the Legion of Merit, the French Croix de Guerre, and seven Purple Hearts.

Born Matty Louis Urbanowitz in Buffalo, New York, on August 25, 1919, he was the third of four sons born to Stanley Urban, a plumbing contractor, and his wife Helen. Growing up on the east side, he exhibited leadership qualities even as a boy. Although an average athlete, he excelled by pushing himself to the limit in football, basketball and track at Buffalo East High School where he graduated in 1937.

He entered Cornell University as part of the Class of 1941, but there was little money for college (the Depression had reduced the family fortune), and Urban worked as a waiter at his fraternity and in a variety of odd jobs to make ends meet. He nonetheless found time for track and boxing, and was All University Boxing Champion two years in a row. With the winds of war stirring in Europe, and for the extra money, Urban joined the ROTC (Reserve Officers' Training Corps).

After his graduation from Cornell with a BA in history and government, Urban was commissioned a second lieutenant (serial no. 0416194) in the U.S. Army on July 2, 1941.

Because he had minored in community recreation, he was assigned as a platoon leader in D Company, Second Battalion, 60th Infantry Regiment of the Ninth Infantry Division (the Go Devils), at Fort Bragg, North Carolina, but he spent most of his time serving as regimental morale officer. He coached the 60th's regimental basketball team to the divisional championship, and was the Ninth Division boxing coach. In addition, he and another officer organized amphibious training for the division's 107,000 men.

As part of the planned amphibious invasion of North Africa (Operation Torch), units of the Ninth began boarding ships in mid-October 1942. Urban boarded a troopship, *Florence Nightingale*, on October 18 at Hampton Roads, Virginia, as part of the 60th Regimental Combat Team under the command of General Patton. The battleship convoy of 850 ships crossed 3,000 miles of sub-infested ocean, arriving at Port Lyautey, French Morocco, on November 8, 1942.

Lt. Col. Matt Urban following the award of the Medal of Honor by President Jimmy Carter in a White House ceremony (White House photograph).

The mission was to seize the port of Casablanca, eliminate enemy air forces, and secure at least one airfield. Port Lyautey was protected by an old Portuguese fort, Fort Kasbah, manned by units of the French Foreign Legion. Because Vichy France was an ally of Germany, planners were unsure of the reception American forces could expect from French troops, and orders were to withhold fire unless fired upon.

The untried American troops met with stiff resistance from the combat veterans of the foreign legion at the November 8 landing. A popular officer, Urban felt his place was with the troops. Ordered to stay aboard ship until the situation was secure, but hearing of heavy casualties, Urban, the regimental special services officer, left the ship with another soldier by raft, against orders, and joined the assault on the Kasbah, taking command of a platoon. After two days of heavy fighting, the French surrendered on November 10.

Once Morocco was secure, Urban resumed his duties as morale officer, organizing USO shows with Martha Raye and Al Jolson, with whom he sang a duet of "Danny Boy." Casablanca was visited by FDR and Churchill, and planners looked east toward the German troops in Tunisia. On February 19, the Ninth Division was ordered to the Tunisian front.

In the Battle of Kasserine Pass on February 21–23, 1943, U.S. forces engaged General Rommel's Afrika Korps along a 52-mile front, stopping the Germans in their tracks. A large part of the credit would go to a young artillery officer, Lt. Col. William C. Westmoreland, in command of the 34th Field Artillery, who would earn the French Legion of Honor.

It was during the Battle of Maknassy Pass in early April of 1943 that Urban received the first two of his seven Purple Hearts. Taking command of F Company when the company commander was wounded, the Second Battalion was holding off a strong German force to the east. Aware that the battalion was at risk from an enemy observation post, he volunteered to put it out of action.

Armed with only a .45 and some hand grenades, Urban crawled alone in the predawn darkness through wadis, slowly drawing parallel with the enemy position. Throwing in his grenades, he quickly followed the explosions, jumping into the position and engaging the fleeing Germans with his .45. Wounded in his right hand by fragments from a grenade tossed by a retreating German, Urban nonetheless cut the communication wires leading into the post and smashed the radio equipment, opening the way for the battalion to advance. During the action, he received a second wound to his left arm.

Refusing evacuation, Urban led his company forward against Djebel Dardyss, a strategically located hill, on Easter morning. Just short of the high ground, the Germans opened fire with mortars and machine-gun fire. With no cover to hide behind, his options were to retreat, surrender or attack. Jumping to his feet, pistol in hand, Urban yelled, "Follow me!" and charged the position, his men close behind. Overcoming a numerically superior German force, Company F took and held the high ground, repelling two German counterattacks. By the time the Germans withdrew the next morning, there were 116 dead Germans. U.S. casualties were 21 dead, 111 wounded.

On May 8, U.S. forces liberated Bizerte, and shortly afterwards, on May 13, Axis forces surrendered and abandoned North Africa. The Ninth Division was tasked with guarding the 150,000 German and Italian prisoners. For his part in the campaign, Urban would earn two Silver Stars, one Bronze Star and two Purple Hearts.

Allied forces next began a campaign of disinformation to convince the Axis forces that the next target was Greece and Sardinia, while making plans for the invasion of Sicily. On July 9, 1943, the Allies staged an amphibious landing at Sicily, beginning the campaign for Italy. Urban and Company F departed North Africa on July 28 aboard the SS *Orizaba*, landing at Palermo on August 1, 1943, with the Second Battalion acting in a flanking movement. The city was declared liberated on August 20, and by the end of 1943, the battalion was back in England at Camp Bushfield, outside Winchester, enjoying a well-deserved rest as veterans of two major campaigns.

Allied planners now turned their attention to the long anticipated invasion of Europe. Codenamed Operation Overlord, the invasion was coordinated by Gen. Dwight Eisenhower, the successful commander of the invasions of North Africa and Italy. Deceived into believing that the invasion would take place at Calais in Northern France, the narrowest point in the English Channel, the Germans were caught unprepared when the Allies landed over 100 miles southwest at Normandy on June 6, 1944. The initial invasion force consisted of 185,000 troops, 18,000 paratroopers, 13,175 aircraft, 4,066 landing craft, 745 ships, 347 minesweepers and 20,000 vehicles.

Urban, now a captain in command of F Company, landed with the Second Battalion at Utah Beach on D-Day plus five (June 11) and began the breakout into the hedgerows of France. When F Company encountered two panzer tanks supporting an enemy position near Renouf, France, Urban grabbed a bazooka and, with another soldier carrying ammunition, engaged and destroyed both tanks. During the action, Urban was wounded by shell fragments in the left calf, but despite requiring a tourniquet, he refused evacuation and continued to command his company while carried on a litter by two GIs. Early the next morning, he was again wounded in the right forearm (his fourth wound) and went reluctantly to the rear only after being given a direct order by the battalion surgeon, Major Weinberg. He was operated on at the field hospital and evacuated to England.

In July, while recovering from his wounds in a hospital in England, he learned that his unit had sustained heavy casualties in the fighting near St. Lo, including the battalion commander, "Black Mike" Kaufman. Convincing his superiors that he was fit for duty, he persuaded them to allow him to train a group of misfits, "the Dirty 40," with the understanding that he would transport them to France and then return. Instead, upon arriving in France, he turned the unit over to another officer, and "hitchhiked 100 miles to the front, rejoining his unit on July 25, 1944."

He arrived at the front near St. Lo to find the Second Battalion pinned down by German artillery fire in the first attack of Operation Cobra. The troops appeared confused and immobile. Limping down the road while using a stick as a cane, he ordered the men to their feet yelling, "Follow me!" S.Sgt Alex Kahn would later describe Urban's actions: "One of the craziest officers suddenly appeared before us, yelling like a madman and waving a gun in his hand.... He got us on our feet, gave us back our confidence, and saved our lives."

Reaching the forward elements of the battalion, he found two American tanks destroyed and another intact but immobile with no commander or gunner. After a lieutenant and sergeant were both killed by heavy enemy fire while attempting to mount the tank, Urban limped forward through intense fire, mounted the tank and ordered it forward. Exposed to enemy fire, he manned the machine gun and placed devastating fire on enemy positions. Energized, the battalion advanced, destroying the enemy.

His valor was witnessed by the battalion commander, Maj. Max Wolf who told Sgt. Earl Evans that he intended to recommend Urban for the Medal of Honor, but he was later killed by artillery fire, and Sergeant Evans was captured. With the death of Major Wolf on August 6, Urban took command of the Second Battalion.

Urban was wounded in the chest by shell fragments on August 2, and disregarding the recommendation of the battalion surgeon, again refused evacuation. In the Champ Du Bout sector on August 7, the battalion held against counterattacks by the Second and 116th Panzer Divisions. On August 15, he was wounded again in the lower back, and still he refused to be evacuated, continuing with his unit north into Belgium.

On September 2, the Second Battalion was tasked with establishing a crossing point on the Meuse River, near Heer, Belgium. Urban with two volunteers scouted, and they entered the city, gaining valuable intelligence. The following day, September 3, Urban personally led a charge across open terrain and was seriously wounded in the throat, mutilating his larynx, his seventh wound. Unable to speak, he refused evacuation until the crossing point was secure.

The battalion surgeon, Major Weinberg, gave Urban little chance of surviving, and the chaplain, Father Timothy Andryziak, administered the last rites. Urban was evacuated to England, where he refused to die and slowly stabilized and recovered his strength.

Incredibly, Urban went AWOL during a five-day pass from the hospital. Disguising his wounds with a scarf and communicating by notes, he made his way to Germany to rejoin his unit, missing a ceremony at the hospital where he was to be awarded a Bronze Star. After a reunion with his men, Urban was convinced by the new battalion commander to return to the hospital in England. For Urban, the war was over.

From England, Urban returned home to New York aboard the *Queen Mary*. After receiving seven telegrams notifying her of his wounds, Urban's mother was relieved to have him home. After a year of outpatient treatments at Veterans Administration hospitals, he recovered his voice to the point that he could whisper. Urban received his delayed promotions to major and lieutenant colonel and was medically retired from the army at Halloran General Hospital in New York on February 27, 1946, a veteran of six major campaigns in 20 months of combat.

Urban remained active in post-war veteran's affairs: testifying before Congress, selling war bonds, and writing a veteran's column for *Liberty Magazine*. He served as recreation director for Port Huron for seven years, followed by 16 years as director of the Monroe Community Center in Michigan, and then took a job as director of the civic and recreation department in Holland, Michigan, where he retired in 1989.

An offhand remark to a friend, an official of the Disabled American Veterans in the early 1970s, led to a request for information and a subsequent investigation by the army's Military Awards Branch, which uncovered a two-page letter dated July 5, 1945, and written by the recently repatriated Sergeant Evans, recommending Urban for the Medal of Honor.

Despite being 35 years after the fact, there was sufficient evidence of Urban's heroism to merit the award, and on July 18, 1980, in a ceremony at the Pentagon, army chief of staff Gen. Edward C. Meyer presented Urban with the Legion of Merit and the French ambassador conferred upon him the Croix de Guerre. The following day, June 19, in a ceremony in the East Room of the White House, Lt. Col. Matt Urban stood at attention as President Jimmy Carter presented him with the Medal of Honor.

After retiring in 1989, Urban traveled nationwide, speaking to veterans organizations and promoting his autobiography, *The Matt Urban Story: Our Most Decorated Combat Soldier* (1989). He died on March 4, 1995, at Holland Community Hospital from complications resulting from a collapsed lung.

He was buried in Section 7A, Grave 40, near the Tomb of the Unknowns, with full military honors.

His Medal of Honor citation reads,

> For conspicuous gallantry and intrepidity at risk of life above and beyond the call of duty: Lieutenant Colonel (then Captain) Matt Urban, 112–22–2414, United States Army, distinguished himself by a series of bold, heroic actions, exemplified by sin-

gularly outstanding combat leadership, personal bravery, and tenacious devotion to duty, during the period 14 June to 3 September 1944 while assigned to the 2nd Battalion, 60th Infantry Regiment, 9th Infantry Division.

SOURCES

Arlington National Cemetery. http://www.arlingtoncemetery.net/murban.htm.
Conrad, Charles, and Matt Urban. *The Matt Urban Story*. Self-published, 1989.
Elliott, J. Michael. "Matt Urban, 75, Much-Decorated War Veteran." *New York Times*, March 7, 1995.
"Medal of Honor." *U.S. News and World Report*, September 15, 1991.

Maynard H. "Snuffy" Smith
First Enlisted Airman Medal of Honor (Europe)

At 0300 hours on the morning of May 1, 1943, crews of the 423rd Bombardment Squadron (Heavy), part of the 306th Bombardment Group, were awakened for a briefing on Mission 53. Their target was the harbor facility at St. Nazaire on the French coast, more specifically, the concrete submarine pens. Following the Casablanca conference between the Allied powers, bombing submarine pens was a "major priority."

At 0845 hours, 18 Boeing B-17 "Flying Fortress" bombers of the 306th took off from their RAF base at Thurleigh, Bedfordshire, England, to rendezvous with 20 bombers of the 91st Bombardment Group, 19 bombers of the 303rd Bombardment Group and 21 bombers of the 305th Bombardment Group for a total of 78 aircraft slated for the mission.

St. Nazaire was not an easy target. Four raids launched by the Eighth Air Force in a six-week period, November 17, 1942, to January 3, 1943, had failed to put the submarine pens out of commission. Referred to by aircrews as "flak city," St. Nazaire was protected by an extensive network of anti-aircraft batteries and fighter aircraft from nearby airfields. Only one additional mission, on February 16, had flown over St. Nazaire since January.

Considered one of the most hazardous routes, St. Nazaire fortifications at Lorient and Brest, were avoided by aircrews returning to England, who would fly west over the Atlantic and then turn east.

As is not uncommon on missions, not all the bombers would make it over the target. The 20 bombers of the 91st were late to the rendezvous and had to fly "full-throttle" across the English Channel to catch up, resulting in five bombers having to abort the mission for mechanical reasons. Of the remaining 15, only two would drop their payload over the target.

An additional six aircraft would abort for mechanical reasons, and 38 would abort because of the weather (cloud cover obscuring the target), leaving the remaining 29 aircraft to drop 57 bombs, each 2,000 pounds, over the target.

The 306th would take the heaviest losses; theirs were three of the seven aircraft shot down in the mission, 33 of the 73 crewmen missing in action, 12 of the 18 wounded in action, and one of the two crewmen killed on the mission.

That foggy morning, B-17 42–29649, part of the 423rd Bombardment Squadron, waited to take off with 1st Lt. Lewis P. Johnson in command as pilot. It was his 25th and final mission before rotating home.

His crew were all veterans who had trained and flown together: 2nd Lt. Robert McCallum, co-pilot; 1st Lt. Stanley N. Kisseberth, bombardier; Sgt. J. C. Melaun, on loan from the 410th as navigator; S.Sgt. William "Bill" Fahrenhold, flight engineer and top turret gunner; S.Sgts Bob Folliard and Joe Bukacek, waist gunners; and Tech. Sgt. Henry Bean, radio operator.

The tenth man, S.Sgt. Maynard "Snuffy" Smith, the ball-turret gunner, was on his first mission.

Smith, five foot six and 130 pounds, was not popular with the men in his unit. Seen as a misfit and malcontent by the men in his unit, few crews wanted to fly with him. But on this, his first flight, Smith's actions would result in the award of the Medal of Honor, the first ever awarded to an enlisted airman in any war.

Born Maynard Harrison Smith, Jr., in Caro, Michigan, on May 19, 1911, he was the great-grandson of Union army major Henry Harrison Smith, a Civil War veteran, and the second child

S.Sgt. Maynard "Snuffy" Smith in flight gear (U.S. Air Force Historical Society photograph).

of Maynard H. Smith Sr., a lawyer and circuit court judge, and Mary (née Gohs) Smith, a schoolteacher. He grew up affluent and spoiled, living a life of privilege during the Depression. Sent to a military academy to instill self-discipline, he appears to have instead developed a love of reading.

Smith worked as a tax agent for the Treasury Department and was an assistant receiver for the Michigan State Banking Commission before "retiring" upon his father's death in 1934, living off his inheritance.

He married Mary France (née Nixon) Smith on March 30, 1941, and they had a son, Richard Keane Smith. He was living in Detroit after their divorce when, given the choice by a Michigan judge of army or jail for failing to support his ex-wife and son, he "enlisted" in the Army Air Corps on August 31, 1942, at the age of 31.

After basic training at Sheppard Field, Texas, Private Smith (serial no. 36523097) then attended aerial gunnery school at Harlington, Texas, starting on September 30 and graduating November 9, 1942. He was given the nickname "Snuffy" after the popular comic strip.

Promoted to sergeant upon graduation, Smith was promoted to staff sergeant on December 1, 1942, shortly after being assigned to the 413th Bomber Squadron, 96th Bombardment Group, at Pocatello, Idaho. On January 1, 1943, he was given further training and attached to the 464th Bombardment Squadron, 331st Bombardment Group, at Casper, Wyoming. On February 7, he was assigned to the First Heavy Bombardment Processing Headquarters in Salinas, Kansas, pending assignment overseas.

Smith was sent overseas to the European theater of operations, departing the United States on March 3, 1943. Upon arriving, he attended a three-week combat crew course at the 11th Combat Crew Replacement Center and then was sent to Thurleigh, England, assigned to the 423rd Bomber Squadron of the 306th Bombardment Group.

The group (the Reich Wreckers) flew its first mission on October 9, 1942, and carried out the first bombing mission into Germany in January 1943. In its 342 missions over Germany and occupied Europe, the 306th dropped over 22,000 tons of bombs on enemy targets.

Smith was assigned as a replacement gunner with the 423rd, in late March 1943, but he flew no missions for almost six weeks, taking off on his first mission that morning of May 1, 1943.

As Andy Rooney, then a sergeant and reporter for *Stars and Stripes*, recalled in his book *My War*, "From the time he entered the Air Force he had been in some kind of trouble over one petty matter or another. 'Snuffy' was, in fact, known by the fourteen other inhabitants of his Nissen hut [as] ... a real fuckup."

His bomber lifted off into the thick cloud cover and headed south over the English Channel, so Smith saw little crammed into the Plexiglas turret in the belly of the B-17.

His view improved somewhat as they neared St. Nazaire. He observed puffs of smoke erupting around the aircraft, and he realized it was flak as tiny bits of shrapnel bounced harmlessly off his turret.

Then he heard the bombardier radio, "Bombs away," and the aircraft lifted slightly with the loss of the weight of the bombs, followed by Lieutenant Johnson declaring, "We're heading home."

The aircraft dropped to 2,000 feet, the crew unaware that the lead navigator had miscalculated and had them turning east too early, bringing them directly into the path of the anti-aircraft guns at Brest. The sky was filled with smoke and deadly accurate 20 mm cannon fire.

As Johnson took the bomber lower to avoid the flak, they came under attack by enemy fighters and took several hits. One hit ruptured the fuel tanks, causing an explosion that set the mid-section of the aircraft ablaze.

Fire broke out in the radio compartment and spread into the waist of the plane, fed by ruptured oxygen lines and isolating the rear section of the aircraft. There was no communication with the pilot and no electricity. Ammunition began catching on fire and exploding.

In the ball turret, with no electricity or communication, there was no way to operate the guns, so Smith hand cranked himself up into the interior of the fuselage, finding a fire forward in the radio room and another fire in the tail section.

The radioman, Bean, dashed past him and dived out the gun hatch, hitting the vertical stabilizer before bouncing off. Both waist gunners, Bukacek and Folliard, unable to stand the intense heat, bailed out, never to be heard from again, although Smith recalled seeing all three chutes open.

Alone in the intense heat and smoke, Smith wrapped a sweater around his face, grabbed an extinguisher and began fighting the fire in the radio room.

Looking back, he saw the tail gunner, Gibson, crawling toward him, seriously wounded and bleeding. Gibson had been shot in the back, his left lung pierced, so Smith rolled him on his left side to prevent blood from filling his right lung, administered a shot of morphine, and went back to fighting the fires.

In the cockpit, and with communication, Johnson sent the engineer, Fahrenhold, back to check on the damage, but the wall of flame and heat he encountered made passage impossible.

In the mid-section, the intense heat had burned large holes in the fuselage, and Smith began tossing everything he could through the openings, both to lessen the weight of the struggling aircraft, and to deny the raging fires fuel. As ammunition boxes began exploding, he tossed them overboard as well.

Enemy fighters continued to pursue the crippled bomber, and through the fuselage, Smith saw a Focke-Wulf Fw-190 fighter positioning for a pass. He dropped the extinguisher to fire the .50-caliber waist guns from both sides before again returning to fighting the fires.

For 90 minutes, in actions that were later characterized as "without regard for his own personal safety," Smith simultaneously fought the fires, provided first aid to the wounded tail gunner, dumped exploding ammo overboard, and manned the bomber's functioning guns to fight off enemy fighters. At one point, the heat was so intense, he had to wrap himself in protective cloth to fight the fire, and with the extinguishers expended, he resorted to urinating on the flames.

By himself, Smith managed to extinguish the fires, drive off the fighters, and stabilize the wounded crewman. Lieutenant Johnson was able to nurse the plane back to England where it broke into two sections upon landing at Predannack. The plane was later found to have over 3,500 bullet and shrapnel holes in the fuselage.

Smith flew four more combat missions before he went before a medical board. Found to be suffering from "operational exhaustion," he was assigned to a non-combat position as an administrative clerk with a reduction in rank to private. He remained with the 306th in the combat zone until March 6, 1945, when he returned to the States.

On July 15, 1943, Secretary of War Henry Stimson arrived in England to present Smith with the Medal of Honor. It would be the first Medal of Honor to be awarded to an enlisted airman in any war, and the first awarded to an airman in the European theater of operations.

For the ceremony, Eighth Air Force commander Gen. Ira Eaker and six other generals were present, the band stood by waiting, 18 bombers prepared for a flyover, and two radio networks were ready to broadcast the ceremony live as reporters and photographers set up. The troops waited in formation in dress uniform

But to the embarrassment of Col. George Robinson, commander of the 306th, Smith was nowhere to be found. Finally located, Smith had to be hustled from KP duty and quickly dressed in an appropriate uniform to accept the award, having been assigned a week of KP for returning late from a pass and missing a mission.

S.Sgt. Maynard "Snuffy" Smith receives the Medal of Honor from Secretary of War Henry Stimson, July 15, 1943 (U.S. Air Force Historical Society photograph).

As General Eaker stated at the ceremony, "Sergeant Smith not only performed his duty, he carried on after others—more experienced than he—had given up. Through his presence of mind, determination and bravery, he saved the lives of six of his crewmates and the Fortress in which he flew."

The man who was cited as "an inspiration to the armed forces of the United States" was honorably discharged, still a private, while assigned to the 1020th Army Air Force Base Unit at Miami Beach, Florida, on May 26, 1945. Besides his Medal of Honor, Smith was also awarded two Air Medals.

He returned home to a hero's welcome and parade but never again achieved the success he'd achieved in uniform, failing both in businesses and marriages.

"To me it was a dream," Smith later declared, recalling his heroism. "I had just done what I had been trained to do. I didn't know what the hell it was all about. I wasn't there to get a medal. Like millions of others, I just wanted to get it over with and get home."

Smith died on May 11, 1984, and is buried in Section 66, Arlington National Cemetery in Virginia.

SOURCES

Astor, Gerald. *The Mighty Eighth: The Air War in Europe as Told by the Men Who Fought It.* New York: Penguin Publishing Group, 2015.

Mikaelian, Allen. *Medal of Honor: Profiles of America's Military Heroes from the Civil War to the Present.* Rockland, MA: Wheeler Pub., 2002.

National Personnel Records Center, St. Louis, MO.

Rooney, Andrew A. *My War.* New York: Crown, 1997.

Sterner, Doug. "Maynard H. "Snuffy" Smith." Home of Heroes. http://www.homeofheroes.com/wings/part2/06_smith.html.

"Teletype Report to Commanding General, First Bombardment Wing dated 1st May 1943." http://www.306bg.us/MISSION_REPORTS/1may43_v2.pdf.

Tillman, Barrett. *Above and Beyond: The Aviation Medals of Honor.* Washington, D.C.: Smithsonian Institution Press, 2002.

Zullo, Allen. *10 True Tales: World War II Heroes.* New York: Scholastic Press, 2015.

Joseph T. O'Callahan
Only Chaplain Awarded Medal of Honor in World War II

On the morning of March 19, 1945, Lt. Cmdr. Joseph Timothy O'Callahan sat down in the wardroom of the USS *Franklin* (CV-13) an Essex-class aircraft carrier currently operating within 50 miles of the Japanese mainland, closer than any carrier during the war.

O'Callahan, the newly assigned chaplain, had just returned from praying for and blessing pilots departing on missions for a fighter sweep over Honshu and a strike on Kobe harbor to disrupt shipping. At 6:05 a.m., when O'Callahan was just sitting down to a breakfast of French toast, he could hear the roar of aircraft taking off. Suddenly there was the sound of a large explosion, knocking out the power and rocking the large ship.

Unseen by O'Callahan, a single plane, most likely a Yokosuka D4Y "Judy" dive bomber or an Aichi D3A "Val" dive bomber had penetrated the *Franklin*'s air defenses to make a low-level run on the ship, dropping two 550-pound semi-armor-piercing bombs.

One bomb penetrated the flight deck centerline, passing through to the hangar deck below, igniting fires through the second and third decks, and knocking out the Combat Information Center and air plot. The second bomb struck aft, tearing through two decks. The *Franklin* had 31 armed and fueled aircraft warming up on her flight deck, and the hangar deck contained 22 additional planes, of which 16 were fueled and five were armed.

The forward gasoline system had been secured, but the aft system was operating. The resulting explosion ignited the fuel tanks of the aircraft on the hangar deck, and gasoline vapor explosions devastated the deck. Only two crewmen survived the fire on the hangar deck.

The explosion also jumbled aircraft together on the flight deck above, causing additional fires and explosions, including the detonation of 12 air-to-surface rockets. The *Franklin* lay dead in the water, 50 miles from the coast of Japan, with no power or communications and with intense heat and smoke from numerous fires.

O'Callahan returned to his quarters to get his helmet and holy oil and then proceeded through the wounded ship, assisting in every way he could. His extraordinary efforts would result in his being awarded the Medal of Honor, the only chaplain of any service to be awarded the Medal of Honor during World War II.[1]

Joseph Timothy O'Callahan was born to a Catholic family in Roxbury, Massachusetts, on May 14, 1905 (his Medal of Honor citation erroneously lists it as 1904). O'Callahan was one of six children (four boys, two girls) of Cornelius and Alice Casey O'Callahan, who ran a produce business in Faneuil Hall in Boston.

After graduating Boston College High School, O'Callahan joined the Jesuit Order in 1922 at the age of 18, completed his philosophical studies at Weston College in 1929 and began teaching physics at Boston College. He was ordained in 1934 and became director of the Mathematics Department at College of the Holy Cross, Worcester, Massachusetts. He earned a master of arts, doctor of philosophy and licentiate in sacred theology from Georgetown University in Washington, D.C. He was teaching math, physics and philosophy when, seeing events in Europe, O'Callahan requested permission to enter the military as a chaplain.

Lieutenant (jg) O'Callahan (serial no. 87280) entered the U.S. Navy Chaplain Corps on November 20, 1940. His basic training was at Naval Air Station Pensacola in Florida. In 1942 he was assigned to the USS *Ranger* (CV-4), an aircraft carrier in the Atlantic Fleet. The

Lt. Cmdr. Joseph Timothy O'Callahan (U.S. Navy photograph).

Ranger, the navy's first aircraft carrier, was commissioned on June 4, 1934, and the sixth U.S. warship to bear the name. The first *Ranger* was the first U.S. warship to fly the Stars and Stripes.

The *Ranger* patrolled the South and North Atlantic, serving as the flagship to two admirals, sailing on missions to Argentina and Trinidad, and saw combat in the invasion of French Morocco in November 1942. She would finish the war training troops and pilots in Hawaii in 1945.

After three years aboard the *Ranger*, O'Callahan was transferred to the Pacific theater at Pearl Harbor in early 1945 and was assigned to the *Franklin*, reporting aboard on March 2, 1945. The *Franklin* (nicknamed Big Ben) was the fifth U.S. warship to bear that name and was commissioned on January 31, 1944, with Lt. Cmdr. Mildred McAfee, commanding officer of the WAVES, serving as the sponsor.

The *Franklin* saw extensive operations and combat in the Pacific, launching air assaults in the Marianas, Iwo Jima, Guam, and Leyte and returning to the Puget Sound Navy Yard in Washington to repair combat damage on November 28, 1944. The *Franklin* departed Bremerton for the Pacific on February 2, 1945, to support the Okinawa landing.

O'Callahan, now a lieutenant commander, reported aboard in Hawaii, assigned as the ship's chaplain. At dawn on March 19, 1945, the *Franklin* had maneuvered to within 50 miles of Kobe. The mission was to launch air attacks on Honshu and its Port of Kobe.

During operations, a Japanese fighter succeeded in piercing the *Franklin*'s air cover, dropping two armor-piercing bombs on target. With fires raging all over, the *Franklin* was dead in the water with no communications and 50 miles off Japan.

O'Callahan's Medal of Honor citation states that,

> calmly braving the perilous barriers of flame and twisted metal to aid his men and his ship, Lieutenant Commander O'Callahan groped his way through smoke-filled corridors to the open flight deck and into the midst of violently exploding bombs, shells, rockets, and other armament. With the ship rocked by incessant explosions, with debris and fragments raining down and fires raging in ever-increasing fury, he ministered to the wounded and dying, comforting and encouraging men of all faiths; he organized and led firefighting crews into the blazing inferno on the flight deck; he directed the jettisoning of live ammunition and the flooding of the magazine; he manned a hose to cool hot, armed bombs rolling dangerously on the listing deck, continuing his efforts, despite searing, suffocating smoke which forced men to fall back gasping and imperiled others who replaced them.

"Father Joe" led rescue parties into the smoke-filled sections of the ship, braving fires and intense heat to rescue trapped, dazed sailors and lead them to safety, encouraging the living, tending the wounded and performing last rites for the dead. The captain of the *Franklin*, Capt. Leslie Gehres, who recommended O'Callahan for the nation's highest award, called him "the bravest man I ever saw."

Despite heavy casualties to the crew of 3,000 officers and men, there were 724 dead and 265 wounded (although figures vary), another 1,000 were in the water, leaving the remaining crew to save the ship. Refusing to quit, and heedless to danger, they were able to restore operations and sail her under her own power to the Brooklyn Navy Yard, earning for her the nickname of "the Ship That Wouldn't Die."

Although not an officer of the line, O'Callahan led from the front, setting the example. After the battle, his example continued. He and other officers gave their bunks to the enlisted men and slept on the hard deck. He personally led parties to retrieve the bodies of the dead, a gruesome task, and then conducted almost non-stop burial services at sea as they sailed toward Hawaii.

Two Medals of Honor, 19 Navy Crosses and 22 Silver Stars would be awarded for that action. O'Callahan would have his medal presented to him by President Harry S. Truman in a White House ceremony on January 23, 1946.

Promoted to the rank of commander in July 1945, O'Callahan served briefly at the Naval Training Station, Newport, Rhode Island, before being reassigned to the USS *Franklin D. Roosevelt* (CVB-42) in October 1945. He was escort chaplain when the body of President Manuel Quezon, the first president of the Philippines, was returned to Manila aboard the USS *Princeton*. He was released from active duty on November 12, 1946, with the rank of full commander. He remained in the navy reserve until November 1, 1953, retiring as a captain.

After the war, O'Callahan returned to Holy Cross, but he suffered a disabling stroke, retiring from teaching in 1950, becoming as he put it, "a man dead in the water." He wrote about his experiences in the book *I Was Chaplain on the* Franklin. He continued to struggle with the health consequences of his stroke until his death in Worcester, Massachusetts, on March 18, 1964.

In a ceremony in Bay City, Michigan, the destroyer escort USS *O'Callahan* (DE-1051) was christened by his sister, Sister Rose Marie Callahan, the first nun ever to sponsor a U.S. Navy ship, and commissioned on July 13, 1968. Sister Rose Marie had been a Maryknoll nun and missionary in the Philippines when it fell to the Japanese and had spent three years as a prisoner in a Japanese detention camp during the war. Only after the war did they learn she was alive.

Cmdr. Joseph O'Callahan (far right) with President Truman and other Medal of Honor awardees (Abie Rowe-National Archives and Records Administration).

Reclassified as a guided missile destroyer (FF-1051) on June 30, 1975, the *O'Callahan* remained in service until it was decommissioned in 1988. It was sold to Pakistan in 1989 and renamed the *Aslat*.

One interesting but unconfirmed story about O'Callahan arises from a photo taken of him administering last rites aboard the *Franklin* during the battle. The story is that the subject of the last rites survived the battle, became an actor, and twenty years later portrayed O'Callahan giving him last rites in a television production.

Note

1. Seven American chaplains have been awarded the Medal of Honor: two Navy chaplains and five Army chaplains. Three were awarded for actions during the Civil War, one during World War II and three during the Vietnam War.

Sources

Dictionary of American Naval Fighting Ships. https://www.history.navy.mil/research/histories/ship-histories/danfs.html.

"Franklin V." *Dictionary of American Naval Fighting Ships.* Navy Department, Naval History & Heritage Command. April 15, 2004.
Hamel, John. "Lieutenant Commander Joseph T. O'Callahan." http://www.johnhamelministries.org/Father_Joe_history.htm.
Hargis, Robert, and Starr Sinton. *World War II Medal of Honor Recipients (1) Navy and USMC.* Oxford: Osprey Publishing, 2003.
O'Callahan, Joseph Timothy. *I Was Chaplain on the* Franklin. New York: Macmillan, 1956.
Satterfield, John R. *Saving Big Ben: The USS* Franklin *and Father Joseph T. O'Callahan.* Annapolis, MD: Naval Institute Press, 2011.

Silvestre S. Herrera
Medal of Honor Awarded to a Mexican National

On September 16, 1940, with the war in Europe and the Pacific threatening to drag the United States into the conflict, President Roosevelt signed the Selective Training and Service Act of 1940 into law, initiating the first peacetime conscription in the history of the United States, requiring all males between the ages of 21 and 36 to register for the draft. Following America's entry into the war, the act was amended and required all males between the ages of 18 and 65 to register. Only those 18–45 were subject to military service.

On June 26, 1942, with the United States now at war, Congress revised the act, deferring married men from the draft, with the intent that families would be left intact as long as possible, exhausting the pool of single men before drafting married men, especially married men with families.

But toward the end of 1943, the manpower needs of the military required drafting married men, and his neighbors on the local draft board sent a letter advising Silvestre Herrera, a 27-year-old farmhand with three children and a pregnant wife, that he was to report for induction into the armed forces by January 1944.

Herrera traveled to El Paso, Texas, to visit his family and make arrangements for his wife and family while he was away in the army, and it was then that his father revealed two startling facts. The man who he believed to be his father was really his uncle, and Silvestre was not an American citizen.

Herrera was born Silvestre Almanza in Camargo, Chihuahua, Mexico, on July 17, 1917, although some sources cite an earlier birth date of December 31, 1916. He was orphaned at the age of one, when his parents died in an influenza epidemic, and he was brought to El Paso by an uncle who raised him until he was ten, when he moved to Phoenix, Arizona, to live with a maternal aunt. It was then that Silvestre took his mother's family name of Herrera.

Now his uncle told him, "Son, you don't have to go. They can't draft you. You aren't an American citizen." Silvestre hoped to become a U.S. citizen and knew that service in the military was a path to citizenship, but his statements in numerous interviews suggest other, more noble motivations: "I didn't want someone else dying in my place," and "I had an American wife and kids with one on the way ... my adopted country had been good to me."

Herrera enlisted in the Texas Army National Guard on January 13, 1944, and reported to Fort McClellan, Alabama, for basic training. He was then assigned to Company E, Second Battalion, 142nd Infantry Regiment, 36th Infantry Division.

By the time Herrera joined his unit in the summer of 1944, the 142nd had already fought its way across Italy, making an amphibious landing at Salerno on September 9, 1943, the first landing by U.S. forces in Europe, and then fought northward up Italy and made a second amphibious landing at Anzio on May 22, 1944.

When Herrera joined Company E, they were preparing for a third amphibious assault, this time in Southern France, and on August 15, 1944, they landed and again began fighting northward, this time toward the German border, and the fighting became even more intense the closer they drew to the border.

The regiment attacked through the foothills of the Vosges Mountains in October and the Foret Domaniale de Champ in November and entered the Alsatian Plains by forcing Sainte Marie Pass on November 25, 1944.

The 142nd Infantry fought at Oberhoffen in northeast France for twelve days (February 1–12) in ferocious combat that earned two soldiers, Tech. Sgt. Edward C. Dahlgren and Sgt. Emile Delau Jr., the Medal of Honor.

On March 15, 1945, Operation Undertone, the Allied invasion of Germany, got under way with a planned assault from the south by the U.S. Seventh and French First Armies of the U.S. Sixth Army Group, with the intent of pushing the Germans back across the Rhine River.

The 142nd was tasked with crossing the Zintzel River at Mertzwiller against determined German resistance. Company E was advancing along a tree-lined road near the town of Mertzwiller when they came under fire from a machine gun positioned in the woods.

As his platoon leader, Lt. Weldon Green, later recalled, "Silvestre was a good soldier. He didn't ever want to slack off." He proved it that March morning.

As his squad dove for cover, PFC Herrera made a one-man frontal assault on the German machine gun, firing his M-1 Garand semi-automatic rifle from the hip until he was close enough to lob two hand grenades. The concussion of the explosions stunned the Germans, and he continued the assault, taking eight Germans prisoner.

After Herrera turned over his prisoners, the platoon began advancing up the road again, only to come under fire from a second machine gun, this one emplaced behind a minefield.

As Herrera recalled in a 2005 interview, "I knew there was a minefield. I had a 2-by-4 and was pushing it ahead of me." Deciding that his progress was too slow, he threw away the board and got to his feet. Despite the danger of unexploded mines, Herrera fearlessly charged forward, firing as he ran.

As he neared the emplacement, he stepped on a land mine and the explosion blew away his foot and lower leg. Despite his wound, he got up and limped forward, pressing the attack, stepping on a second land mine, destroying his other foot. Still, Herrera continued fighting.

As his Medal of Honor citation noted, "Despite intense pain and unchecked loss of blood, he pinned down the enemy with accurate rifle fire while a friendly squad captured the enemy gun by skirting the minefield and rushing in from the flank."

As Herrera later described it, "I was protecting my squad from a machinegun. I was trying to draw their fire. I stepped on one (land mine), it blew me up. Then I stepped on another one with another foot. I was fighting them on my knees."

Herrera was evacuated to an aid station, still conscious, then to a field hospital where he remained for two months before being returned stateside to Bushnell General Military Hospital in Brigham City, Utah, which operated from August 1942 to June 1946. The facility was a World War II army hospital that specialized in treating amputations and fitting prosthetics, or artificial limbs.

Herrera was on a 90-day furlough home to Phoenix when he learned he was going to be awarded the Medal of Honor, the nation's highest award for valor. Although awarding the Medal of Honor to non-citizens was unusual, it was not without precedent, and a greater concern was whether Herrera's health would permit his traveling to Washington, D.C.

Herrera was honored locally when Arizona governor Sidney Osborne declared August 14, 1945, as Herrera Day and held a hero's parade to welcome him home. And with the help of his uncle, who took time off from work, Herrera was present on the lawn of the White House on August 23, 1945, when President Truman bent over his wheelchair and presented him with the Medal of Honor.

Honorably discharged from the army as a sergeant in 1946, a drive, supported by numerous national figures, resulted in Herrera being granted U.S. citizenship. That same year, Mexico awarded Herrera the Premier Merito Militar, that nation's highest military honor, making Herrera only the second individual in history to be awarded both the Medal of Honor and the Premier Merito Militar.

The citizens of Arizona also raised $14,000 to help Herrera buy a house. Herrera, his wife Ramona, and his children, who would eventually number seven, settled in Phoenix where Herrera, now fitted with prosthetic feet, made a living as an artisan, working in leather and silver.

Herrera was active in the community and a popular speaker at schools, clubs and civil organizations. He frequently served as the grand marshal of the Phoenix Veterans Day Parade.

Although modest about his accomplishments, the honors continued over the years, with an elementary school in Phoenix named after him in 1956, recognition by the U.S. House of Representatives in March 1996, and an army reserve center in Mesa, Arizona, named in his honor in 1998.

Silvestre Herrera passed away peacefully in his sleep at home on November 26, 2007, at the age of 90, survived by five children, 11 grandchildren and 17 great-grandchildren. His wife had died in 1991.

On a sunny afternoon on Saturday, December 8, Herrera was laid to rest at the West Resthaven Park Cemetery in Glendale, Arizona, with full military honors and was buried beside his beloved Ramona.

Herrera rarely spoke about his disability. "I didn't want anybody to feel sorry for me. I lived a very happy life."

Sources

Cossel, Benjamin. "Profile in Heroism: Medal of Honor Recipient Silvestre Herrera, DVIDS." https://www.dvidshub.net/news/14280/profile-heroism-medal-honor-recipient-silvestre-herrera.

Johnson, Jim. "Local Veteran Remembers Medal of Honor Recipient." *Eastern Arizona Courier*, December 2, 2007.

McLellan, Dennis. "Silvestre Herrera 1916–2007." *Los Angeles Times*, December 3, 2007.

Sterner, Doug. "Silvestre S. Herrera, Medal of Honor, World War II." http://www.home ofheroes.com/profiles/profiles_herrera.html.

Texas Military Forces Museum. "142nd Lineage and Honors." http://www.texasmilitary forcesmuseum.org/36division/archives/142/142lin.htm.

Tillman, Barrett. *Heroes: US Army Medal of Honor Recipients.* New York: Tekno Books, Penguin Group, 2006.

Isadore S. Jachman

Native-Born German Who Won the Medal of Honor

By early December 1944, the Allied forces were advancing toward Germany, fighting town by town, village by village as they pushed the Germans back. Many believed the war to be almost over.

In what was to be Hitler's last attempt to stop the momentum, he ordered his armies to advance through the wooded area of the Ardennes in Luxembourg and Belgium in order to divide the Allied armies in two and then push onwards to the port of Antwerp, a vital Allied stronghold.

On December 16, 1944, the Germans began the Ardennes Offensive (December 16, 1944–January 16, 1945), which the Germans named Unternehmen Wacht am Rhein (Operation Watch on the Rhine), often referred to by the Americans as the Battle of the Bulge. It would be the largest battle in U.S. military history, involving over 600,000 American troops.

Although there were indications from German prisoners that there was a buildup of troops and equipment in the Ardennes area, British general Bernard Montgomery assured General Eisenhower, the Allied supreme commander, that the Germans would be incapable of staging "major offensive operations."

Before dawn on the morning of December 16, the Germans began their last major offensive of the war. The attack came as a complete surprise to the Allied command. The response was slow and confused. Thick snow and heavy fog complicated things and prevented the Americans from employing their airpower.

The Germans advanced in force, with 250,000 men of the Fifth and Sixth Panzer Armies, and drove a wedge into the American line, the origin of the name Battle of the Bulge. Germans, dressed in American uniforms and driving captured U.S. jeeps, caused confusion, and within five days the Germans had surrounded almost 20,000 Americans at the crossroads of Bastogne.

The situation was desperate, but when the German commander gave Brig. Gen. Anthony McAuliffe, the American commander at Bastogne, the chance to surrender, McAuliffe answered with a single word—"Nuts."

But 8,000 U.S. soldiers near the town of St. Vith were forced to surrender, the largest surrender of U.S. troops since the American Civil War, 80 years earlier.

As the Allied command scrambled to solidify the line, circumstances improved when the weather cleared up on December 23, allowing the Allies to deploy their airpower, and bombers destroyed the German supplies in the rear, while P-47 fighters strafed German troops on the road, and supplies of food, medicine and ammunition were air-dropped into Bastogne.

By the next day, the German advance had been halted at the Meuse River, as the Germans had overextended their supply lines and were suffering critical shortages of fuel and ammunition.

Many of the American troops would see their first combat in this battle, including Staff Sergeant Isadore S. "Izzy" Jachman (serial no. 13136814), a squad leader in Company B, First Battalion, 513th Parachute Infantry Regiment, 17th Airborne Division.

As Sergeant Jachman's unit advanced, he drew nearer and nearer the place of his birth. Isadore Jachman was born in Berlin, Germany, on December 14, 1922, the first son of Leo and Lotte Jachmann. Leo had moved to Berlin some years earlier from the family home in Kalisz, Poland, where his name had been Jachimowicz.

In 1924, when Isadore was two years old, his family emigrated to the United States, settling in Baltimore, where his father Americanized his name by dropping the second "n." A younger brother and sister, Joe and Sylvia, were both born in the United States after the family immigrated.

Raised in Baltimore, Jachman attended high school at Baltimore City College, graduating in 1939. Jachman, who was Jewish, had relatives who remained in Germany, many of whom died in the Holocaust, including six aunts and uncles.

With America's entry into World War II, following Japan's attack on the U.S. fleet at Pearl Harbor, Hawaii, Jachman, now a naturalized citizen, enlisted in the U.S. Army. At the time of his enlistment on November 17, 1942, his induction papers listed him as a 22-year-old citizen, single with no dependents, with one year of college, and working as a skilled mechanic/repairman.

Assigned as a private in the cavalry, after basic training, Jachman was sent to Company B, 513th Parachute Infantry Regiment. The 513th was constituted on December 26, 1942, and assigned to the 13th Airborne Division.

It was activated January 11, 1943, at Fort Benning, Georgia, and moved to Fort Bragg, North Carolina, on November 1, 1943, and then to Camp Mackall, North Carolina, on January 15, 1944.

On March 4, the 513th relocated to the Tennessee Maneuver Area, where the regiment was transferred from the 13th Airborne Division and formally assigned to the 17th Airborne Division on March 10. The unit relocated to Camp Forrest, Tennessee, on March 24; staged at Camp Myles Standish, Massachusetts, on August 13; and departed from the Boston Port of Embarkation on August 20, 1944.

The 513th Parachute Infantry Regiment arrived in England under the command of Col. James W. Coutts, the former assistant commandant at the Fort Benning Parachute School. The regiment was transported to Camp Chiseldon, the 17th Airborne Division staging area, on August 28, 1944. Flight and tactical training continued, as well as night maneuvers. When Operation Market Garden was initiated, the 17th Airborne was still in training and was held in strategic reserve.

Then came the surprise German offensive through the Ardennes forests on December 16. The 82nd and 101st Airborne Divisions, in Sissone, France, were rushed by truck to contain the bulge in the Allied lines. To help reinforce the siege at Bastogne, the entire 17th Airborne Division was finally committed to combat in the European theater of operations on December 23.

The 513th was flown into the Reims area in France in night flights and then hastily trucked into Belgium. Upon arrival, the 513th and the other elements of the 17th Airborne Division were attached to Patton's Third Army and ordered to immediately close in at Mourmelon.

After taking over the defense of the Meuse River sector from Givet to Verdun on December 25, the 17th moved to Neufchateau, Belgium, and then marched through the snow to Morhet, relieving the 28th Infantry Division on January 3, 1945.

General Patton had ordered the 17th Airborne to capture the Belgian village of Flamierge where the 11th Armor and the 87th Infantry Divisions had encountered stiff, almost fanatical resistance from the Germans. In the subsequent fighting, the 513th would have its baptism of fire. Patton told Gen. William "Bud" Miley, commander of the 17th Airborne Division, there would be little resistance. His assessment proved to be inaccurate.

Lacking time to make an effective reconnaissance, the division went blindly into the attack and suffered dearly.

The plan called for the 513th Parachute Infantry Regiment to push forward on the right while the 194th Glider Infantry Regiment would be abreast of the 513th on the left. Almost immediately the regiments came under relentless mortar fire.

The First Battalion reached Cochleval but was pinned down by heavy machine-gun and mortar fire. When two German tanks broke out of the dense fog and threatened to overrun the 513th's position, Sergeant Jachman went into action.

Al Bryant, also in B Company, recalled,

> Our anti-tank weapons were useless. When our bazookas fired it might knock off a little metal but no real harm was done. We had a trooper dug in with a bazooka about 40 feet in front of us. He fired his bazooka at a Tiger tank, the tank fired back and our trooper was directly hit by an 88-millimeter shell.

After heavy German machine-gun fire put both of B Company's bazooka teams out of action, Jachman, despite heavy and sustained enemy fire, charged across an open field and picked up a bazooka dropped by one of the men.

Loading the weapon, he fired, knocking out the lead enemy tank. As he prepared to fire at a second tank, he was cut down by machine-gun fire, dying from his wounds. He was 22 years old.

For his actions, Jachman was awarded posthumously the Distinguished Service Cross.

After the war, a neighbor of Jachman's parents, hearing of his courage, wrote to Maryland senator Herbert R. O'Conor, who in turn wrote to the adjutant general, asking for a review of his case.

Rather than the Distinguished Service Cross, on June 9, 1950, President Truman signed papers authorizing the award of the Medal of Honor for "conspicuous gallantry and intrepidity," and the medal was presented to Jachman's mother and father.

Years later, the village of Flamierge erected a statue at the site where an unknown brave American soldier had stood fighting to save the village. A subsequent search of army records established that this was Sergeant Jachman, and his name was added to the statue.

The Staff Sgt. Isadore Jachman Armory, named in his honor, is located at 12100 Greenspring Avenue, Owings Mills, Maryland.

SOURCES

Congressional [sic] Medal of Honor Society. "Citation for Isadore Jachman." http://www.cmohs.org/recipient-detail/2800/jachman-isadore-s.php.Cordero, Dave. "Paratroopers Recall Brutal Battle of the Bulge." *USA Today.* https://www.stargazette.com/story/news/2015/01/06/vault-paratroopers-recall-brutal-battle-bulge/21321469/.

Devlin, Gerald M. *Paratrooper: Saga of Parachute and Glider Combat Troops during World War II.* London: Robson Books, 1979.

"The 513th Parachute Infantry Regiment Unit History." http://www.ww2-airborne.us/units/513/513.html.

MacDonald, Charles B. *United States Army in WWII–Europe: The Last Offensive.* Atlanta: Whitman Publishing, 2012.

Richard Nott Antrim

*Only Medal of Honor Awarded
to a POW During World War II*

In April 1942, the war in the Pacific was still new, but already some Americans were learning hard lessons about the character of the enemy they were facing. This included the crew of the destroyer USS *Pope* (DD-225), prisoners of the Japanese since three days after their ship was sent to the bottom on March 1, and already they were showing the effects of their captivity.

Life in a Japanese prisoner of war camp was not easy, as the 150 crewmen of the *Pope* would discover. Interned at the Makassar POW Camp, Celebes Island, Dutch East Indies (known today as Indonesia), the 2,700-plus prisoners were mostly Dutch and colonial troops but included American sailors from the USS *Pope* and the submarine USS *Perch* (SS-176), which was scuttled after being damaged by Japanese destroyers, and British sailors from the HMS *Exeter* and HMS *Encounter*.

Roll call was 5:30 a.m., with work beginning at 7 a.m. and continuing until 6 p.m., with a half-hour lunch, consisting of cold rice and dry fish. Work was conducted at Makassar harbor, a lime factory, Mandai airfield, and later, nickel mines. Last roll call was at 9 p.m.

Beds consisted of bare boards, the men's feet pointed toward the center, with straw bricks as pillows and two blankets, summer and winter. Pneumonia took one prisoner a day the first winter. No medicine or medical supplies were available. Fleas, rats and lice were endemic, and there was no soap. Dysentery was rampant, and religious services rarely permitted. There was no mail, no newspapers, no news of any kind, only rumors.

Most deadly was the discipline, which could be characterized as severe at best and homicidal at worst, with beatings common and executions not uncommon, sometimes for the slightest of infractions. The Japanese code of Bushido made it shameful to be taken prisoner, and thus guards considered their prisoners to have forfeited their honor and were cowards and unworthy of respect. Many guards used this as an excuse for sadism. The capricious application of discipline made it all the more frightening.

On that April morning, Lt. (jg) Allen Jack Fisher failed to bow low enough to one of his guards, which caused the guard to fly into a violent rage, venting his anger by striking Fisher with a series of brutal blows with his swagger stick, knocking the bleeding officer to the ground where other guards joined in, kicking Fisher senseless.

As the prisoners watched frozen, afraid of attracting the wrath of the already frenzied guards, the executive officer of the *Pope*, Lt. Richard Antrim, to the awe of both the Japanese and the prisoners, stepped forward. What he said and what he did would earn him the award of the Medal of Honor.

Richard Nott Antrim was born in Peru, Indiana, on December 17, 1907, one of three children born to Sergeant Nott W. Antrim and his wife Mary Margaret, a schoolteacher. His father would retire as a master sergeant after service with Company C, 361st Engineer Regiment during World War II.

Antrim attended public schools in Peru and played football in high school, winning the Wabash Valley Football Conference in 1924 and graduating in June 1926. He enlisted in the U.S. Navy Reserve on June 28, 1926, and was appointed to the U.S. Naval Academy on June 20, 1927, where he played varsity football for three years, graduating on June 4, 1931, with a commission as an ensign.

After brief duty with the 11th Naval District, Antrim reported aboard the battleship USS *New York* (BB-34) as the fire control officer in August 1931. In April

Ens. Richard Antrim, circa 1931 (U.S. Naval Historical Center).

1932, Antrim was sent to Naval Air Station Pensacola, in Florida, for flight training. Between June and November 1932, Antrim served aboard the USS *Salinas* (AO-19), a Patoka-class replenishment oiler; USS *Nitro* (AE-2), an ammunition ship; and USS *Trenton* (CL-11), a light cruiser.

Ordered to the Bethlehem Steel shipyard in Quincy, Massachusetts, in November, he assisted in fitting out the heavy cruiser USS *Portland* (CA-33) and served as a division officer following her commissioning on February 23, 1933, until April 1936. He then transferred to the destroyer USS *Crowninshield* (DD-134), where he served until June when he was sent to Naval Air Station Lakehurst, New Jersey, for instruction in lighter-than-air aviation. Antrim was on duty and narrowly escaped injury on May 6, 1937, when the German passenger airship LZ 129 *Hindenburg* caught fire and was destroyed during its attempt to dock.

Now certified to fly airships, kites and free-balloon aircraft, Antrim reported aboard the USS *Bittern* (AM-36), a Lapwing-class minesweeper, serving as its executive officer from May 1938 until December 1939, when he became executive officer of the USS *Pope* (DD-225), a Clemson-class destroyer, an aging "four-stacker" commissioned in October 1920 and assigned to the Asiatic Fleet.

The *Pope* was part of the Yangtze River Patrol in 1923 and spent most of her service in the Far East, primarily China, especially after Japan invaded Manchuria. She was in the Philippines when the Japanese attacked Pearl Harbor on December 7, 1941, and while most of the Asiatic Fleet was withdrawn, the *Pope* was among the few ordered to sail to the Dutch East Indies four days later, on December 11.

The *Pope* saw significant action in the early days of the war, taking part in two major engagements fought by the Asiatic Fleet destroyers; the Battle of Balikpapan and the Battle of Badung Strait.

On January 9, 1942, the *Pope* departed Darwin, Australia, heading for Surabaya, Java, as part of an escort for the transport *Bloemfontein*, carrying desperately needed U.S. Army artillery units to reinforce Dutch, British and Australian troops to repel the expected Japanese invasion of Java. The *Pope*, along with the destroyers USS *Stewart* (DD-224), USS *Bulmer* (DD-222), USS *Parrott* (DD-218) and USS *Barker* (DD-213), along with two light cruisers, USS *Boise* (CL-47) and USS *Marblehead* (CL-12) saw the troops safely to Java.

On January 11, 1942, just 35 days after the outbreak of war with Japan, the Second Battalion, 132 Field Artillery disembarked on Java, the only U.S. ground combat unit to reach the Netherlands East Indies before the Dutch capitulated to the Japanese. The survivors became among the earliest American prisoners of the Japanese when, on March 8, Dutch general Hein ter Poorten, commander of all American, British, Dutch and Australian (ABDA) troops on Java surrendered unconditionally.

For the next two weeks, the *Pope* and other American warships joined with ships of the British, Australian and Royal Netherlands Navy in patrolling the waters surrounding the Netherlands East Indies and screening Allied shipping moving south from the Philippines.

The oilfields of Balikpapan on the island of Borneo became a prime target of the Japanese following their failure to capture the oilfields at Tarakan before they were destroyed. On January 22, the Japanese fleet was sighted moving south. The next day, the 23rd, formations of nine Dutch Martin B-10 bombers escorted by 20 Brewster Buffalo fighters, attacked the convoy from the sky, sinking the transport *Tatsugami Maru*. That same day, a Dutch submarine sank the transport *Tsunuga Maru*. Despite this, they couldn't prevent the successful landing of troops southeast of the airfield early on the morning of January 24.

The landing was not without cost. The 59th Destroyer Division, composed of the *Pope* and the destroyers USS *Paul Jones* (DD-230), USS *John D. Ford* (DD-228), and USS *Parrott* (DD-218), savaged the convoy of 12 transports and three patrol boats (World War I destroyers) acting as escorts, sinking four transports—*Kuretake Maru*, *Nana Maru*, *Sumanoura Maru* and *Tatsugami Maru*—and patrol boat P-37 and damaging two other transports.

Despite the success at Balikpapan, the Japanese offensive relentlessly advanced, with Kendari falling on January 24, Ceram on January 31, Makassar on February 8 and Banjarmasin on February 10. The Japanese completed their occupation of Borneo and Celebes and set their sights on Java.

On February 18, two transports carrying units of the Japanese 48th Infantry Division, escorted by one light cruiser and eight destroyers, landed troops on Bali, Dutch East Indies. Capture of the island would give the Japanese an airbase within range of the ABDA naval base at Surabaya. The threat could not be ignored.

Two submarines, the USS *Seawolf* (SS-197) and HMS *Truant*, attacked the convoy but did no damage and were driven off by Japanese destroyers. An attack later in the day by some 20 U.S. AAF B-17s managed to damage only the transport *Sagami Maru*.

Dutch admiral Karl Doorman, in tactical command of the ABDA strike force, had his naval resources dispersed and was forced to engage the Japanese in three waves rather than in one combined force, one group following the next.

Group 1, sailing from Tjilatjap and made up of Royal Netherlands Navy light cruisers *De Ruyter* and *Java*, Dutch destroyers *Kotenaer* and *Piet Hein* and two U.S. Navy destroyers, *Pope* and *John D. Ford*, would engage first and inflict maximum damage with gunfire and torpedoes, then withdraw to the north. The second wave would consist of the Dutch light cruiser *Tromp* and U.S. destroyers *Stewart, Parrott, John D. Edwards*, and *Pillsbury*.

Aware of the danger of additional attacks, the Japanese hurried the landing, with most of the escort force departing, leaving only the two transports, *Sasago Maru* and the damaged *Sagami Maru*, and four destroyers, *Asashio, Oshio, Arashio*, and *Michishio*. Shortly before midnight the last of the Japanese ships departed the anchorage at Sanur Roads.

It was a dark and cloudy night, making visibility difficult. At 10:25 p.m., the Japanese were spotted, and the cruiser *Java* opened fire. The opposing vessels fired upon each other with no effect as they maneuvered to gain better positions. The Dutch destroyer *Piet Hein* launched a torpedo and opened fire while making a turn back to the south. The sharp turn threw a crewman against the Make Smoke button, and the resulting smoke confused the U.S. destroyer captains and blocked their visibility even more.

At 10:40 p.m., *Piet Hein* was hit by a torpedo from *Asashio*, sinking almost immediately. The *Ford* began laying smoke as the American destroyers withdrew. The *Pope* was able to fire off five torpedoes, but none struck home. After an exchange of gunfire with the *Asashio* and *Oshio*, *John D. Ford* and *Pope* retired to the southwest, separated from the cruisers heading northeast.

The second wave did little better, with only damage to the Dutch cruiser *Tromp*, which had to return to Australia for repairs, and the Japanese destroyer *Michishio*, which had to be towed from the battle. The third wave of eight Dutch motor torpedo boats arrived at 6 a.m. on February 20 but didn't encounter any Japanese ships. The Battle of Badung Strait was over.

Following the action, *Pope*'s commanding officer, Cmdr. Welford C. Blinn, in his report noted that his executive officer, Antrim, was "highly deserving of commendation for the meritorious performance of his several duties before and throughout the action," citing him for his performance in navigation fire control and torpedo fire and recommending him for a "decoration deemed appropriate."

The Bali garrison of approximately 600 Indonesian militia surrendered with no resistance, and the airfield was captured intact. The four

Japanese destroyers, outnumbered and outgunned, had driven off the much larger Allied force, sinking the destroyer *Piet Hein* and damaging the cruiser *Tromp*, while sustaining little damage.

The Japanese advanced on Timor, capturing it on February 23, and advanced on Java with a large force of cruisers and destroyers to encircle the small island. As the Japanese amphibious forces prepared to strike at Java on February 27, 1942, the main Allied naval force, under Dutch admiral Doorman, sailed northeast from Surabaya to intercept a convoy of the Eastern Invasion Force approaching from the Makassar Strait.

Doorman's force consisted of a heavy cruiser, HMS *Exeter*, four light cruisers, USS *Houston* (CL-81), His Netherland Majesty's ship (HNLMS) *De Ruyter*, HNLMS *Java*, HMAS *Perth*, and ten destroyers: HMS *Electra*, HMS *Encounter*, HMS *Jupiter*, HNLMS *Kortenaer*, HNLMS *Witte de With*, USS *Alden*, USS *John D. Edwards*, USS *John D. Ford*, USS *Paul Jones* and USS *Pope*.

The Japanese task force protecting the convoy, commanded by Rear Admiral Takeo Takagi, consisted of two heavy cruisers, *Nachi* and *Haguro*, and two light cruisers, *Naka* and *Jintsū*, and 14 destroyers, *Yūdachi*, *Samidare*, *Murasame*, *Harusame*, *Minegumo*, *Asagumo*, *Yukikaze*, *Tokitsukaze*, *Amatsukaze*, *Hatsukaze*, *Yamakaze*, *Kawakaze*, *Sazanami*, and *Ushio*.

The Allied force engaged the Japanese in the Java Sea, and the battle raged sporadically from mid-afternoon to midnight as the Allies tried to reach and attack the troop transports of the Java invasion fleet, but they were driven off by superior firepower, with the result of heavy losses to the Allies, including 10 ships, and approximately 2,173 sailors.

The *Pope* was not in the battle but tied up dockside at Surabaya, undergoing emergency repairs to the evaporators, necessary for making fresh water essential to the ship's operation.

At 1700 hours on the evening of February 28, Commander Blinn was ordered to report to Capt. O. L. Gordon aboard the HMS *Exeter* and was informed that *Pope*, along with the HMS *Encounter*, would escort *Exeter*, damaged in the previous day's action and capable of a speed of only 16 knots, from the area and to Ceylon, India, for repairs.

At 1900 hours, the three Allied ships departed Surabaya, attempting to slip out and escape through the closing noose, heading north, hoping to round Bawean Island, then head west to pass through the Sunda Strait between Java and Sumatra.

At 0730 on the morning of March 1, they were spotted by a single enemy aircraft, but the *Exeter*'s anti-aircraft guns shot her down. Shortly afterwards, first contact was made with a Japanese force consisting of two heavy Ashigara-class cruisers, the *Nachi* and *Haguro*, escorted by a heavy destroyer, approaching from the south. The two forces began exchanging gunfire, with the larger eight-inch guns of the Japanese cruisers having the advantage over the four-inch guns of *Pope* and *Encounter*.

At 1050 hours, the Japanese were reinforced by three more destroyers and two additional heavy cruisers, the *Ashigara* and *Myōkō*. Closing in on either side of the fleeing Allied ships, the cruisers opened fire as they came in range. Outnumbered and outgunned, the ships were now fighting to survive.

At 1120 hours, *Exeter* took a major hit in her one remaining boiler room, resulting in a loss of power and slowing her until she was dead in the water, unable to maneuver. As the four Japanese cruisers closed in on *Exeter*, *Encounter* and *Pope* were ordered to "make a run for it" but the *Pope* circled the *Exeter*, laying down smoke to better enable the crew to safely abandon ship, even while they were under heavy enemy fire, and then she headed for a nearby rain squall, attempting to shake off pursuit.

With *Exeter* at a standstill, the destroyer *Inazuma* closed in for a torpedo attack, hitting *Exeter* with two torpedoes on her starboard side. *Exeter* sank at approximately 1140 hours, and at about the same time, the *Encounter* took a hit in the ammunition magazine and blew up, sinking almost immediately.

Hidden temporarily by the rain squall, *Pope* tried to make a run for it, but the outdated "four-stacker" that the crew joked was "old enough to vote" couldn't outrun her pursuers. Desperate, *Pope* fired all her torpedoes, and dumped her depth charges to lighten the ship and gain speed, as the cruisers closed to finish her off.

Spotted at 1230, *Pope* came under attack by six cruiser-borne dive bombers, each making two attacks, with the 11th attack, a near miss, putting a hole on the port side aft and below the waterline, damaging the port engine as water flooded into the after engine room.

The *Pope* also survived an attack by six Mitsubishi Type 97 Ki-21 heavy bombers from about 3,000 feet whose bombs all missed, but the flooding couldn't be controlled. The stern was settling fast, and the order was given to stand by to abandon ship.

By all accounts, the executive officer, Lieutenant Antrim, was everywhere, despite being wounded in the earlier action. He was seeing that all watertight doors and hatches were opened, preparing the motor whale boat and life rafts for lowering, seeing to the destruction of confidential materials and secret, underwater sound gear on the bridge, and setting demolition charges there and in the forward engine room.

Several crewmen were injured in the battle, but the only fatality occurred when a piece of metal entered the chest of the Fire Control Talker Howard Davis, Yeoman Second Class, after shrapnel from the demolition charge pierced the chart house bulkhead, killing him instantly.

The motor whale boat, the wherry (a large rowboat) and three cork rafts were lowered into the water, with the wounded put aboard the whale boat. Antrim, along with two volunteers, Mathews and Penninger, remained aboard until the crew was safely over the side, then set off the last demolition charges. The *Pope* had already begun sinking when a salvo from one of the cruisers finished the job, sending her to the bottom.

As Antrim later wrote in an action report,

> The [whale boat] circled around until it located the three life rafts, the damaged wherry which was repaired the next day, and lashed all to the side of the boat. At about 2000, a muster was held and all personnel, with the exception of Davis, Y2c, who had been killed, 151 in all, were found present. The officers and men were divided into six watches, allowing one watch (plus the wounded) in the boat for about thirty minutes at a time. This procedure was modified later as conditions became more desperate ... it was hoped that an American submarine might possibly pick up survivors. A flare was set off at 2200.
>
> In the afternoon of the second day an enemy plane circled the boat. After sundown, in the interest of morale, since all men were becoming restless, the motor was started, and the rafts were towed in the direction of Java. The repaired wherry was used to pick up stragglers who became detached from the greatly overcrowded life rafts. During the night two Japanese destroyers approached within several miles of the boat whereupon we stopped the motor in order to avoid detection.
>
> After the gasoline ran out about noon of the third day, a sail was rigged with a blanket at the bow to point the boat in a southerly direction and the strongest officers and men rowed in relays with all available paddles and oars. An enemy plane again circled us during this afternoon. By nightfall life jackets had become so waterlogged as to become almost useless, many men were almost completely exhausted, and it was feared some unobserved stragglers would be lost this night.
>
> At 2230 (about) a Japanese destroyer hove into sight, picked the boat up in her searchlight beam, and hailed us. Lt. Wilson, who spoke Japanese, answered them. All personnel were then taken on board, sprayed with a solution of carbolic acid, searched, and made captive. There was no loss of life in the water.

For his "coolly, calmly, efficiently, with contempt for danger and with remarkable judgement in carrying out his vital battle tasks of navigation, fire direction and damage control with a preciseness that left nothing to be desired" during the battle, and for his later "extraordinary heroism and perseverance in his immediate task of supervising the abandoning of the ship" and for "courageously exposing himself to low flying enemy bombers [as] he directed the men over the side in such a manner that group targets would not be offered to the enemy from the air, at the same time supervising the removal of the wounded from the ship," Antrim would be awarded the Navy Cross.

Known as the Second Battle of the Java Sea, it was the last naval action of the Netherlands East Indies campaign of 1941–1942, and 800 crewmen were taken into captivity, including 151 sailors of the *Pope*.

Now, in April 1942, as Antrim stood in formation with his fellow prisoners, watching Lieutenant Fisher being beat nearly to death for failing to not bow low enough, he felt compelled to step forward to intervene. As three guards kicked the bleeding, semi-conscious officer, Antrim stepped out of ranks and using broken Japanese and gesturing, he tried to convey that the officer meant no disrespect and that they were all unfamiliar with the Japanese customs.

There is a question as to who was more shocked by Antrim's audacity, the Japanese guards who ceased the beating, perhaps dumbfounded at his foolishness, or the 2,700 or so POWs who watched silently amazed and certain that Antrim would be the next victim of the guards' homicidal rage. In the weeks of their captivity, they had lived in fear, watching their fellow prisoners being broken and abused by sadistic guards. Deaths were not uncommon.

As Antrim pleaded for mercy for the officer, the camp commandant stepped forward, and Antrim made his case directly as the commandant listened. After some consideration, the commandant declared that there would be no mercy, and that Fisher's punishment would be 50 lashes with a hawser, a thick naval rope.

The beating resumed. Blow after blow landed on the now-unconscious Fisher, and it was obvious that he would die if the beating continued. Then, to the amazement of all, Antrim again stepped forward on the 15th lash and shouted, "Enough! I'll take the rest." As the guards watched, astonished, he repeated, "I'll take the rest of this man's beating." Some accounts give his words as, "If there is to be 50 lashes, I will take the rest of them for him." It matters little.

There was an astonished silence, the Japanese guards shocked, or perhaps impressed, by his courage. They looked over at where the commandant stood, also uncertain about what to do.

A low roar among the POWs erupted into a long, deafening cheer, acknowledging Antrim's bravery, courage and boldness. The commandant gestured for Fisher to be taken away to the dispensary and then strode purposefully to stand before Antrim.

It was so silent that one could hear the flies buzzing in the tropical heat as all eyes watched, waiting to see what his punishment would be, many expecting summary execution. Keeping eye contact with Antrim, the commandant bowed in an act of respect, and again the prisoners broke out in cheers. Executing a precise about-face, he strode away leaving an astonished Antrim.

His family learned he was still alive only when on January 17, 1943, Tokyo radio station JLG4 broadcast a message read by a Japanese announcer written by Antrim: "Dear mother, the Japanese have given me permission to send a message and I am sending you my love. I am treated fine and am in good health."

It would be another two and a half years before Antrim would see his family, after being liberated in September 1945, but not before Antrim would accomplish one more act of audacious courage, right under the nose of his captors.

Ordered to take charge of a labor party assigned the task of constructing slit trenches for protection from bombs during air raids, he obtained approval from the Japanese to alter the construction plan, causing to be constructed, under the watchful eyes of his captors, a large "US" visible from above and clearly identifying the occupants as Americans. Had his act been discovered, Antrim would have been beheaded. This act was credited for saving hundreds of prisoners' lives for which he was later awarded a Bronze Star with a "V" device, denoting valor.

Antrim remained in the navy after the war, taking rehabilitation leave until March 1946 and a Repatriated POW refresher course at the Washington Navy Yard in Washington, D.C., in May 1946, before taking a pilot refresher course at Lakehurst, New Jersey, and completing a course at the Naval War College, Newport, Rhode Island from June 1946 to June 1947.

On January 30, 1947, in a ceremony at the White House, President Truman presented

Capt. Richard Antrim (U.S. Navy).

Antrim with the Medal of Honor and Bronze Star. The citation stated, "By his fearless leadership and valiant concern for the welfare of another, he not only saved the life of a fellow officer and stunned the Japanese into sparing his own life but also brought about a new respect for American officers and men and a great improvement in camp living conditions."

Antrim continued in the navy, commanding the destroyer USS *Turner* (DD-834) from July 1947 until October 1948, and later the attack transport USS *Montrose* (APA-212) August 1952 until June 1953, during the Korean War. This was interspaced with shore assignments at the Pentagon, as a policy advisor to the State Department, and as head of the Naval Amphibious Warfare section in the Office of the Chief of Naval Operations until August 1953.

Poor health, most certainly a result of three and a half years as a Japanese POW caused his admission to the U.S. Naval Hospital at Bethesda, Maryland, from where he was medically retired on April 1, 1954, and advanced to rear admiral on the retired list.

Admiral Antrim retired to Mountain Home, Arkansas, where he passed away on March 7, 1969. A modest man, most who knew him never knew that he had been awarded the Medal of Honor until reading his obituary. He was buried with full military honors at Arlington National Cemetery.

On September 26, 1981, Antrim's widow, Mary Jean, and other family members were present in Seattle, Washington, for the commissioning of the guided missile frigate USS *Antrim* (FFG-20).

Perhaps Antrim's character was best summed up by President Truman, who upon presenting the Medal of Honor, said simply, "You did a mighty fine thing."

Sources

"Action Report: U.S.S. POPE (DD225)," March 1, 1942. https://www.ibiblio.org/hyperwar/USN/ships/logs/DD/dd225-Java.html.
Adkins, Jim. "Hoosier Hero Richard Antrim." http://www.wordandwork.org/2012/09/hoosier-hero-richard-antrim/.
Hargis, R., and S. Sinton. *World War II Medal of Honor Recipients*. Oxford: Osprey Publishing, 2003.
La Forte, Robert Sherman, and Ronald E. Marcello, eds. *Building the Death Railway: The Ordeal of American POWs in Burma, 1942–1945*. Lanham, MD: Rowman & Littlefield, 1993.
O'Hara, Vincent P. "Battle of Badung Strait—February 18/19, 1942." http://www.microworks.net/pacific/battles/badung_strait.htm.
Penninger, William. "The USS *Pope*'s Last Action." http://www.asiaticfleet.com/usspope/usspope.htm.
Roscoe, Theodore. *United States Destroyers Operations in WWII*. Annapolis, MD: Naval Institute Press, 1994.
Sterner, Douglas. "Richard Nott Antrim." Home of Heroes. www.homeofheroes.com/brotherhood/antrim.html.

Roddie Edmonds

*First U.S. Serviceman Named
"Righteous Among the Nations"*

It was a cold winter morning in Ziegenhain, Germany, on January 27, 1945. Outside their barracks at Stalag IX-A prisoner-of-war camp, 1,275 American enlisted servicemen stood in ranks trying to keep warm while waiting for the morning roll call. They stood in defiance of their German captors. Standing at their front was the senior NCO, M.Sgt. Roddie Edmonds.

Earlier, orders had been given for only the Jewish POWs to fall out for morning roll call. The prisoners were not unaware of the rumors regarding the Germans' murdering of Jewish prisoners. At five foot six and 143 pounds, Edmonds was not an especially imposing figure, but his moral authority was universally respected.

"We're not going to do that," he is remembered as having said more than 70 years later by witnesses to the event. "The Geneva Convention affords only name, rank and serial number, and so that's what we're going to do. All of us are falling out."

When the camp commandant saw all the Americans formed in ranks, he stormed up to Edmonds, furious, and demanded to know what was going on. "All of you can't be Jewish!"

Edmonds calmly replied, "We are all Jews here."

Infuriated, the commandant placed a pistol at Edmond's head and threatened to shoot him if he didn't order the non-Jews back to the barracks.

Calmly, Edmunds responded, "If you are going to shoot, you are going to have to shoot all of us because we know who you are, and you'll be tried for war crimes when we win the war."

Frustrated, the commandant stalked away, and Edmonds was subsequently credited with saving the lives of an estimated 200 Jewish soldiers, an act for which he was named as "Righteous Among the Nations" by Yad Vashem, Israel's official memorial to victims of the Holocaust, and Israel's highest honor to non-Jews, in February 2016. He is one of only five Americans to be so honored and the only U.S. serviceman.

Roddie W. Edmonds was born in Knoxville, Tennessee, on August 20, 1919, to Thomas C. and Jennie Mary Sexton Edmonds, one of four brothers. His mother died when he was three, and his father worked hard to provide modestly for the family. Edmonds graduated from Knoxville High School in 1938.

He resided for a time in Dooley County, Georgia, where he married and had a daughter, but the marriage ended in divorce sometime after Edmonds enlisted in the U.S. Army as a private (serial no. 34039247) at Fort Oglethorpe, Tennessee, on March 17, 1941, nine months before the attack on Pearl Harbor.

Little is known of his early military service, except that by the time of his capture, he was one of the youngest master sergeants in the U.S. Army and was well respected by the men he served with.

The 422nd Infantry Regiment, 106th Infantry Division, was formed on March 15, 1943 at Fort Jackson, South Carolina. Edmonds was assigned to it, and they arrived in France on December 6, 1944, following 19 days of training in England. The unit to this point had seen no combat.

The 422nd Infantry went into combat in the Schnee-Eifel area of Germany on December 10, 1944, as the 106th Division was put into the line to relieve the Second Infantry Division. According to the U.S. Army Service Manual, one division should not be responsible for more than one mile of front. The 106th was responsible for a front of almost 26 miles and almost the whole division was green troops.

On the morning of December 16, German troops, believed to be on the defensive, launched a surprise attack, the last major German offensive of the war, to drive through the densely forested Ardennes of Belgium, with the goal of crossing the Meuse River to capture the port city of Antwerp. The resulting Battle of the Bulge (December 16, 1944–January 25, 1945) was the costliest action ever fought by the U.S. Army, which suffered over 100,000 casualties.

The assault began at dawn with a 90-minute barrage from 1,600 artillery pieces, and the 422nd found themselves facing the battle-hardened veterans of the Second SS Panzer Division. By December 19,

422nd Infantry Regiment officers and NCOs, Fort Jackson, 1943 (Edmunds bottom row, second from left) (U.S. Army photograph).

out of ammunition and surrounded, both the 422nd and the 423rd surrendered, the largest mass U.S. surrender of World War II.

Edmunds was taken prisoner early in the battle, the International Red Cross reporting his capture on December 16, and with other prisoners, he arrived at Stalag IX-B, a prisoner-of-war compound southeast of the town of Bad Orb in Hesse, Germany, on Christmas Day, 1944.

By this time, alerted by rumors, most of the Jewish prisoners had discarded their dog tags and anything else that would identify them as Jewish.

Thirty days later, they were separated by rank, with 1,275 NCOs, sergeant and above, being sent to Stalag IX-A near Ziegenhain, with privates and corporals remaining at the IX-B camp. Edmunds as senior NCO was in command of the prisoners. It was there, on January 27 that Edmonds took his stand. It was not the only time Edmunds would stand up to his German captors.

Extraordinary over-crowding, appalling conditions and starvation diets were responsible for high death rates through starvation, disease and overexposure in the camps. Guards brutalized their captives, and in late March, the prisoners were ordered to march east.

Informed toward the end of the war that they were going to be moved east, further into Germany, Edmond believed that his men, sick and starving, were too weak and wouldn't survive, and he instructed his men to act sick and refuse to leave the barracks.

Again threatened with being shot and by attack dogs, Edmund stood his ground and again the commandant yielded, throwing up his hands and declaring, "You win. You can have the camp," and they were left behind. With difficulty, Edmonds persuaded the men to remain in camp to await the advancing Allies.

The following day, April 2, 1945, the Second Battalion, 114th Infantry Regiment, supported by the tanks and armored cars of the 106th Cavalry Group and the 776th Tank Destroyer Battalion, liberated Stalag IX, which in a sense was already "self-liberated."

Edmonds survived 100 days as a POW to return home after the war, and he served again during the Korean War. Following his second return home from a war, he met and married Mary Ann Watson, with whom he had two sons, Mike and Chris, but he never mentioned that day in Stalag IX-A, telling his son, "There are some things I'd rather not talk about," and he took that "secret" to his grave, passing away on August 8, 1985, at the age of 65.

It was only by chance that the story came to light.

While researching his father online, Edmond's son Chris, now a Baptist pastor, found a *New York Times* article from 2008 in which a man named Lester Tanner was interviewed about his sale of his Manhattan townhome to former president Richard Nixon.

In the article, Tanner reflected on his experiences as a Jewish prisoner of war during World War II and specifically, how he had been saved from likely death owing to the bravery of Roddie Edmonds. Chris Edmonds was later able to get in touch with Tanner and about a few other men who were there and pieced together the amazing story using their memories and his father's war diary, which included undated notations he had previously been unable to decipher. Only the notation "Before the Commander" referred to the event.

As President Barack Obama described him at the ceremony held on January 27, 2016, at the Israeli embassy in Washington, D.C., "Faced with a choice of giving up his fellow soldiers or saving his own life, Roddie looked evil in the eye and dared a Nazi to shoot. His moral compass never wavered."

On March 23, 2016, H.R. 4863 was introduced in the U.S. House of Representatives, 114th Congress, by Representatives Duncan and Cohen of Tennessee to award the Medal of Honor to Master Sergeant Roddie Edmonds posthumously. The bill, at this writing, is currently referred to the Committee on Armed Services.

Asked why he thought his father had never mentioned it, Chris answered, "I just think he thought it was part of his responsibility, his duty, not only as a soldier of the US Army to protect his men but also as a Christian, a man of faith, to do the right thing for his fellow man."

Sources

Lee, Joseph Andrew. "POW Recalls Battle of the Bulge." *On Patrol*, January 7, 2011.

Matthew, Joseph C. "What Happened to the 422 Before and After." 106th Infantry Division Association. http://www.106thinfdivassn.org/the422.html.

Shearer, John. "Recently Recognized World War II Veteran Came through Fort Oglethorpe." Chattanoogan.com, January 30, 2016.

Tucker, Melanie. "Leader Among Men." *Daily Times*, Maryville, TN. December 19, 2015.

Charles Valentine August
Twice a POW in the Same War

Only a small percentage of any army end up as prisoners in a war. Sixteen million Americans served in the military during World War II. Of these, over 120,000 lived out part of the war behind barbed wire. In the European theater, 93,941 Americans were held as prisoners of war, while another estimated 27,000 were prisoners of the Japanese. Of American prisoners in Japanese camps, 40 percent died according to the U.S. Congressional Research Service, compared to just 1 percent of American prisoners in German POW camps.

An even smaller percentage of soldiers and sailors were taken prisoner twice in two wars. But Charles Valentine August has the distinction of being the only American servicemember to be awarded two Prisoner of War Medals for the same war.

Very little information is available about August's early life. He graduated the University of California and enlisted in the Naval Aviation program and earned his wings of gold and a commission as an ensign.

In November of 1942, August, now a lieutenant (jg), was a pilot in Fighter Squadron 41 (VF-41) aboard the aircraft carrier USS *Ranger* (CV-4) as part of Carrier Air Group Four.

The *Ranger*, one of the fleet's earliest aircraft carriers, and the first to be designed from the keel up as an aircraft carrier, was launched in 1933. *Ranger* was already patrolling the Atlantic and escorting British troop ships, when she returned to Norfolk Naval Yard on December 7, 1941, and learned about the Japanese attack at Pearl Harbor.

The *Ranger* operated around Bermuda on training cruises until March 1942 and then made two cruises carrying army P-40 Warhawk fighters to Africa's Gold Coast for service further east with the American

Volunteer Group Flying Tigers, in China. By November, the *Ranger* was part of Operation Torch, the invasion of North Africa.

Under pressure from the Soviet Union to open a second front in Europe to reduce German pressure in the east, Britain and the United States agreed to an invasion of French North Africa, which began November 8, 1942. It was the first major operation involving American troops in the European or North African theater of operations.

Under the command of General Eisenhower, the Allies planned to invade Morocco, Algeria and Tunisia, territory under the control of the Vichy French government. With much of North Africa already under Allied control, this would allow the Allies to carry out a pincer operation against Axis forces in North Africa. The Vichy French forces included 60,000 troops in Morocco, 15,000 in Tunisia, and 50,000 in Algeria, with coastal artillery, and a small number of tanks and aircraft. In addition, there were 10 or so warships and 11 submarines at Casablanca.

The Allies believed, or at least hoped, that the Vichy French forces would not fight, partly because of information supplied by the American consul in Algiers, Robert Daniel Murphy. The French were former allies of the United States, and the American troops were instructed not to fire unless they were fired upon.

Ranger had been joined by four new Sangamon-class escort carriers, USS *Sangamon* (CVE-2), USS *Suwannee* (CVE-27), USS *Chenango* (CVE-28), and USS *Santee* (CVE-29). Leading this carrier force, *Ranger* provided air superiority for the Operation Torch landings in French Morocco.

The real question confounding the commanders of the invasion was, would the French resist the invasion, and if yes, to what degree? Although the ground and naval forces would find their own answers to that question, August found his answer in the skies over Morocco.

On the morning of November 8, the first day of Operation Torch, Lieutenant August was among a group of 18 fighters that attacked the Cazes Airdrome, and as the citation for his Silver Star medal noted, "[August] inflicted heavy damage to aircraft on the ground and to anti-aircraft batteries near the airport."

Outnumbered by French Curtiss 75A Hawk fighters, known in the United States as the P-36 Hawk, August, flying a F4F Wildcat, was nonetheless able to shoot down two hostiles before damage to his aircraft forced him to parachute from the plane. He hit the tail of his plane bailing out, and his parachute barely had time to open before he hit the ground. Stunned, August was captured shortly after.

Lt. (jg) Charles Shield of VF-41, attacked by four 75As suffered the same fate, as did Ens. C. E. "Nick the Greek" Mikronis, and the squadron executive officer, Lt. Malcolm T. Wordell, all of whom were taken prisoner by the Vichy French forces.

Six *Ranger* airmen, none from VF-41, were killed during the attack: Lt. (jg) Stanton M. Amesbury, Lt. Edward Micka, Ens. Thomas Wilhoite, Aviation Radioman George Biggs, Ens. Charles E. Duffy and Aviation Radioman Aubra Patterson, while *Ranger* fighters accounted for 16 French aircraft shot down.

The naval aviators were held as POWs until the armistice on November 11, earning August and the others the Prisoner of War Medal.

With Casablanca's surrender to American forces on November 11, the *Ranger* departed the following day for Norfolk. Upon arrival, *Ranger* underwent an overhaul from December 16, 1942, to February 7, 1943.

On March 30, 1943, a late winter storm blew into New England as the *Ranger* was off the coast of Massachusetts heading toward the Boston Navy Yard for refitting. As a precaution, the ship's aircraft were to fly inland to the Quonset Point Naval Air Station in Rhode Island, but first they were to stop at Squantum Naval Air Station in Quincy, Massachusetts, and obtain an updated weather forecast. If it was favorable, they were to proceed to Quonset. If not, they were to wait at Squantum.

Through an error in communication, this information was not relayed to the pilots, and all 30 aircraft—25 F4F Wildcat fighters, four SBD Dauntless dive bombers, and one TBF Avenger torpedo bomber, headed directly for Quonset and flew head-on into the storm.

Visibility dropped to zero, with cloud cover beginning at 200 feet and extending all the way up to 7,000 feet, in icing conditions. The storm also interfered with radio communication, and it wasn't long before the aircraft got separated.

The first aircraft in trouble was an SBD Dauntless, piloted by Lt. Luke M. Boykin. His carburetor iced over, and he was forced down into the icy water off Swampscott, Massachusetts. As the plane began to sink, Boykin and his radioman, H. H. Reed, scrambled into an inflatable life raft, and were rescued a short time later by a Coast Guard boat from nearby Winter Island.

Lt. Theodore A. Grell, a Wildcat pilot, experienced engine trouble over a rural section of northern Fall River, Massachusetts. As the plane quickly lost altitude, he knew he was going to crash, and he bailed out even though he was now below a safe altitude to do so.

His chute had only half opened when he crashed into the top of a tree, which broke his fall. His plane crashed and exploded about a half mile away. Lying seriously injured in the falling snow, local residents came to his aid, caring for him until an ambulance arrived and took him to a hospital.

August and two other *Ranger* pilots, Lt. Keene G. Hammond and Lt. (jg) Dee Jones, had managed to stay together, but they soon realized they were lost. With no visual reference points, they had veered off course and were now heading over western Massachusetts toward upstate New York.

About ten miles west of Poughkeepsie, over the small town of New Paltz, their fuel low, they began circling, looking for a place to land. With no airport available, they were forced to try for a rough landing in an open field. Lieutenant Hammond came in first and made a pancake landing with his wheels up, causing minor damage to the plane, but he emerged uninjured.

The next to land was August who managed the same feat. Lieutenant Jones wasn't as lucky. Upon landing, his plane caught in the snow and nosed over onto its back, trapping him inside. Although he was relatively unhurt, he was in danger should his fuel ignite.

The landings were noticed by two civil defense aircraft spotters stationed in an observation tower, who notified authorities. Townspeople rushed to the scene and dug him out. Despite the accidents, by the end of the day all of the *Ranger*'s airmen had been accounted for except for Lt. (jg) Arthur Cassidy. He went missing and is unaccounted for to this day, no wreckage or body ever found.

By mid-1944, August, now a full lieutenant, was flying a F6F-5 Hellcat, assigned to VF-44 Crusaders aboard the USS *Langley* (CVL-27), part of Task Force 58 under the command of Rear Admiral Marc Mitscher, which arrived in the Marshall Islands on January 29, 1944, after seeing combat in New Guinea, Saipan, and on June 19–20, the Battle of the Philippine Sea.

By October, *Langley* was operating in the Philippines, fighting in the Battle of Leyte Gulf (October 23–26) in support of the amphibious invasion of the Gulf of Leyte by American forces and Filipino guerrillas under the command of Gen. Douglas MacArthur.

On November 3, 1944, August was shot down, his third aircraft loss, over Manila, but he was recovered uninjured and returned to duty and continued to fly combat missions.

On December 15, 1944, in actions that would subsequently earn him the award of a Distinguished Flying Cross, Lieutenant August led a flight of eight Hellcat fighters of VF-44 in aerial combat between the islands of Luzon and Formosa. August led a coordinated attack, through intense anti-aircraft fire, against a Japanese destroyer that official records list as "probably sunk," and additionally led a low-level attack on a Japanese floatplane, destroying it.

August's luck ran out on January 4, 1945. Taking off from the *Langley* at 0715 hours, part of a flight led by Cmdr. Malcolm Wordell, they were escorting six Grumman TBF Avenger torpedo bombers on an attack of the Kobi Airfield on Formosa.

Over the target at 1020 hours, August's Hellcat suffered an engine failure, and he made a forced landing near the field. The crash was reported immediately, and August was quickly captured, although he would be carried as missing on the squadron's roster.

August was transported to Japan and held as a POW at the Omori prison camp. Built on a manmade island between Tokyo and Yokohama, Omori became notorious for starving its prisoners while forcing them to perform manual labor, like unloading cargo from ships. August survived until the end of the war and was liberated on September 8, returned to military control, and sent home.

The inhumane conditions at Omori were later detailed in the book *Unbroken: A World War II Story of Survival, Resilience, and Redemption*, a 2010 non-fiction book by Laura Hillenbrand.

Lieutenant Commander August was subsequently awarded a second Prisoner of War Medal, the only individual to hold the distinction of being taken prisoner by two different countries in the same war. Little is known of August following the war, except that he was still in the navy in 1946.

His F6F-5 Hellcat fighter, bureau no. 71441, has its own interesting story. The wreckage of August's fighter was recovered largely intact by personnel from Kobi Airfield and it was displayed at Kobi Shrine for a period of time before being transported to Japan.

A Japanese rising-sun insignia was painted over the American markings and it operated for a time out of Yokosuka Airfield before being found abandoned at the end of the war by U.S. forces, lying on its belly, most likely after having made a forced landing. The aircraft had been stripped, with the propeller and engine cowling removed, fabric surfaces missing and cockpit canopy missing.

After discovery, the wreckage was moved and subjected to further removal of parts. Ultimately, it was most likely scrapped.

SOURCES

Ignasher, Jim. "The Disappearance of Lieutenant Jg. Arthur J. Cassidy Jr.—March 30, 1943." *New England Aviation History*. https://www.newenglandaviationhistory.com/the-disappearance-of-lieutenant-jg-arthur-j-cassidy-jr-march-30-1943/.

National Archives. "WW II Prisoner of War Data Files." https://aad.archives.gov/aad/record-detail.jsp?dt=466&mtch=1&cat=all&tf=F&q=Charles+August&bc=sd&rpp=10&pg=1&rid=124955.

PacificWrecks.Com. "F6F-5 Hellcat Bureau Number 71441." http://www.pacificwrecks.com/aircraft/f6f/71441.html.

Wordell, Malcolm T., and Edwin N. Seiler. *"Wildcats" Over Casablanca: U.S. Navy Fighters in Operation Torch.* Washington, D.C.: Potomac Books, 2007.

Virginia Hall
World War II's Most Dangerous Spy

During her long career, she was known by many names: Agent Heckler, Marie Monin, Marcelle Montagne, Germaine, Marie of Lyon and Camille. To the French, she was "la dame qui boite." To the Germans, she was Artemis. To the Gestapo, the Nazi secret police, she was "the lady with the limp" and was considered the "most dangerous of Allied spies." To the British Special Operations Executive (SOE), she was Diane. To the CIA, she was Virginia Hall Goillot.

Despite being limited with a wooden leg, being hunted by the Gestapo (Geheime Staatspolizei, the German secret police), and earning the personal attention of Gestapo chief Klaus Barbie, the Butcher of Lyon, Hall was able to evade capture for over 36 months while operating behind the lines in occupied France.

As Peter Earnest, the executive director of the International Spy Museum in Washington, D.C., himself a 35-year veteran of the CIA, stated of Hall, "She was in imminent danger of being arrested virtually the whole time she was in France. She was very aware of the consequences if the Germans picked her up."

Born in Baltimore, Maryland, on April 6, 1906, Virginia Hall was the older of two children of Edwin Lee Hall and Barbara Virginia (née Hammel). Her family was well off, with a maternal grandfather who made a fortune in shipping. The family took European vacations, and Hall, and her brother John, attended private schools.

A good student at Roland Park Country School, she showed an early talent for leadership, being elected class president, editor of the school newspaper, and captain of the field hockey team. She is remembered in the yearbook as "the most original of our class."

She also demonstrated an aptitude for languages, eventually gaining fluency in German, Italian and French and a little Russian, and she aspired for a career in the diplomatic corps.

She studied languages at Barnard College (Columbia University) in New York, and Radcliffe University in Cambridge, Massachusetts, both exclusive all-female institutions, before traveling abroad in 1926 to finish her education.

She took classes at the Ecole des Sciences Politiques at the Sorbonne in Paris and earned a degree in economics and international law at the Konsularakademie in Vienna, Austria. She also took classes at the universities in Strasbourg and Grenoble.

Hall returned to the United States in 1929 and enrolled in French classes at George Washington University in Washington, D.C.

In 1931, Hall accepted a position with the U.S. State Department as a consular service clerk at the U.S. embassy in Warsaw, Poland. She also worked for a time at the U.S. consulate in Izmir, Turkey.

It was at Izmir, in December 1933, that a hunting accident changed the course of Hall's life. While hunting Gallinago, a marsh bird native to the Gediz Peninsula, she accidently shot herself in the left foot. It turned gangrenous, requiring amputation below her left knee.

She returned home to Baltimore to recover and be fitted with a wooden prosthesis with rubber-covered foot and then resumed work in December 1934 as a clerk at the U.S. consulate in Venice, Italy. While preparing for the Foreign Service examination in 1937, Hall learned that her amputation disqualified her for a Foreign Service career.

She transferred to the legation at Tallin, Estonia, in June 1938, but when her final appeal was denied and a career in the Foreign Service no longer possible, she lost interest in the work and resigned from the State Department in May 1939. She was in Paris on September 3, 1939, when England and France declared war following Germany's invasion of Poland.

Hall volunteered for the French Army, serving at the front as an ambulance driver, private second class, from the end of the "Phony War" on May 10 until France surrendered on June 22, 1940.

Hitler dictated that the French capitulation take place at Compiegne, a forest north of Paris, and ordered that the signing ceremony take place in the same railroad car that hosted the surrender 22 years earlier.

Under the terms of the armistice, two-thirds of France was occupied by the Germans, and the French Army was disbanded. Because of her U.S. passport, Hall was able to make her way to England, via neutral Spain in

August 1940, and took a job as a code clerk for the military attaché at the U.S. embassy in London in September.

After surviving the German Luftwaffe's round-the-clock bombings of London between July and October 1940, during the Battle of Britain, Virginia became convinced that she needed to take part in the war against the Germans.

Hall came to the attention of Col. Maurice Buckmaster, the head of Section F of the SOE, an agency formed by the minister of Economic Warfare, Hugh Dalton, on July 22, 1940, to conduct espionage, sabotage and reconnaissance in occupied Europe and to aid local resistance movements. Section F was responsible for France.

Recruited into the SOE by Vera Atkins, a special assistant to Buckmaster, Hall resigned from the embassy on February 26, 1941, stating only that she had found other employment. Hall undertook agent training, completing all but the parachute training, and then she was sent to France, with the cover of being a correspondent for the *New York Post.*

Hall arrived in Vichy, the capitol of unoccupied France on August 23, 1941, and after registering with the embassy, took an apartment in the city of Lyon to begin her work as part of the Heckler network. Being American, with the United States still neutral, Hall could travel freely throughout unoccupied France.

Lyon was a center for the occupying Germans and a stronghold for the French Resistance, and Hall was advised by her English handlers to avoid the U.S. embassy, as several of the staff were suspected of being pro-German.

Her stories in the *Post* provided valuable intelligence, whether it was reporting on the evacuation of German children as bombings intensified, verifying the effectiveness of the bombing campaign, or reporting on French workers relocating to Germany to find work ("One likes to eat. To eat, one must work. To work, one must go to Germany").

More importantly, for the next 14 months, using pseudonyms such as Bridgette LeContre, Marie, Philomene, and Germaine, Hall served as a contact for incoming agents, recruited contacts, helped downed fliers escape, served as a courier and obtained supplies for the network, all under the nose of the Gestapo which, having penetrated other networks, was avidly intent on capturing "the lady with a limp."

On November 9, 1942, following the Allied invasion of North Africa, Germany responded by occupying the unoccupied zone, and because the knowledge she possessed made her capture risky, Hall was ordered back to England.

In December 1942, Hall escaped into Spain by walking across the snow-covered Pyrenees. She was arrested in San Juan de las Abasedas while trying to board a train to Barcelona. After being detained for 20 days, she was released and returned to England.

Back in England, Hall requested to return to France, but the SOE denied her request, deeming it too risky, especially with her likeness on wanted posters across the country. Instead, she was posted to Madrid in May 1943, acting as a foreign correspondent for the *Chicago Times* but secretly paid by the SOE.

In the year she spent in Madrid, Hall felt she accomplished little, and frequently requested a more "operational" assignment, complaining, "When I came out here, I thought I would be able to help ... but I don't and can't. I am simply living pleasantly and wasting time ... my neck is my own. If I am willing to get a crick in it, I think that's my prerogative." Her requests were denied, in the belief that she was too well known to risk capture by the Gestapo.

Instead, Hall was returned to London, assigned as a briefing officer, debriefing returning agents and briefing the "new boys" on what they could expect to encounter in occupied territory.

She also attended Special Training School at Thame Park in Oxfordshire, where she was instructed in the use wireless radios. But even with the shortage of trained operators, the SOE was reluctant to return her to France.

Frustrated, Hall heard of a new American organization, the OSS, that was conducting missions in cooperation with the SOE in supporting resistance operations. Developing contacts within the agency, she transferred to the OSS on March 10, 1944, with the understanding that she would be sent back into France.

At the end of March 1944, Hall crossed the English Channel and returned to France. Since it was impractical to parachute her in with a wooden leg, Hall was taken to the coast of Bretagne by a wooden British torpedo boat under the cover of darkness, where she and another agent were put ashore in a rubber boat.

Using the name Marcelle Montagne, codename "Diane," Hall was assigned as a radio operator in the Haute-Loire region of central France. She disguised herself as an elderly farmhand, dying her hair gray, wearing clothes that made her look heavier, and shuffling her feet to conceal her limp.

After transiting through Paris, Hall set up operations in Maidou, a village south of Paris, but the Germans had sophisticated radio-detection equipment, and when the Gestapo began to close in, Hall moved further south to the town of Cosne, where she set up operations in May 1944.

Moving from location to location to avoid being detected by the Gestapo tracking her radio signals, Hall coordinated drop zones for arms and supplies, served as a courier and radio operator for the underground, and reported on German troop movements. Despite several close calls, Hall managed to evade capture.

After the D-Day invasion at Normandy on June 6, 1944, Hall worked with a Jedburgh team, codenamed "Jeremy," that arrived from Algiers in mid-August to sabotage German troop movements, disrupt communications and train resistance fighters.

Jedburgh teams were personnel from the SOE, the OSS, the Free French and the Dutch and Belgian Armies that were dropped by parachute into occupied France, the Netherlands and Belgium. They operated clandestinely to conduct sabotage and guerrilla warfare and assist the local Resistance forces in fighting the Germans.

Hall's teams destroyed bridges, derailed trains, tore up track and downed telephone lines, as well as killing or capturing over 600 Germans. Paris was liberated on August 25, 1944, as Allied troops pushed the Germans east.

On September 4, 1944, one of the men who arrived as part of the airdrop was a French American lieutenant, Paul Goillot, who was immediately attracted to Hall, and it was mutual. Eight years her junior, Goillot would marry Hall in 1950.

With resistance ended in their sector, Hall, Goillot and their team reported to Paris on September 25, were congratulated and pulled from the field.

Hall and Goillot volunteered for another hazardous assignment, this time behind German lines in Austria. On April 25, Hall's new OSS team was poised at the border of Switzerland, waiting for orders to cross the border. But on May 2, the mission was canceled, and six days later, Germany surrendered to the Allies. After almost six years, the war in Europe was finally over.

On May 12, 1945, Maj. Gen. William "Wild Bill" Donovan, director of the OSS sent a memo to President Truman advising him that Hall had been awarded the Distinguished Service Cross, the only civilian female so honored during World War II.

Although President Truman wanted to present the award to her at a public ceremony, Hall declined, insisting that she was still operational and that the publicity might jeopardize her effectiveness. Instead, in a private ceremony in his office on September 23, 1945, attended only by Hall and her mother, Donovan, himself a recipient of the Medal of Honor and Distinguished Service Cross, presented Hall her medal. Her response: "Not bad for a girl from Baltimore."

Her citation reads that the medal was

> for extraordinary heroism in connection with military operations against an armed enemy while serving as an American Civilian Intelligence Officer in the employ of the Special Operations Branch, Office of Strategic Services, [and one] who entered voluntarily and served in enemy-occupied France from March to September 1944. Despite the fact that she was well known to the Gestapo because of previous activities, Miss Hall established and maintained radio communications with London headquarters, supplying valuable operational and intelligence information. With the help of a Jedburgh team, she organized, armed, and trained three battalions of French resistance forces in the Department of the Haute Loire. Working in a region

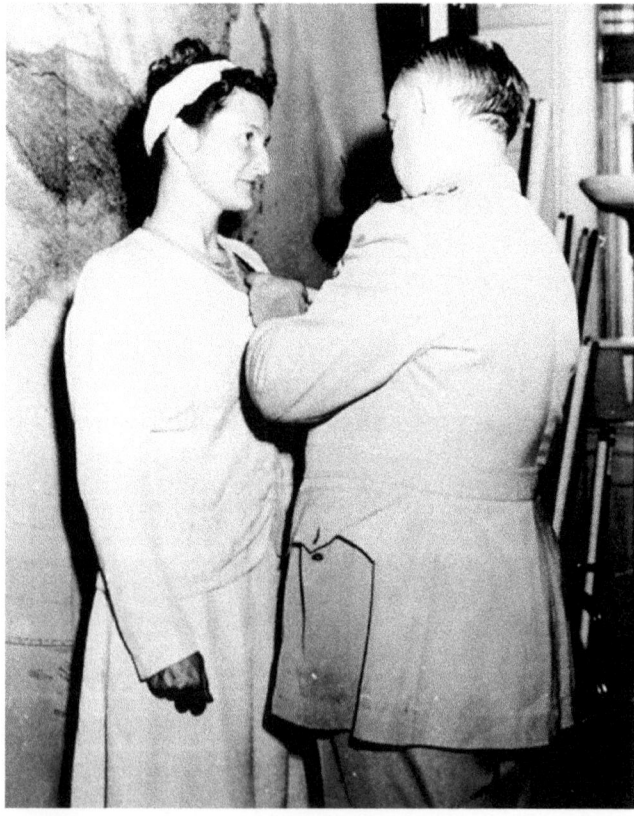

Maj. Gen. William "Wild Bill" Donovan presents Virginia Hall with the Distinguished Service Cross (Central Intelligence Agency).

infested with enemy troops and continually at the risk of capture, torture, and death, she directed the resistance forces with extraordinary success in acts of sabotage and guerrilla warfare against enemy troops, installations, and communications. Miss Hall displayed rare courage, perseverance, and ingenuity. Her efforts contributed materially to the successful operations of the resistance forces in support of the Allied Expeditionary Forces in the liberation of France.

On September 30, 1945, President Truman disbanded the OSS, but Hall obtained a position with the newly created Central Intelligence Group, the forerunner of the CIA.

Hall spent a majority of 1947 and 1948 working in the field in Europe. Because she spoke Italian fluently, she was sent to Venice, where she collected and transmitted economic, financial, and political intelligence, focusing on the communist movement and its leaders.

After her return to the United States, Hall worked for the National Committee for Free Europe, a CIA front, in New York City, where she lived with her long-time lover, later husband, Paul Goillot, who also took a job with the agency. Her official start date with the CIA was December 3, 1951.

Hall wanted a field assignment, but she was put to work as an analyst in the Office of Policy Coordination in Washington, D.C. She worked at a variety of positions within the agency, and was the first woman to become a member of the CIA's career staff in 1956.

Hall retired from the CIA as a GS-14 in 1966, upon reaching the mandatory retirement age of sixty. She enjoyed reading, was an avid birdwatcher, gardened, and kept pet poodles on her farm in Barnestown, Maryland. She died on July 12, 1982, in Rockville, Maryland, at the age of 76 and is buried beside her husband in the Druid Ridge Cemetery, Pikesville, Maryland.

In 1988, Virginia Hall was inducted into Military Intelligence Hall of Fame at Fort Huachuca, Arizona, and a dining facility at the U.S. Army Intelligence Center there was named after her in 1994.

In 2006, the British ambassador to the United States presented Hall's niece, Lorna Catling, with a warrant installing Hall as a Member of the Order of the British Empire, signed by King George VI in 1943, which Hall had refused to accept, as it would have jeopardized her cover.

Modestly summing up her time during the war, she said simply, "It was just six years of my life."

Sources

Binney, Marcus. *The Women Who Lived for Danger: Behind Enemy Lines during WW II.* New York: Harper-Collins, 2003.

Gralley, Craig R. "A Climb to Freedom: A Personal Journey in Virginia Hall's Steps." *Studies in Intelligence* 61 (1) (March 2017).

Jones, Liane. *A Quiet Courage: Women Agents in the French Resistance*. New York: Bantam Press, 1990.

Lineberry, Cate. "Wanted: The Limping Lady." Smithsonian.com, February 2007. http://www.smithsonianmag.com/history/wanted-the-limping-lady-146541513/.

McIntosh, Elizabeth P. *Sisterhood of Spies: The Women of the OSS*. Annapolis, MD: Naval Institute Press, 1998.

"Not Bad for a Girl from Baltimore: The Story of Virginia Hall. https://photos.state.gov/libraries/estonia/99874/History%20stories/Not-Bad-for-a-Girl-from-Baltimore.pdf.

Pearson, Judith. *The Wolves at the Door: The True Story of America's Greatest Female Spy*. Lyon Press, CT, 2005.

Moe Berg
*Catcher, Scholar,
Intelligence Officer*

In November and December of 1934, even as war clouds were gathering in the Pacific and relations between the United States and Japan were strained, American baseball players visited Japan on a goodwill tour.

The 1934 All-American Tour was a 12-city, 18-game series and featured such future Hall-of-Famers as Lou Gehrig, Lefty Gomez, Jimmie Fox, Connie Mack, Earl Averill, Charlie Gehringer and Babe Ruth. It was also all-American in the sense that the National League forbade its players from participating.

So what was Moe Berg, a relief catcher hitting .251, doing touring with legends like Ruth and Gehrig? Was there another purpose for the "home movies" he took on the tour, including shots of the Tokyo skyline from the roof of a hospital? Was there an ulterior motive for including the charming and erudite Berg on the tour, a man legendary Yankee manager Casey Stengel once described as "the strangest man ever to play baseball."

In his 17 major league seasons, Berg played just 662 games, with a lifetime average of .243, inspiring teammates to observe, "He can speak seven languages, but he can't hit in any of them."

Born in a New York City cold-water tenement on East 121st St. in Manhattan on March 2, 1902, Berg grew up the youngest of three children of Bernard and Rose Berg, Russian Jewish immigrants. The family moved to Newark, New Jersey, in 1906, and his father opened a pharmacy. In 1910, the family moved to the suburb of Roseville, and at the age of seven, Berg began playing on a Roseville Methodist Episcopal Church's baseball team, using the name "Runt Wolf" to hide his Jewish roots.

He was a star on the Barrington High School baseball team, where he graduated with honors at age 16. After two semesters at New York University, Berg entered Princeton University in September of 1919, majoring in modern languages. While at Princeton, Berg played shortstop for the Tigers, the university's champion baseball team, where he showed a talent for the game.

When Berg graduated Princeton magna cum laude in 1923, he was ranked 24 in a class of 211, and he was offered a job as a teacher of languages at Princeton. He was courted by both the New York Giants and the Brooklyn Robins, both major league teams. Berg began his professional baseball career with the Brooklyn Robins, figuring he'd have more opportunity to play with the mediocre Robins. (The team later changed its name to Dodgers). He made his major league debut on June 27, 1923.

1933 Goudey baseball card of Moe Berg of the Washington Senators, #158.

After completing the 1923 season in October, Berg moved to the Latin quarter of Paris in France and attended Sorbonne University, studying linguistics and philosophy, taking 22 classes in the two years he was there.

In 1925, Berg missed spring training with the Chicago White Sox and the first part of the season so that he could complete his first year of law school at Columbia University in New York.

In May 1926, unable to make the same arrangement with White Sox owner Charles Comiskey, who ordered Berg to choose between baseball or the law, Berg took a leave of absence from Columbia, played the season with the White Sox, and then took extra classes in the post-season to catch up. It was during this period that Berg changed his position from shortstop to catcher.

Berg graduated Columbia with a law degree on February 26, 1930. He was dropped from the White Sox roster after he twisted his knee. He worked briefly as an attorney for Satterlee and Canfield, but by spring training in 1931, he was on the roster of the Cleveland Indians.

In 1932, Berg moved to the Washington Senators team, where he performed adequately enough, but his real value to the team was his popularity with the sports writers and the public, becoming known as the "brainiest man in baseball."

In 1933, Berg visited Japan for the first time, where he studied Japanese while teaching baseball at Japanese universities. Because he spoke the language, Berg was immensely popular with the Japanese public. After his teaching assignment, he returned to the United States via Japanese-controlled Manchuria, Peking, Shanghai, Saigon, Bangkok, India, Egypt, Palestine, Athens, Vienna, Berlin (around the time of the rise of Hitler) and Paris, returning in time for 1933 spring training.

He was dropped by the Senators in 1934 but was again picked up by the Indians, and after the 1934 season, Berg returned to Japan as part of the American all-star baseball team.

Relations with Japan were difficult during this period, as the militarists took control of the government and the secret police were almost paranoid toward foreigners. Despite this, baseball was very popular, as was Berg, and he freely roamed Tokyo with a 16 mm Bell & Howell movie camera, filming a "documentary."

On November 29, 1934, dressed in native clothes and able to speak the language, Berg, while visiting the American ambassador's daughter, covertly gained access to the roof of St. Luke's Hospital, where he filmed Tokyo Bay. Some sources claim he later made the film available to U.S. military intelligence for bombing missions.

After games in Shanghai and the Philippines, the team disbanded and returned home, but Berg traveled through Asia on his own, until he was arrested and deported by Russian authorities. He returned home in April 1935. He promptly began spring training for the Boston Red Sox.

Berg continued to play ball through the Great Depression but also pursued other interests. In 1939, he was so successful on the radio trivia show *Information Please* that he was invited back twice.

Berg's last major league appearance was on September 1, 1939, the Reds losing to the Detroit Tigers 14–10. Across the world in Europe, Germany invaded Poland, starting World War II.

In February 1940, Berg was dropped from the Red Sox roster as a player, but he stayed with the team as a coach, where he remained through 1941.

Berg left the Red Sox a week after the attack on Pearl Harbor on

December 7, 1941, and took a position with Nelson Rockefeller, who was coordinator of the Office of Inter-American Affairs. The mission was to bolster the war effort by encouraging friendly relations between the United States and Latin American countries while countering Axis influence. He was sworn in on January 21, 1942.

Berg's first mission was for the OSS, making a propaganda broadcast (in Japanese) for broadcast in Japan. In April 1942, Berg made a tour of U.S. military bases in Latin America, gathering intelligence on Italy and on the various governments' attitude toward the Allies. He visited Costa Rica, Peru, Guatemala, Honduras, Panama, Colombia, Venezuela, Trinidad and Brazil. His tour over, he kept his ears open for useful information before returning to the States in February 1943. His mission complete, Berg resigned from the Office of Inter-American Affairs to enlist in the OSS on August 2, 1943, assigned to the Special Operations Branch.

Berg was an ideal candidate for the OSS. He was highly intelligent, well-traveled, educated and conversant in many languages, among them Greek, French, Spanish, Italian, German, Japanese, Russian, Hebrew, Yiddish, and Sanskrit, and he read Latin.

Sworn in, Berg was assigned in September to the Secret Intelligence Branch, on the Balkans desk in Washington, D.C. In this role, Berg parachuted into occupied Yugoslavia and met with Draža Mihailović and Tito to evaluate the strength of their partisan forces. Berg determined Tito to have the stronger force. Around the end of 1943, he was recruited for a special mission.

In December 1942, the Chicago lab of the Manhattan Project achieved the first controlled nuclear chain reaction, a significant advance in the race with Germany to develop the atomic bomb. Werner Heisenberg, a leading physicist, was in charge of the German effort, and the OSS mounted Operation Azusa to determine the state of Germany's research and development capability. Berg was assigned to the mission.

While awaiting orders to travel overseas to Italy, which had surrendered in mid- 1943 and then been occupied by its former German allies, Berg brushed up on his knowledge of nuclear physics. On May 4, 1944, Berg left Washington, D.C., for London to meet with intelligence officers, attending briefings and then disappearing for short periods. He visited Algiers before arriving in Italy on June 5.

When Rome was liberated, Berg rushed to the city to attempt contact with Italian scientists, meeting with Edoardo Amaldi and Gian Carlo Wick and learning that Heisenberg was now in southern Germany. He continued to gather intelligence until he returned to London in September 1944.

Berg endured the London Blitz bombings while gradually reaching the conclusion that there was no risk from the German nuclear program. Intelligence learned that Heisenberg was planning to give a lecture in Zurich on December 18, and Berg was assigned to attend the lecture, disguised as a graduate student. He was armed with a pistol. He had orders to kill Heisenberg if Berg determined that the Germans were making advances.

Berg stated that his poor German and inadequate understanding of the finer points of nuclear fission made it difficult to be sure if there was a risk, and he decided not to shoot. This may have been fortunate since post-war indications suggest that Heisenberg, although a brilliant physicist, was a poor administrator whose ineptitude actually impeded Germany's progress in developing the bomb.

The Allies continued their mopping up operations as they advanced into Germany. OSS agents were often in advance of the liberating troops, snatching German scientists ahead of the Russians. After breakfast with General Donovan on April 13, 1945, Berg returned briefly to the States but by May was back in Europe.

In September 1945, the OSS was disbanded, succeeded by the Strategic Services Unit, which was concerned with assessing the state of Russian intelligence in Europe. Berg participated in various operations and was awarded the Medal of Freedom in October 1946, but he declined to accept it. His sister accepted it for him after his death.

The citation was by necessity vague, due to the nature of his assignments, and stated only that the award was made for "studies and analyses vital to the mounting of American operations." He was discharged from the Strategic Services Unit in April 1947.

Berg did contract work for the CIA into the early 1950s and traveled throughout Europe in 1952, meeting with old contacts and gathering information on Soviet and East German nuclear research. His contract was terminated in 1954.

From that point until his death, Berg's later life remains as shrouded in mist as his career. He never again owned a home or car, never again held a job and spent the remainder of his life visiting family and friends across the world. When asked what he was up to, he would often respond with a mysterious wink. He lived for 17 years with his brother, Samuel, and his last years were spent living with his sister, Ethyl, at her home in Belleville, New Jersey.

In May 1972, Berg, now 70, fell from his bed and was admitted to the hospital in Belleville. He died on May 29, and his last words were to his nurse, asking how the Mets (baseball team) were doing. He passed away before she could answer. Scholar, scientist, athlete, linguist, intelligence officer, and one of the most colorful figures of the 20th century, Moe Berg passed into legend.

His baseball card is on display in the CIA's lobby at its headquarters at Langley, Virginia.

Sources

Acocella, Nick. "Moe Berg: Catcher and Spy." ESPN. http://www.espn.com/classic/biography/s/Berg_Moe.html.

Dawidoff, Nicholas. *The Catcher Was a Spy: The Mysterious Life of Moe Berg*. New York: Vintage Reprint, 1995.

Kaufman, Louis. *Moe Berg: Athlete, Scholar, Spy*. Boston: Little, Brown, 1975.

Bert Shepard
One-Legged Major League Pitcher

It was a hot, muggy Saturday at Griffith Stadium in Washington, D.C., on August 4, 1945, as 13,000 fans filled the seats to watch the Washington Senators battle the Boston Red Sox. The war in Europe was over, and amid rumors of an upcoming invasion of Japan, a top-secret mission was already under way to end the war in the Pacific.

But the fans were concerned with a different battle as the home-team Senators trailed the Red Sox 14–2 in the top of the fourth inning with bases loaded. Manager Ozzie Bluege sent in Bert Shepard, a recently returned veteran, as a relief pitcher, making baseball history.

The only pitcher to play Major League Baseball with an artificial leg, Bert Robert Shepard was born in Dana, Indiana, on June 28, 1920, the second of six boys. His father, John, worked as a laborer, and the family grew up in a home of "modest" means during the depression. The family moved to Clinton, Indiana, and Shepard worked for the Civilian Conservation Corps during high school. He graduated Clinton High School in 1940, where he had played on the basketball team, there being no baseball team. He learned to play sandlot ball.

After high school, Shepard got a position with the Wisconsin Rapids, a D-class minor league team of the Chicago White Sox but was released as "untrained" after a couple of months. Shepard learned to play first base, play the outfield, and to pitch as he believed that this would increase his potential to be "picked up" by another club. He played the 1941 season in the Texas-Arizona League.

With war on the horizon, Shepard took the pilot exam and was awaiting the results when he was drafted on May 26, 1942. He was sent to Fort Benjamin Harris, Indiana, for processing. After his induction into the

Army Air Corps, he was sent for eight weeks of basic training at Keesler Field, Mississippi, which he recalled as "hotter than hell."

After basic, Shepard was sent to Daniel Field, Georgia, to await further orders. He remained there from July until the end of November, playing on the camp baseball and football teams. Late in November, Shepard was accepted for pilot training, and Private Shepard became Cadet Shepard.

Ordered to Santa Ana, California, for pre-flight training, he graduated in February 1943 and was sent first to King City Air Base in California for primary flight training, then to Gardiner Field near Bakersfield in April for basic flight training. On June 1, Shepard was transferred to Williams Field, Arizona, for fighter training with the P-38 "Lightning," which the Germans later named Der Gabelschwanz Teufel (the Forked-Tail Devil).

Upon completing training on August 30, 1943, Shepard was awarded his wings and a commission as a second lieutenant (serial no. O-754558). He was sent to Edwards Air Base near Huron for additional training in advanced aerobatics and formation flying. Following this, he was sent to a base outside Salinas in October for training in night flying.

Shepard recalled one occasion when the training was a bit too real. He was flying at 11,000 feet when he was called in because it was too foggy. One by one, the planes dropped to land. Shepard was the last, and by this time, the fog was too dense to land. He was ordered to fly north until he could find a field open enough to land. Failing this, he would have to bail out over Monterey Bay. (Because it was during wartime, blackout conditions prohibited fields from turning on their runway lights.)

Running low on fuel, he finally saw a light below, and staying in a tight turn to avoid the mountains, he dropped low enough to see the dim outlines of planes in a hanger. After making a very difficult landing, he found that he was at Hollister Navy Base, and had come close to being targeted as an enemy plane. Being unfamiliar with the P-38, the admiral in charge requested that Shepard "buzz" the base the next morning, and he happily complied, climbing to 5,000 feet and diving in at 500 mph.

He continued to train to obtain the needed 100 hours before qualifying for overseas duty. In the middle of November, he went to Lomita, California, for more training and finally received orders for combat, embarking on Christmas Eve. He took a train to New York, and from Fort Hamilton, he departed on a troopship from Pier 88 on January 3, 1944.

He arrived in Greenwich, England, on January 9, six days later. The normal four-day crossing took longer because the troopship, sailing alone without escort, used evasive tactics to avoid enemy submarines. Shepard took four weeks of ground school at Shrewsbury, England, then flew a few orientation flights at Goxhill. The need for trained mechanics was great, and Shepard was less than comforted when his mechanic admitted that he was "still studying."

Sent to Nuthamstead, England, Shepard was assigned to the 38th Fighter Squadron, 55th Fighter Group. (The P-38 would play a vital part in the coming invasion of Europe. Because of its unique silhouette, it was easily identifiable as an Allied plane, and so it would be selected to fly "top cover" during the invasion.) On his third mission, March 4, 1944, he flew escort on the first daylight bombing raid into Berlin. The majority of his missions were escorting bombers or making strafing runs, and in 33 missions, Shepard never got in a dogfight or downed an enemy plane. He attributed this to "a lot of luck."

On May 21, 1944, Shepard was flying his 34th mission over Germany with orders for an "all out strafing of all targets of opportunities" (radio stations, power plants, trains, etc.) He was flying at an altitude of about 200 feet when his P-38 fighter was struck numerous times by enemy ground fire, resulting in several wounds and loss of control of his plane. He radioed the leader to tell him he was hit and then told him he'd call back, but he never did. He was hit in the chin by flak, and he lost consciousness. His plane crash landed outside Ludwigslust, halfway between Hamburg and Berlin.

Shepard was saved by an Austrian doctor drafted into the Luftwaffe (German air force), who pulled the unconscious pilot from his craft, at great risk since the plane could explode at any moment. The doctor had been helping German soldiers wounded in the raid when he was ordered to check out the crash. Seeing Shepard unconscious in the cockpit, he pulled him out and then protected him from angry townsmen, pulling his pistol at one point when they threatened him with axes and pitchforks. The local hospital refused to accept him (some U.S. pilots had engaged in "dirty straf-

Lt. Bert Shepard, U.S. AAF (U.S. Air Force).

ing," i.e., firing on civilian targets) until the doctor called the high command, and Shepard was ordered admitted.

Shepard regained consciousness more than a week later to find his right leg amputated 11 inches below the knee. The unknown Samaritan had remained long enough to ensure that Shepard was stable before returning to his unit. Shepard never learned his name.

While Shepard was interned at Luft Stalag 9C in Meningen (June 24, 1944–January 21, 1945), a camp for wounded POWs, a Canadian medic, Don Erry, fashioned an artificial leg from scrap iron, wood and leather. Shepard actively pitched cricket with the other prisoners, learning to adjust to the leg. After eight months' captivity, Shepard was among a group of Americans in a prisoner exchange on January 21, 1945, and he returned to the United States on February 21, arriving in New York City.

He was fitted for a new leg on March 10, and was one of four former POWs invited to Washington for a press release on the treatment of POWs. There was great concern in the United States as to how the Axis powers were treating prisoners.

Arriving in Washington, D.C., the group was greeted at the Pentagon by Robert P. Patterson, the undersecretary of War. During the conversation, Shepard was asked what he hoped to do, and he answered that he wanted to play professional baseball.

Patterson called his friend Clark Griffith, owner of the Washington Senators, and arranged for a tryout for Shepard. Shepard proved he could throw hard and his pitching was sufficiently unaffected by his artificial leg. He moved around so well that it was difficult to tell he even wore an artificial leg.

Griffith was impressed, and on March 29, 1945, he signed Shepard to a major-league contract and he was signed as a batting practice pitcher and coach. He played while on medical leave.

On July 2, 1945, Shepard was honorably discharged from the air corps as a first lieutenant, earning the Distinguished Service Cross, the Air Medal and a Purple Heart. Shepard was placed on the Senators' regular roster.

On July 10, in an exhibition game with the Brooklyn Dodgers, Shepard was the starting pitcher. Before the game, Gen. Omar Bradley presented Shepard with the Air Medal at home plate. Pitching four innings, Shepard gave up only one hit. Impressed, management moved him to the active roster after the game.

On August 4, 1945, before more than 13,000 fans in Griffith Stadium, Shepard made his major league debut against the Boston Red Sox. The

Senators were behind 14–2 in the fourth inning of the first game of a doubleheader when Shepard was brought in as a relief pitcher. With bases full for the Reds, he struck out the batter to end the inning.

He pitched five and a third innings, allowing only three hits and one run. He struck out two, one of them "Catfish" Metkovich, who retired the inning with bases loaded. Shepard finished the game, but this was to be his only appearance in the major leagues. The Senators were in a pennant race with the Detroit Tigers, and Bluege was reluctant to take a chance with Shepard.

Shepard would step on to a Major League field again only when, between doubleheaders, he was presented with the Distinguished Service Cross, second only to the Medal of Honor. He was released from the team on September 30.

However, Shepard's baseball career and his military career were far from over.

On November 29, 1945, Lieutenant Shepard was recalled to active duty, by Patterson, now secretary of War, to make a training film for amputees titled *Half a Chance*, which followed his rehabilitation. He agreed, with the proviso that he be released in time for spring training. Upon completing the film, newly promoted Capt. Shepard toured the country's seven regional occupational training centers. He was released from active duty on March 9, 1946, in time to join spring training with the Senators, as agreed.

In July of 1946, he failed to make the roster, competing with players returned from the war, but he was hired as a coach. He requested to be "sent down" to the AA league Chattanooga Lookouts, where he played five games. Shepard recalls that his leg must not have bothered him too bad, since in one game against the Little Rock Travelers, he was able to score from second base on a hit to left field, no easy task for a man with two legs.

In 1948, Shepard managed the class B Waterbury Timers in Connecticut, and in 1949 stole five bases while playing with the team. After leaving baseball in 1954, he worked construction jobs, for companies like Fleur and Hughes Aircraft, both in the states and overseas in Venezuela for two and a half years. In 1980, Shepard, a safety engineer, helped develop an improved artificial leg, but despite spending $10,000 of his own money, he was unable to persuade the bureaucracy at the Veterans Administration to accept the concept. He retired in 1983, less from desire than lack of work.

Shepard always wondered about the man who had saved his life. He made some attempts to locate him, but Ludwigslust was in East Germany, and access was limited. In 1992, a conversation between a British businessman and an Austrian doctor while both were on a hunting vacation in Hungary led to the doctor, Ladislaus Loidl, searching for and finding Shepard. The two men had a reunion at Loidl's home in Parndorf, Austria, on May 21, 1993, exactly 49 years to the day after being shot down. Shepard (72) was able to personally thank Loidl (76) and recalls that it was an "emotional moment" as they hugged each other. He realized that these were the same arms that pulled him from the plane.

Shepard retired to Hesperia, California. He suffered a stroke and died on June 16, 2008, while a resident of a nursing home in Highland, California, at the age of 87. He was survived by his former wife Betty, who he'd divorced before his death, after 48 years of marriage, and by two sons, Justin and Preston, and two daughters, Penny and Karen, and nine grandchildren.

As to the wartime experiences that cost him a leg, Shepard had no bitterness toward Germans. Rather, he was grateful for the care he was given while unconscious and a prisoner. "They saved my life."

Sources

Bohn, Terry. "Bert Shepard." Society for American Baseball Research (SABR). https://sabr.org/bioproj/person/8cb03c17.

Eriksmoen, Curt. "Loss of Leg Didn't Stop Baseball Player." *Bismarck (ND) Tribune*, September 29, 2013.

Eriksmoen, Curt. "One-Legged Baseball Player Defies the Odds." *Bismarck (ND) Tribune*, September 22, 2013.

Finoli, David. *For the Good of the Country: World War II Baseball in the Major and Minor Leagues.* Jefferson, NC: McFarland, 2002.

Newell, Rob. *From Playing Field to Battlefield: Great Athletes Who Served in World War II.* Annapolis, MD: Naval Institute Press, 2006.

Wolter, Tim. *POW Baseball in World War II: The National Pastime Behind Barbed Wire.* Jefferson, NC: McFarland, 2002.

William Augustus Read, Jr.
Coconuts and the Navy Cross

On the morning of October 19, 1944, a U.S. Navy PB4Y heavy bomber, "Miller's High Life," took off from Wama Airfield on Morotai in the Maluku Islands bound for the South China Sea. The PB4Y, the navy version of the B-24 Liberator was from Patrol Squadron 101 (VP-101), the "Black Cats," only recently redesignated Patrol Bombing Squadron 29 (VPB-29) on October 1.

Piloting the bomber was the squadron commander, Cmdr. Justin Miller, a 1931 graduate of the Naval Academy, with Ens. Hector McDaniel as co-pilot and Ens. George H. Martin as the navigator. The crew included Chief Ordnanceman J. W. Eckfield, Radioman First Class Curtis Ford, Radioman Second Class Francis M. Ford, Machinist Mate First Class Peter A. Villa, Ordnanceman Third Class Harry A. Rummersfeld, Ordnanceman Second Class John Coshow, and Ordnanceman Third Class Dean W. Doering. Also aboard was Lt. William Read Jr., the squadron's gunnery officer, who had volunteered to go on the mission as the nose turret gunner.

At about 1515 hours, while returning from a 1,000-mile patrol, Miller diverted from his route home to attack a Japanese seaplane base at Puerto Princessa. Coming in low, at 100 feet, they dropped ten 100-pound bombs on two ships and strafed the packed airfield where over 40 aircraft sat parked.

As the navigator, Martin, later recalled, "We came in as intended and dropped our bombs in perfect order. Two of the ships were definitely destroyed. And then we swept down on the runway a little to the right ... we saw the fire from eight planes and more were probably damaged."

Miller was wise enough not to risk a second pass, but the plane was struck by anti-aircraft fire from harbor defenses as they departed the area. The aircraft was crippled, with damaged controls and an engine on fire.

Miller and McDaniel fought to keep the bomber level and airborne to escape the area and succeeded for several minutes before crashing into the ocean six miles north of Puerto Princessa, in Honda Bay. The plane broke in half on impact.

Martin and Villa were both wounded by gunfire, Martin in his right leg and Villa more seriously in his right knee. The impact of hitting the water threw Miller, still strapped in his seat, through the windshield, with McDaniel also exiting that route, working to get Miller free. Martin exited through the waist hatch. Curtis Ford, trying to free a raft, was hurled forward and escaped through the top turret. The others escaped into the sea from where the two sections separated. All 11 of the crew escaped the aircraft, all injured to some degree.

Their bomber had been equipped with extra fuel tanks to extend the range of their patrols, which turned out to be fortunate. The empty tanks, broke loose on impact and now floated in the water. Curtis Ford and Coshow managed to catch one and Read the other.

Villa, weak from loss of blood, was unable to hold on and slipped under the waves. Eckfield escaped the plane, but injured, drowned. Doering was last seen in a life jacket, but he disappeared.

The other eight airmen, using the tanks as floatation devices, made their way to an island, three miles distant. The island, Pandan Island or Ramesamey Island depending on the source, was approximately seven miles from Puerto Princessa on Palawan Island, and its 3,000-yard circumference encompassed dense vegetation and mangrove swamps, and the only source of nourishment was coconut trees.

Finding a previously used crude thatch shelter made of palm fronds, they put Martin and Francis Ford, the most seriously injured, under cover and waited, expecting to be either rescued or taken prisoner by the Japanese.

As Lieutenant Read sat on that barren sand, one must wonder if he regretted volunteering for that mission.

William Augustus Read, Jr., was born at home on Beacon Street, Boston on May 16, 1918, the oldest of nine children to William Augustus Sr. and Edith Fabyan Read. He grew up in Purchase, New York, and attended St. Paul's School in New England, but from his earliest days, he dreamed of being a navy pilot. No surprise, given his lineage.

His father had been a cavalryman with General Pershing in Mexico when the United States entered World War I, and he considered joining the Army Air Corps, but when he learned his three younger brothers had already entered naval aviation, he changed to the navy. He flew combat sorties during World War I, remained in the reserves after the war, and was called to active duty as a captain during World War II, serving on Admiral Marc Mitscher's staff, and retiring as a vice admiral.

His three uncles were all pioneers of naval aviation, and all flew combat missions in Europe during the war. One uncle, Ens. Curtiss Seaman Read, was killed in a seaplane crash in France. Capt. Duncan Hicks Read flew from bases on the Italian coast, and Lt. (jg) Russell Bartow Read was awarded the Navy Cross for his wartime service. Flying was in the Read family blood.

Read earned his pilot's license by the age of 16, and despite weak eyesight that required wearing spectacles, he was an expert marksman, an avid hunter and skeet shooter, talents that would serve him well.

After war broke out in December 1941, Read wanted to be a fighter pilot but was disqualified because of his eyesight. He considered going to Canada and joining the Royal Canadian Air Force, where he said the physical requirements were "can you see lightning and hear thunder?" His father persuaded him to apply for the Aviation Volunteer Specialist program. He was granted a waiver for his eyesight and accepted into the program.

He completed officer training school at Fort Skylar, north of New York City, and graduated as an ensign in 1942, after which he was sent to the Naval Aerial Gunnery Instructor School at Pensacola, Florida, where he finished as the top student. He quickly mastered the .30- and .50-caliber machine guns and used every opportunity to perfect his marksmanship.

Read was ordered to San Diego, where he instructed and served as range officer, teaching fundamental marksmanship and aerial gunnery techniques. Cmdr. Justin Miller, the commanding officer of VP-101, cycling through training in October 1943, was impressed with Read. Needing a squadron gunnery officer, Miller offered the position to Read, who immediately accepted, wanting to get into the war. VP-101 had been the first squadron to fly the PB4Y Liberator in combat.

He was sent through Air-to-Air Gunnery School at El Centro, California, and the Norden Bomb-Sight School. With training complete, the squadron departed San Diego in April 1944, bound for Kaneohe, Hawaii, and ultimately combat in the Pacific.

The squadron first flew from Momote Airfield on Los Negros in the Admiralty Islands from May until August 19, when they moved to Owl

Airfield on Schouten Island, Biak, off the northwestern coast of the island of New Guinea.

The squadron advanced to Wama Airfield on Morotai on October 18 and flew their first mission the following morning. From the beginning, Read would volunteer, offering to take the place of the nose turret gunner, who willingly accepted the opportunity for a day off. When Read climbed aboard Miller's High Life on October 19, he was on his 25th mission.

Now, as the first night approached for the eight surviving airmen marooned on the small island off Palawan Island, many concerns filled their thoughts; discovery and capture by the Japanese, medical treatment for their injuries, food and water, rescue. All their equipment had gone down with the aircraft; their only weapons were two knives.

The next afternoon, at about 1435 hours they heard a PB4Y Liberator approaching. Those sailors able to stand went into the open, waving and trying to get the pilot's or crew's attention.

As fate would have it, a Japanese G4M Betty bomber was taking off from Puerto Princessa, although some sources say it was a transport plane. In any event, it was shot down by Lt. Hamilton Dawes of VPB-115, hit the water and ricocheted onto the island, crashing into their camp.

Francis Ford was crushed by the fuselage, which narrowly missed McDaniel, and Curtis Ford and Coshow suffered facial lacerations. Read's right leg had a compound fracture, a deep gash and severed muscles.

Despite his injuries, Read was advancing on the wreckage, smoke curling up from the flaming aircraft, and he could hear the screams of dying Japanese, when an officer emerged uninjured from the wreckage and, brandishing a knife, advanced on the prone McDaniel.

Unarmed, Read used the only weapon available. Scooping up a coconut, he hurled it, barely missing the man's head. Picking up a second coconut, the two screamed and menaced each other, Read gesturing that there were lots of other Americans. Curtis Ford joined Read, brandishing a stick.

Outnumbered, the officer retreated to the beach, stealing the fuel tank and paddling out to sea. There is little doubt Read's actions saved McDaniel's life.

They scavenged the downed aircraft, retrieving two Nambu pistols, several swords, life vests, parachutes, tarps, and a small amount of tinned fish and rice, but they subsisted almost entirely on coconuts.

On October 21, McDaniel attempted to swim to Palawan, but he was too weak and returned to the island. On October 25, Miller's 35th birthday, they began constructing a raft. Two days later, Miller and McDaniel paddled out, reaching another small island before collapsing from fatigue. After resting several days, they set off again, and island-hopping from one small island to the next, they finally made Palawan on November 2.

Making contact with friendly natives, Miller arranged for his injured crewman to be brought to Palawan in dugout canoes and carried ashore to the village while a runner was sent to contact the Filipino American guerrillas further north.

Contact was made with "Col." Jacinto Cutaran, a U.S. Army sergeant who had promoted himself to "work more efficiently" with the Filipino guerrillas, not an uncommon practice. He commanded the Palawan Special Battalion, mostly former members of the Philippine Army. Once their identity was confirmed, Cutaran radioed Australia and requested a pickup.

In addition to the seven members of the Miller's High Life crew, four additional downed airmen had been rescued by the guerrillas: Lt. (jg) Everett Ross Bunch, Jr., and his radioman, AOM (Aviation Ordnance Man) 3c Edwin D. Cunningham, and Lt. (jg) Ralph Harvey Beatle and his radioman, AOM2c Ralph Albert Johnson.

On the morning of September 24, the aircraft carrier USS *Intrepid* (CV-11), "The Fighting I," and aircraft of Bombing Squadron 18 (VB-18), "Sunday Punchers," launched an air strike on Culion Island. Two Curtiss SB2C Helldiver dive bombers were shot down and their crews rescued by Filipino guerrillas.

Arrangements were made to extract the airmen by a PBY Catalina Flying Boat, but the attempt had to be aborted twice because of heavy presence of Japanese fighters in the area. Finally, the decision was made to extract them by submarine.

By this point in the war, the amount of Japanese shipping had declined to the point that the mission of submarines was expanded to acting as "lifeguards" on airstrike missions and rescuing downed airmen.

The USS *Gunnel* (SS-253), a Gato-class submarine launched in May 1942 was on her seventh war patrol, under the command of Lt. Cmdr. Guy O'Neil Jr., U.S. Naval Academy Class of 1937, who had taken over command of the sub from her previous skipper, Lt. Cmdr. John S. McCain Jr., later an admiral and father to the U.S. senator.

The *Gunnel* had departed Freemantle, Australia, on October 21 and had already sunk three ships when alerted for the rescue on December 1. As the ship's patrol journal for December 1 records,

> 2249 [hours]: Received instructions to pick up a party of eleven Naval Aviators led by Commander Miller, USN. We were to rendezvous with a sailboat in position 10 miles bearing 117°(T) from Flechas Point, Palawan which plotted as Latitude 10–18

N., Longitude 119–43 E. We were to be in position at dusk of 2 December. The boat or boats were to show a torch at ten-minute intervals and shout the password "BALLAST."

At dusk on December 2, the correct signal fires were lit, a small boat sailed alongside the surfaced submarine and the eleven airmen were taken aboard at 2019 hours without incident. They enjoyed pie and ice cream in the wardroom, and Colonel Cutaran and his deputy, Maj. Pablo Muyco, Philippine Army, who had come aboard with the airmen, were presented with automatic weapons, ammunition, medical supplies, clothing and tinned food when they departed.

The voyage back to Saipan was not without incident. The sub proceeded on the surface for greater speed but frequently had to dive to avoid enemy aircraft and had to fight both heavy seas and a typhoon that sank four nearby destroyers. The captain recorded in his log, "[it was] a monstrous typhoon, the worst I've ever seen, and the boat did everything but an outside loop. The waves were over thirty feet high and the wind well over 60 knots from the Northeast, and increasing."

Despite the hazards, O'Neil brought the *Gunnel* safely into Saipan on December 16 and unloaded the passengers before being resupplied and departing for Pearl Harbor the next day.

Read and the others were flown to Townsville, then to Sydney, Australia, for medical treatment, and their families were notified that their loved ones were no longer missing in action.

For their actions, Lieutenant Read, Commander Miller, Ensign McDaniel and Lieutenant Commander O'Neil were all awarded the Navy Cross, the navy's second-highest award for valor.

VPB-101 had completed their combat tour by the time Read rejoined them in Hawaii, and he returned stateside aboard a small aircraft carrier, assigned to the Naval Gunnery School in San Diego. Meeting an old friend, Lt. Cmdr. J. E. Muldrew, now commanding a PB4Y squadron, he was offered the gunnery officer slot with the squadron, but he declined as he was scheduled for follow-up surgery. It was a fortunate choice, as Muldrew and his crew were later shot down with no survivors. "I probably would have been with him," Read later recalled.

Read finished the war as a lieutenant and retired as a full commander in the naval reserve, having flown 25 combat missions. His decorations include two Air Medals and two Purple Hearts in addition to the Navy Cross. Read, his father and five brothers all fought during World War II, and all survived.

After the war, Read was a partner at Phelps, Fenn, a municipal bonds firm in New York City. In 1959, he married Isabel Collier. They retired to Florida, where she passed away in 2008 after nearly 50 years of marriage.

His interest in marksmanship continued, earning him multiple honors and titles, including an Olympic Gold Medal in International Skeet, Veterans Class, and inclusion in the Trap Shooting Hall of Fame.

Despite his war experiences, Read never held a grudge with the Japanese. "I wasn't after the individual Japanese, I was after the machines of war. I knew they were individuals like myself, and they were under orders like I was."

William A. Read passed away on October 28, 2011, at the age of 93, and he was buried with full military honors at Hillcrest Memorial Park in West Palm Beach, Florida.

Once when asked by a niece what it was like to be a bow-turret gunner, he replied, "I'd always liked hunting, the ammunition was free, and there was no bag limit."

Sources

Campbell, Douglas E. *Save Our Souls: Rescues Made by U.S. Submarines during World War II*. Lulu.com, 2016.

Ford, James E. "The Last Mission of the *Miller's High Life*: The Story of Francis Ford, Patrol Bombing Squadron 101, and World War II in the Philippine Islands." https://www.amazon.com/Last-Mission-Millers-High-Life/dp/197462207X.

Paine, Ralph D. *The First Yale Unit*. Cambridge, MA: Riverside Press, 1925.

Tillman, Barrett. "Two Coconuts and a Navy Cross." *Naval History Magazine*, U.S. Naval Institute, February 2010.

"USS *Gunnel* SS-253: Seventh War Patrol, October 21, 1944–December 28, 1944." http://www.jmlavelle.com/gunnel/patrol7.htm.

"William A. Read Jr. Obituary." Hillcrest Memorial Park. http://obits.dignitymemorial.com/dignity-memorial/obituary.aspx?n=William-Read&lc=0758&pid=154437937&mid=4870848.

Bruce Ward Carr

*Departed in a Mustang,
Returned in a Focke-Wulf*

Col. Bruce Carr was a legendary fighter pilot who was once almost court-martialed for being "too aggressive," and stories abound of his leading flights into battle against overwhelming odds As a veteran of three wars, he certainly saw his share of combat and had countless war stories.

One, involving him being shot down and stealing an enemy fighter to return to friendly lines, has both its champions and its debunkers, but it is just improbable enough to be true.

Bruce Ward Carr was born in Union Springs, New York, on January 28, 1924, and grew up there. He was a licensed pilot, having learned to fly at 15. His instructor, Johnny Burns, would coincidentally be his military flight instructor.

On September 3, 1942, at 18, Carr enlisted as a private in the U.S. Army and was enrolled in the aviation cadet program. Already a skilled pilot, he and four others were put through an accelerated program with the Curtiss P-40 Warhawk fighter plane for six weeks of combat training.

By the time he graduated flight training at Spence Field, Georgia, on August 30, 1943, he had 243 hours of military flight time. He was commissioned a flight officer, the precursor to the modern-day rank of warrant officer.

After additional training, he was sent overseas to England, assigned to the 380th Fighter Squadron, 363rd Fighter Group, Ninth Air Force at RAF Keevil, reporting in on February 4, 1944, the same month the unit began flying combat assignments.

He was assigned a North American P-51 Mustang fighter, which he named "Angel's Playmate," and he recalled being impressed with the aircraft. "It flew like an airplane. I just flew the P-40, but in the P-51, I was part of the airplane. And it was part of me. There was a world of difference."

On March 8, 1944, he scored his, and the squadron's, first kill, when he shot down a Bf-109 Messerschmitt approximately 30 miles south of Berlin. He recalled,

> We were roaring around within a few feet of the ground, and he pulls up to go over some trees, so I just pull the trigger and keep it down ... one bullet, a tracer, came tumbling out ... and hit him in the left wing. He pulled up, off came the canopy, and he jumped out, but too low for the chute to open and the airplane crashed. I didn't shoot him down, I scared him to death with one bullet hole in his left wing. My first victory wasn't a kill, it was more of a suicide.

Back at the squadron, Carr was criticized as being "overaggressive," while he expressed the opinion that the squadron was not being led aggressively enough. Avoiding a court-martial, Carr was transferred to the 353rd Fighter Squadron, 354th Fighter Group, in May, which although nominally assigned to the Ninth Air Force, was operating with the Eighth Air Force.

The 353rd "Fighting Cobras" flew mission 93 on June 6, 1944, during D-Day, the Normandy Invasion, escorting C-47 transport planes, as part of Operation Overlord.

On June 14, Carr scored a "likely" kill, on another Messerschmitt, and his first with his new squadron, en route to Caen, followed by a half credit on a Focke-Wulf-190 Wurger, on June 17. He was promoted to second lieutenant on August 18.

On September 12, while leading a flight on a fighter sweep, Carr observed seven Junkers Ju-88 bombers parked in a group on an airfield south of Linburg, Germany. He led the flight in an attack, destroying several on the ground and igniting aviation fuel. Ground attacks were the most dangerous, and one pass, hard and fast, was the norm since alerted anti-aircraft guns would quickly find their range on subsequent passes.

Carr resumed his patrol, taking the flight up to ten thousand feet. North of Frankfort, they spotted a group of 30-plus Fw-190s 2,000 feet below, and they attacked, diving at high speed. Credited with downing three Focke-Wulfs, as well as escorting a badly damaged aircraft back to friendly territory, Carr was awarded the Silver Star.

A little more than a month later, on October 29, Carr was leading his flight on a dive bombing and strafing mission against enemy airfields near Bockingen, Germany, when they were attacked by a large number of enemy aircraft. In 35 minutes of aerial combat, Carr destroyed two Messerschmitts and damaged another, while sustaining damage to his own aircraft.

The flight was credited with 24 kills, and four aircraft lost. With kills number five and six, Carr was officially an ace, and on November 13, Carr was awarded the Distinguished Flying Cross for his "brilliant leadership and tactical technique."

It was his most famous exploit that has recently been called into question, involving stealing and crashing a Messerschmitt fighter. The fact that he stole and crashed an Me-109 is undeniable, but the circumstances as to exactly how and when are in dispute.

On November 2, 1944, Carr was leading a flight over Czechoslovakia and on a sweep over a Luftwaffe airfield when his aircraft was struck by anti-aircraft fire. He was forced to bail out, but he took note of the terrain and the location of the nearby airfield.

Different versions of the tale have him evading the enemy for several days with a dead chicken and waiting in the woods outside the airfield, intending to surrender in the morning. Then he observed a crew servicing a Fw-190, fueling and arming it.

Once they departed, he snuck up to the aircraft and spent the night in the cockpit, taking off at first light for friendly lines 200 miles distant, hoping to avoid American fighters. Unable to get the landing gear down and hoping to avoid "friendly" anti-aircraft fire, Carr came in fast and low, belly-landing the plane among the surprised Americans.

Critics have posted undated photographs of airmen standing around a damaged German Fw-190 aircraft at an airfield in Ansbach, Germany. The aircraft had just been belly-landed without landing gear by U.S. Lt. Bruce Carr, who they claim had taken it from a German airfield near Linz, Austria, after the war.

On November 15, 1944, Carr was promoted to first lieutenant and went on leave, returning to destroy an Fw-190 on March 9, 1945, and another four Me-109 Messerschmitt fighters northwest of Limburg, but his victories were not officially confirmed owing to a defective gun camera.

On April 1, Carr got a half credit in downing a Junkers Ju-188 near Wurzburg-Kassel. The following day, April 2, Carr was leading four aircraft on an armed reconnaissance mission in the area of Schweinfurt, Germany, when he "observed more than sixty enemy fighters flying high above. Completely disregarding his personal safety and the enemy's overwhelming numerical superiority and tactical advantage of altitude, he led his element in a direct attack on the hostile force, personally destroying five enemy aircraft and damaging still another." For his actions that day he was awarded the Distinguished Service Cross on May 27, 1945.

By shooting down five aircraft, two Fw-190s and three Me-109s, in one action, Carr earned the distinction of being the war's last "Ace in a Day." His flight downed a total of 15 aircraft.

On April 9, Carr was promoted to captain. He celebrated by shooting down a Messerschmitt the next day and destroyed a Heinkel He-111 bomber on April 15, as the bomber was landing at Mensdorf airfield. His final aerial combat, during a strafing mission on April 25, netted him a Ju-88 bomber and an Fw-190.

Carr finished the war as a "triple-ace" and one of the highest-scoring pilots in the 353rd Fighter Squadron, itself the highest-scoring fighter unit in the war, and U.S. military history, with 701 kills. In his 172 combat missions, Carr had 15 confirmed kills, three unconfirmed, and 7½ destroyed on the ground.

Following the war, Carr was assigned as a pilot with the Acrojets, the first U.S. Air Force jet-powered aerobatic demonstration team. Created at the Williams Air Force Base combat school, outside Chandler, Arizona, the team flew Lockheed F-80A Shooting Star fighter jets. The Acrojets first performed the now well-known bomb-burst maneuver followed by a crossing maneuver, which the Thunderbirds, a later demonstration team, adopted as its trademark.

Like most fighter pilots, Carr, now a major, received orders for Korea and was assigned to combat missions toward the end of the war. While assigned to the 336th Fighter Interceptor Squadron (336th FDS) "Rocketeers," flying an F-86 Sabre, Carr racked up another 57 combat missions, primarily air superiority missions, and served as the squadron's commanding officer from January 1, 1955, until August 6, 1956.

Promoted to lieutenant colonel on March 25, 1958, and colonel on November 3, 1968, Carr deployed to war for the third time when he reported in as the assistant deputy commander for operations with the 31st Tactical Fighter Wing at Tuy Hoa Airbase, Republic of Vietnam.

The wing primarily flew air support and air interdiction missions. Carr flew 286 combat missions in the North American F-100 Super Sabre fighter jet and was awarded an additional three Distinguished Flying Crosses.

Carr was piloting an F-100 about 20 miles northwest of Saigon on March 11, 1969, when he received a call to support troops on the ground. As his second Distinguished Flying Cross citation recounted, Carr "flew in support of friendly ground forces in close contact with a hostile force.

In spite of extremely poor visibility and the absolute necessity for accuracy caused by the close proximity of the friendly force to the target, Colonel Carr placed all his ordnance exactly on target, resulting in heavy losses to the hostile troops and forcing their retreat."

He was awarded a third Distinguished Flying Cross for his actions on July 8, 1969, 11 miles northwest of Tay Ninh City, when he

> was diverted to strike hostile automatic weapons positions which had directed intense fire at friendly ground and air forces. On his first bombing pass both he and the Forward Air Controller received heavy defensive fire from these positions.
> Colonel Carr pressed the attack in spite of tracer fire that narrowly missed his aircraft. Disregarding his own safety, he made another bombing attack in the face of heavy fire and six additional bombing and strafing attacks completely destroying five gun sites and killing the hostile gunners.

Carr's fourth and final Distinguished Flying Cross was awarded for actions that had occurred earlier, on December 28, 1968. While piloting an F-100 on a mission southwest of Bin Thuy, Carr had "relentlessly attacked an unknown size hostile force that was defending a base camp and supply area. Attacking under conditions of an immediate hostile threat, Colonel Carr bombed the hostile positions with deadly accuracy, destroying the base camp and supply area."

Carr was also awarded a Legion of Merit medal for his leadership as deputy commander of operations for the 31st Tactical Wing from November 27, 1968, to November 19, 1969.

Carr retired from the air force in 1973, having flown a total of 509 combat missions. Along with the Distinguished Service Cross, Silver Star, Legion of Merit and four Distinguished Flying Crosses, Carr was awarded 31 Air Medals.

Asked once how he'd chosen the name for his plane, Carr recalled, "On my first long-range mission, we just kept climbing, and I'd never had an airplane above about 10,000 feet before. Then we were at 30,000 feet and I couldn't believe it! I'd gone to church as a kid, and I knew that's where the angels were and that's when I named my airplane 'Angel's Playmate.'"

The pilot known as "Peck's Bad Boy" passed away in St. Cloud, Florida, of prostate cancer on April 25, 1998, at age 74, and was buried with full military honors at Arlington National Cemetery.

Sources

Eielson Air Force Base, 353rd Training Squadron website. http://www.eielson.af.mil/About-Us/Fact-Sheets/Display/Article/382389/353rd-combat-training-squadron/.

Hammel, Eric. *Aces Against Germany: The American Aces Speak*. Pacifica, CA: Pacifica Military History, 2007.

Hess, William. *Down to Earth: Strafing Pilots of the Eighth Air Force.* Oxford: Osprey Publishing, 2012.
Hess, William. *354th Fighter Group.* Oxford: Osprey Publishing, 2012.
Parra, Laurant. "Bruce Ward Carr." http://www.cieldegloire.com/014_carr_b_w.php.
Sterner, Doug. Home of Heroes. http://www.homeofheroes.com/.
Treadwell, Terry. *Great Escapes.* Charleston, SC: History Press, 2011.

Chips
U.S. Army War Dog Awarded the Distinguished Service Cross

On November 19, 1943, at a churchyard in Pietravairano, Italy, soldiers of the Third Infantry Division stood at attention as their commander, Maj. Gen. Lucian Truscott, presented the award of the Silver Star and Purple Heart Medals to one of their own.

An excerpt from the citation read, "For a special brand of courage, arising from love of master and duty, Chips' courageous act, single-handedly eliminating a dangerous machine-gun nest, reflects the highest credit on himself and the military service."

The recipient, a three-year old, 100-pound German shepherd, collie, husky mix named Chips, a member of the recently created K-9 Corps, sat patiently while the general pinned the ribbons to his collar. This act would generate debate in the War Department, the U.S. Congress and the American public.

Dogs had always been a part of the American army since the nation's founding, but they had always served unofficially. Following America's entry into World War II, in January 1942, members of the American Kennel Club and other dog lovers formed a civilian organization called Dogs for Defense. They offered to train dogs to perform sentry duty for the army along the coast of the United States.

The army quartermaster general, Maj. Gen. Edmund B. Gregory suggested to Undersecretary of War Robert P. Patterson that the army use the sentry dogs at supply depots. Patterson gave his approval to an experimental program, and on March 13, 1942, the K-9 Corps was created as part of the Quartermaster Corps.

In August 1942, the Quartermaster Corps established the first War

Dog Reception and Training Center at Front Royal, Virginia. Later locations included Fort Robinson, Nebraska; Gulfport, Mississippi; Camp Rimini, near Helena, Montana; and San Carlos, California.

The 8- to 12-week program included "basic training" to become accustomed to life in the military, and the dogs were tested for reactions when exposed to noise or gunfire, disease, poor sense of smell, or temperament. Then the dogs were assigned to a specialized program for training as sentry dogs, scout or patrol dogs, messenger dogs, or mine detection dogs.

Of the 18,000 dogs admitted to the training centers, almost 8,000 of those animals failed exams given at the centers and were rejected for military service. Although the K-9 Corps initially accepted 32 breeds of dogs, eventually the list was reduced to seven: German shepherds, Doberman pinschers, Belgian sheepdogs, Siberian huskies, collies, Eskimo dogs, and malamutes.

During World War II, 10,425 dogs served in the military, most as sentry dogs at supply depots, military installations and along America's coastline. However, approximately 1,000 dogs were trained as scout dogs. Chips was one of those dogs.

The Quartermaster Corps created 15 War Dog Platoons for service overseas with seven sent to Europe and eight to the Pacific theater. Each platoon was commanded by a lieutenant, with a technical sergeant serving as the platoon sergeant, with three squads and a veterinary sergeant. Each squad consisted of eight handlers, a sergeant and seven T/5s (technician fifth grade), and eight dogs, four scout dogs and four messenger dogs. The platoons were attached at the corps or division level.

Chips was "enlisted" by Mr. and Mrs. Edward J. Wren of Pleasantville, New York, on August 31, 1942, and was one of the first dogs to graduate Front Royal. Chips and his handler, Pvt. John P. Rowell, were assigned to Third Military Police Platoon attached to I Company, 30th Infantry Regiment, Third Infantry Division.

They departed Norfolk, Virginia, aboard a troopship bound for North Africa and Operation Torch, the invasion of French Morocco. The mission of Operation Torch was to secure French North Africa for the Allied forces in order to conduct operations on the European continent. Chips and his handler landed on November 8, 1942, under fire.

Most of the landing areas were defended by Vichy French troops who had declared loyalty to Germany after France fell. The invasion would take place in three places: Casablanca, an Atlantic port city in Morocco, and the Algerian port cities of Oran and Algiers. After three days of intense fighting, the French agreed to a cease-fire and joined the Allied forces.

With Casablanca secured, the Allies could now move men and matériel into the Mediterranean Sea without fear of the Strait of Gibraltar being cut off.

From January 14 to January 24, 1943, the Allied powers held a conference at Casablanca, Morocco, where the British prime minister Winston Churchill and President Roosevelt met with their generals and admirals to coordinate Allied military strategy against the Axis powers for the following year.

Among the outcomes was an agreement to concentrate their efforts against Germany to draw German forces away from the eastern front, relieving the pressure on the Red Army, and to increase shipments of supplies to the Soviet Union.

They also agreed to build up forces in England for the eventual landing in Northern France, but they would first concentrate their efforts in the Mediterranean by launching an invasion of Sicily and the Italian mainland designed to knock Italy out of the war. They also agreed to strengthen their strategic bombing campaign against Germany. Finally, they agreed on a policy of "unconditional surrender."

Chips served as a sentry dog during the conference, guarding Winston Churchill's and Franklin Roosevelt's quarters, meeting both the great men. After the conference, Chips moved east with the Third Division in support of the British forces attacking Tunisia. During this time, Chips struck up a relationship with another war dog, Mena, who was sent home after delivering nine puppies.

One of Chips's handlers, Cpl. William Haulk, maintained correspondence with the Wren family and wrote them that Chips was now a father and was "lovesick" when he was shipped out for the Sicily invasion.

The Allied invasion of Sicily, codenamed Operation Husky, was a large amphibious and airborne operation, followed by a six-week land campaign, which was the beginning of the Italian campaign that would, using Churchill's words, attack Europe's "soft underbelly."

Operation Husky began on the night of July 9–10, 1943, and by the time it ended on August 17, many of the goals established at Casablanca had been achieved. The taking of Sicily opened the Mediterranean Sea to Allied merchant ships for the first time since 1941. Benito Mussolini was toppled from power in Italy, and the way was opened for the Allied invasion of Italy. Adolf Hitler canceled a major offensive at Kursk after only a week, in part to divert forces to Italy, resulting in a reduction of German strength on the eastern front.

It was during Operation Husky that Chips would distinguish himself. In the predawn hours of July 10, 1943, Maj. Gen. Lucian Truscott's Third Infantry Division landed on the shore of southern Sicily near Licata.

Private Rowell and Chips and the Third Military Police Platoon landed at dawn and were among the first American troops to set foot, and paw, on Italian soil. As they moved inland, they came under machine-gun fire from a bunker, camouflaged as a peasant hut.

As the platoon dove for cover, Chips broke away from his handler and attacked. Dashing forward across open terrain under fire, he charged into the bunker. The machine gun went suddenly silent. There were shouts and yells and a pistol shot, and then one Italian emerged with Chips at his throat, followed by three more Italians with their hands raised.

As Rowell later described it for the newspapers, "There was an awful lot of noise and the firing stopped. Then I saw one soldier come out of the door with Chips at his throat. I called him off before he could kill the man."

Chips suffered a scalp wound and powder burns, but returned to duty that night, and alerted on ten Italian infiltrators trying to sneak into camp, resulting in their capture. Chips' deeds became known throughout the division.

On September 9, 1943, Capt. Edward G. Parr, the platoon commander, recommended Chips for the Distinguished Service Cross citing his "courageous action in single-handedly eliminating a dangerous machine gun nest and causing the surrender of its crew."

On October 24, 1943, Third Infantry Division Headquarters issued General Order 79, authorizing the award of the Silver Star and Purple Heart to Chips. On November 19, 1943, waiving War Department regulations prohibiting the award of medals to animals, Truscott presented Chips with the Silver Star and Purple Heart, affixing them to his collar.

A United Press story dated January 14, 1944, under the headline "Chips, Canine Hero Given Distinguished Service Cross," reported that General Truscott "added the ribbon to Chips' collar, which already carried the Silver Star and Purple Heart," making Chips the first, and only, dog so honored.

The following day, William Thomas, national commander of the Order of the Purple Heart, fired off protests to the White House, the secretary of War, the War Department and Congress, stating that awarding medals to dogs was "demeaning" to all men awarded the Purple Heart.

His complaints resulted in a three-month investigation, the outcome being a law restricting medals of valor to humans, but that "appropriate citations may be published in unit general orders." Many sources state that Chips's medals were revoked.

However, the February 28, 1944, issue of *Time* magazine reported that "the Army Adjutant General, Major General James A. Ulio, ruled, following protests, that Chips could keep his medals, but no more medals would be awarded to dogs."

It was much ado about nothing to Chips, who unaware of the controversy, continued to do his duty, serving with Third Infantry Division throughout the campaigns in Italy, France and Germany until the end of the war.

Chips was personally promoted to PFC by General Eisenhower when the two met in Italy in 1945, and Chips nipped the supreme commander when he tried to pet him, with handler Pvt. Morris Owens explaining that Chips was trained to bite anyone he didn't recognize.

Chips meets Gen. Dwight Eisenhower, 1945 (U.S. Army photograph).

Shortly before he was honorably discharged and returned home to the Wren family in New York, on December 11, 1945, his platoon unofficially awarded him a Theater Ribbon with arrowhead for an assault landing and eight battle stars.

Like many returning veterans, Chips had difficulty adjusting to a return to civilian life, and six reporters and photographers accompanied Chips home, where his owner reported that "he doesn't wag his tail as much" and suspected battle fatigue. The war took its toll, and Chips passed away from kidney failure seven months after returning home. He is buried at the Peaceable Kingdom Pet Cemetery in Hartsdale, New York.

In March 1990, Walt Disney television released *Chips, the War Dog*, a 92-minute made-for-TV movie loosely based on Chips's life.

On January 15, 2018, the 75th anniversary of the Casablanca conference, Chips was posthumously awarded Great Britain's PDSA Dicken Medal, often called the animal Victoria Cross. The medal, named for Maria Dicken, founder of the British veterinary charity, was established in 1917 to honor acts of valor by animals.

The presentation was made at the Churchill War Rooms in London, and the medal was accepted by John Wren, 76, the son of the family who donated Chips to the military in 1942, and Ayron, a USAF German shepherd and his handler, Staff Sergeant Jeremy Mayorhoffer.

Chips is the 70th recipient of the Dicken Medal. Since 1917, the medal has been awarded to 32 dogs, 32 messenger pigeons, four horses and a cat.

After World War II, the Military Police Corps took over responsibility for training military dogs. The army employed 1,500 dogs during the Korean War and 4,000 in the Vietnam War. Currently, the army has approximately 578 dog teams, which have seen service in Iraq and Afghanistan.

Sources

Bergeron, Arthur W., Jr. *War Dogs: The Birth of the K-9 Corps*. U.S. Army Military History Institute, February 14, 2008. https://www.army.mil/article/7463/war_dogs_the_birth_of_the_k_9_corps.
"CHIPS—THE Famous 3rd Infantry Division Sentry Dog." http://ww2awartobewon.com/wwii-articles/chips-3rd-infantry-division-sentry-dog/.
Derr, Mark. *A Dog's History of America*. New York: Overlook Press, 2016.
"Honoring the First Dog to Be Awarded the Purple Heart." National Constitution Center. https://constitutioncenter.org/blog/honoring-the-only-dog-to-be-awarded-the-purple-heart.
Kistler, John M. *Animals in the Military: From Hannibal's Elephants to Dolphins in the US Navy*. Santa Barbara, CA: ABC-CLIO, 2011.
Zimmerman, Dwight John. *Chips: War Dog Hero of the 3rd Infantry Division*. Defense Media Network. https://www.defensemedianetwork.com/stories/chips-war-dog-hero-of-the-3rd-infantry-division/.

Index

Aggerholm, Harold 80
Arlington National Cemetery 38, 56, 85, 137, 163, 206

USS *Barb* (SS-220) 86–96
Barker, Joseph 20–21
Bataan 14–16, 18, 20–21
Battle of the Bulge 102, 148, 149, 165
Bradley, Omar 192

Carlson, Evans F. 24, 27–38
Casablanca 45, 56, 67, 125, 126, 131, 170, 171, 209, 210, 213
Central Intelligence Agency (CIA) 26, 180, 181
Churchill, Winston 5, 44, 126, 210, 213
Clark, Mark 63, 69
Clark Field 18

Dachau Concentration Camp 98
Daladier, Edouard 98, 99, 103
Darlan, Jean François 51, 53
Distinguished Service Cross 22, 74, 108, 151, 179, 180, 192, 193, 205, 206, 208, 211
Donovan, William "Wild Bill" 26, 110, 179, 180, 187
Dostler, Anton 109, 115–117, 119–122

Eaker, Ira 135, 136
Eisenhower, Dwight D. 1, 45, 51, 52, 58, 110, 127, 148, 170, 212
Elliott, George 10–13
USS *Enterprise* (CV-6) 10
Epperson, Harold G. 80

Fort Bragg 22, 55, 56, 125, 150
Fort McKinley 3
Fort Shafter 8

442nd Infantry Regiment 74, 81
USS *Franklin* (CV-13) 138

Gangl, Josef "Sepp" 97, 99–106, 108
Gehrig, Lou 183
Gilbert Islands 24, 29
Great Marianas Turkey Shoot 79
Guadalcanal 11, 28, 29, 36, 39, 40, 61, 65

Hamilton, Alexander 46
Harvard University 24, 46, 50
Heisenberg, Werner 186
Henderson Field 11, 41, 61
Hickam Field 10, 11
Holcomb, Thomas 26
Homma, Masaharu 14, 20

USS *Juneau* (CL-52) 63, 65

Kasserine Pass 126
King, Ernest 27, 93
Koso, Abe 35

Lockard, Joseph 10–13

MacArthur, Douglas 14, 18, 20–22, 172
Makin Island 24, 29, 36–38
Manhattan Project 186
McAuliffe, Anthony 149
McCain, John S., Jr. 199
McCard, Robert H. 79
McCarthy, Joseph 36
MGM Studios 25, 41
Midway, Battle of 29, 61, 89, 91, 93, 95
Montgomery, Bernard 148
Mountbatten, Louis 26, 47

Navajo Code Talkers 79
Naval War College 162

Navy Cross 1, 28, 29, 31, 34, 35, 52, 84, 87, 89–91, 95, 141, 161, 200
USS *Nevada* (BB-36) 88
Nimitz, Chester 27, 95
Ninth Infantry Division 45, 125
Normandy (D-Day) 45, 51, 55–58, 61, 62, 72, 102, 127, 179, 203

Obama, Barack 167
Obara, Yoshio, 35
Office of Strategic Services (OSS) 26, 110, 123, 180
Okinawa 6, 36, 140
Omori Prison Camp 173
Operation Barbarossa 49
Operation Husky 210
Operation Torch 1, 44, 50, 125, 170, 209

Patch, Alexander 73
Patton, George S. 45, 47, 69, 125, 150
Pearl Harbor 1, 5, 10–12, 14, 18, 24, 27, 29, 34, 36, 47, 60, 62, 66, 81, 88, 93, 140, 149, 155, 165, 169, 185, 200
Puller, Lewis "Chesty" 41, 42

Quezon, Manuel Luis 20, 141

Randolph Field 9, 34
USS *Ranger* (CV-4) 139
Roberts Commission 12
Rommel, Erwin 49, 126
Rooney, Andy 133, 137
Roosevelt, Eleanor 24, 37
Roosevelt, Franklin D. 3, 20, 24, 40, 44, 50, 53, 62, 66, 75, 110, 144, 210

Roosevelt, Theodore, Jr. 57
Ruth, "Babe" 183

Saint Nazaire 131
Saipan 1, 78–85, 90, 172, 200
Second Marine Division 25, 27, 78, 80, 81, 84
Segundo, Fidel 16, 19
Smith, Holland "Howling Mad" 79
Special Operations Executive (SOE) 110, 175, 177–179
Stengel, Casey 183
Stimson, Henry 135, 136
Sullivan Brothers 65

Thomason, Clyde 30, 31, 34, 37
Thorpe, Claude 21
Timmerman, Grant F. 80
Truman, Harry S. 141, 142, 147, 151, 162, 163, 179, 181
Truscott, Lucian 45, 47, 49–53, 208, 211

U.S. Naval Academy (Annapolis) 3, 4, 87, 88, 96

Vandegrift, Alexander 62

Wainwright, Jonathan 16, 18, 20
War Plan Orange 14
Warren, Earl 36
West Point (USMA) 20, 48, 50
Westmoreland, William C. 126
Wheeler Field 8, 10–11, 16, 48

Zamparini, Louis 35

www.ingramcontent.com/pod-product-compliance
Ingram Content Group UK Ltd.
Pitfield, Milton Keynes, MK11 3LW, UK
UKHW041955140426
5217IPUK00015B/815